SACREDSPACE

SACREDSPACE
the prayer book 2007

from the web site www.sacredspace.ie

Jesuit Communication Centre, Ireland

ave maria press AMP Notre Dame, Indiana

acknowledgment

The publisher would like to thank Gerry Bourke SJ and Alan McGuckian SJ for their kind assistance in making this book possible. Gerry Bourke SJ can be contacted at feedback@jesuit.ie

Unless otherwise noted, the Scripture quotations contained herein are from the *New Revised Standard Version Bible*, copyright © 1989 by the Division of Christian Education of the National Council of the Churches of Christ in the United States of America. Used by permission. All rights reserved.

First published in Australia 2006 by
Michelle Anderson Publishing Pty Ltd

Founded in 1865, Ave Maria Press is a ministry of the Indiana Province of Holy Cross.

www.avemariapress.com

ISBN-13 978-1-59471-097-1 ISBN-10 1-59471-097-X

Cover and text design: K.H. Coney

Printed and bound in the United States of America.

how to use this book

We invite you to make a sacred space in your day and spend ten minutes praying here and now, wherever you are, with the help of a prayer guide and scripture chosen specially for each day. Every place is a sacred space so you may wish to have this book in your desk at work or available to be picked up and read at any time of the day, whilst traveling or on your bedside table, a park bench . . . Remember that God is everywhere, all around us, constantly reaching out to us, even in the most unlikely situations. When we know this, and with a bit of practice, we can pray anywhere.

The following pages will guide you through a session of prayer stages.

Something to think and pray about each day this week
The Presence of God
Freedom
Consciousness
The Word (leads you to the daily scripture and provides help
   with the text)
Conversation
Conclusion

It is most important to come back to these pages each day of the week as they are an integral part of each day's prayer and lead to the scripture and inspiration points.

Although written in the first person, the prayers are for "doing" rather than for reading out. Each stage is a kind of exercise or mediation aimed at helping you to get in touch with God and God's presence in your life.

We hope that you will join the many people around the world praying with us in our sacred space.

The Presence of God

Bless all who worship you, almighty God,
from the rising of the sun to its setting:
from your goodness enrich us,
by your love inspire us,
by your Spirit guide us,
by your power protect us,
in your mercy receive us,
now and always.

contents

december 3–9

Something to think and pray about each day this week:

Reading the future

Judaism provided the early church with rich images to describe the final coming of God as the Lord of all history and creation. The gospels drew on that imagery to encourage the early Christians—and us today—to look forward to the day when the Son of Man comes. That day is imminent; be vigilant, watchful in how you live, and confident in your suffering.

For the Christian, the return of Jesus is not a time to be feared; the end is not the end at all but a time of hope, of liberation, of rebirth, of new life. Until that day, Jesus exhorts us to watch and wait, to live a life that stands out from those we live among. "Be on watch and pray always" (Luke 21:36).

The Presence of God
I remind myself that, as I sit here now,
God is gazing on me with love and holding me in being.
I pause for a moment and think of this.

Freedom
I will ask God's help,
to be free from my own preoccupations,
to be open to God in this time of prayer,
to come to love and serve him more.

Consciousness
I exist in a web of relationships—links to nature, people, God.
I trace out these links, giving thanks for the life that flows
through them.
Some links are twisted or broken: I may feel regret, anger,
disappointment.
I pray for the gift of acceptance and forgiveness.

The Word
God speaks to each one of us individually. I need to listen to
what he is saying to me. (Please turn to your scripture on the following pages. Inspiration points are there should you need
them. When you are ready, return here to continue.)

Conversation
Remembering that I am still in God's presence,
I imagine Jesus himself standing or sitting beside me,
and say whatever is on my mind, whatever is in my heart,
speaking as one friend to another.

Conclusion
Glory be to the Father, and to the Son, and to the Holy Spirit,
As it was in the beginning, is now and ever shall be,
World without end. Amen

Sunday 3rd December, First Sunday of Advent
Jeremiah 33:14–16

"The days are surely coming," says the Lord, "when I will fulfill the promise I made to the house of Israel and the house of Judah. In those days and at that time I will cause a righteous Branch to spring up for David; and he shall execute justice and righteousness in the land. In those days Judah will be saved and Jerusalem will live in safety. And this is the name by which it will be called: "The Lord is our righteousness.""

* Advent tells us that we have a marvelous future awaiting us.
* What are my reactions to God's promise of great things? Do I flow easily with it? Is it drowned out by other feelings, other voices? Do my current circumstances make it hard for me to trust the promise?
* Can I listen keenly to the promise, "the days are surely coming," and step out with confidence?

Monday 4th December   Matthew 8:5–11

When Jesus entered Capernaum, a centurion came to him, appealing to him and saying, "Lord, my servant is lying at home paralyzed, in terrible distress." And he said to him, "I will come and cure him." The centurion answered, "Lord, I am not worthy to have you come under my roof; but only speak the word, and my servant will be healed. For I also am a man under authority, with soldiers under me; and I say to one, 'Go,' and he goes, and to another, 'Come,' and he comes, and to my slave, 'Do this,' and the slave does it." When Jesus heard him, he was amazed and said to those who followed him, "Truly I tell you, in no one in Israel have I found such faith. I tell you, many will come from east and west and will eat with Abraham and Isaac and Jacob in the kingdom of heaven."

- The centurion made an extraordinary leap from his own culture, position, and pride to recognize Jesus' power. Jesus was amazed at his faith.
- Have I the insight to perceive holiness and God's hand at work around me, or am I imprisoned in the stereotypes of my culture?

Tuesday 5th December　　　　　　　　　　　　Luke 10:22

At that same hour Jesus rejoiced in the Holy Spirit and said, "All things have been handed over to me by my Father; and no one knows who the Son is except the Father, or who the Father is except the Son and anyone to whom the Son chooses to reveal him."

- William Barclay writes: "We believe in evolution, the slow climb upward of man from the level of the beasts. Jesus is the end and climax of the evolutionary process, because in him man meets God; he is at once the perfection of manhood and the fullness of godhead."

Wednesday 6th December　　　　　　　　　Matthew 15:29–37

Jesus went on from there and reached the shores of the Sea of Galilee, and he went up into the hills. He sat there, and large crowds came to him bringing the lame, the crippled, the blind, the dumb and many others. The crowds were astonished to see the dumb speaking, the cripples whole again, the lame walking and the blind with their sight, and they praised the God of Israel. But Jesus called his disciples to him and said, "I feel sorry for all these people; they have been with me for three days now and have nothing to eat. I do not want to send them off hungry, they might collapse on the way." The disciples said to him: "Where could we get enough bread in this deserted place to feed such a crowd?" Jesus said to them: "How many loaves have you? Seven, they said, and a few small fish." Then he instructed the crowd to sit down on the ground, and he took the seven loaves and the fish, and he gave thanks and broke them and handed them to the disciples who gave them to the crowds. They all ate as much as they wanted, and they collected what was left of the scraps, seven baskets full.

- Jesus felt compassion, which carries a weight of meaning. It is not a modern word, but fits the full-bodied response of Jesus. His was not just a warm feeling. Compassion means that action follows the "heart" response.
- Jesus started with what the apostles already had on hand, seven loaves and a few small fish. Can I learn to use everything I am given?

Thursday 7th December   Matthew 7:21, 24–27

Jesus said to his disciples, "Not everyone who says to me, 'Lord, Lord,' will enter the kingdom of heaven, but only the one who does the will of my Father in heaven. Everyone then who hears these words of mine and acts on them will be like a wise man who built his house on rock. The rain fell, the floods came, and the winds blew and beat on that house, but it did not fall, because it had been founded on rock. And everyone who hears these words of mine and does not act on them will be like a foolish man who built his house on sand. The rain fell, and the floods came, and the winds blew and beat against that house, and it fell—and great was its fall!"

- It is not enough to hear the words of Jesus. They only have power when we act on them.

- What does "acting" on the words of Jesus mean in my life? Can I actually see where my action grows out of faith and prayer?

- Do Jesus' words challenge me about times of procrastination or lack of direction when I dodge the call?

- Can I be open, right now, to hearing the will of the Father, calling me, in ways small and great, into life?

Friday 8th December, The Immaculate Conception of the Blessed Virgin Mary   Luke 1:26–38

In the sixth month the angel Gabriel was sent by God to a town in Galilee called Nazareth, to a virgin engaged to a man whose name was Joseph, of the house of David. The virgin's name was Mary. And he came to her and said, "Greetings, favored one! The Lord is with you." But she was much perplexed by his words and pondered what sort of greeting this might be. The angel said to her, "Do not be afraid, Mary, for you have found favor with God. And now, you will conceive in your womb and bear a son, and you will name him Jesus. He will be great, and will be called the Son of the Most High, and the Lord God will give to him the throne of his ancestor David. He will reign over the house of Jacob forever, and of his kingdom there will be no end." Mary said to the angel, "How can this be, since I am a virgin?" The angel said to her, "The Holy Spirit will come upon you, and the power of the Most High will overshadow you; therefore the child to be born will be holy; he will be called Son of God. And now, your relative Elizabeth in her old age has also conceived a son; and this is the sixth month for her who was said to be barren. For nothing will be impossible with God." Then Mary said, "Here am I, the servant of the Lord; let it be with me according to your word." Then the angel departed from her.

- By her yes, Mary first bore the Son of God in her heart, and then in her body.

- Can I watch the scene? A young woman, who could have had no idea of what was being asked or where it might lead, made a leap of trust, of faith, and of hope.

- How does Mary's experience touch me? Am I called to "bear" God in my heart? What issues of surrender and trust arise in my case?

Saturday 9th December   Isaiah 30:19–21

Truly, O people in Zion, inhabitants of Jerusalem, you shall weep no more. He will surely be gracious to you at the sound of your cry; when he hears it, he will answer you. Though the Lord may give you the bread of adversity and the water of affliction, yet your Teacher will not hide himself any more, but your eyes shall see your Teacher. And when you turn to the right or when you turn to the left, your ears shall hear a word behind you, saying, "This is the way; walk in it."

- Does the promise that God will be gracious to me in my distress touch a chord with me?

- Do I feel I have been given the "bread of adversity" and the "water of affliction"? Do I feel for others in their affliction?

- As I listen to the Lord's promises, in what space do they find me? Buoyant and responsive? Weighed down and cynical? Vulnerable?

- Wherever I am today can I hear the Lord's words of consolation and offer of guidance?

Something to think and pray about each day this week:

Spiritual muscle

"The Spirit helps us in our weakness." Even when we do not know how to pray, the Holy Spirit, whose temple we are, maintains an unceasing dialogue with the Father on our behalf. Our spiritual progress depends not so much on muscular effort as on removing the obstacles to God—our selfishness and silliness— and on allowing God to shape us, giving space to the good seed of Jesus' parable. *Sacred Space* is one such space, where we set time aside for God's word to grow in us.

The Presence of God
God is with me, but more,
God is within me, giving me existence.
Let me dwell for a moment on God's life-giving presence
in my body, my mind, my heart
and in the whole of my life.

Freedom
God is not foreign to my freedom.
Instead the Spirit breathes life into my most intimate desires,
gently nudging me towards all that is good.
I ask for the grace to let myself be enfolded by the Spirit.

Consciousness
In God's loving presence I unwind the past day,
starting from now and looking back, moment by moment.
I gather in all the goodness and light, in gratitude.
I attend to the shadows and what they say to me,
seeking healing, courage, forgiveness.

The Word
I read the Word of God slowly, a few times over, and I listen to
what God is saying to me. (Please turn to your scripture on the
following pages. Inspiration points are there should you need
them. When you are ready, return here to continue.)

Conversation
How has God's Word moved me? Has it left me cold?
Has it consoled me or moved me to act in a new way?
I imagine Jesus standing or sitting beside me,
I turn and share my feelings with him.

Conclusion
Glory be to the Father, and to the Son, and to the Holy Spirit,
As it was in the beginning, is now and ever shall be,
World without end. Amen

Sunday 10th December, Second Sunday of Advent
Luke 3:1–6

In the fifteenth year of the reign of Emperor Tiberius, when Pontius Pilate was governor of Judea, and Herod was ruler of Galilee, and his brother Philip ruler of the region of Ituraea and Trachonitis, and Lysanias ruler of Abilene, during the high priesthood of Annas and Caiaphas, the word of God came to John son of Zechariah in the wilderness. He went into all the region around the Jordan, proclaiming a baptism of repentance for the forgiveness of sins, as it is written in the book of the words of the prophet Isaiah, "The voice of one crying out in the wilderness: 'Prepare the way of the Lord, make his paths straight. Every valley shall be filled, and every mountain and hill shall be made low, and the crooked shall be made straight, and the rough ways made smooth; and all flesh shall see the salvation of God.'"

- Who is active here? Who takes the initiative?
- If the Word of God "came" to me, would I be able to hear? What would block my hearing?

Monday 11th December　　　　　　　　**Luke 5:17–26**

One day, as Jesus was teaching, there were Pharisees and teachers of the Law sitting by, who had come from every village of Galilee and Judea and from Jerusalem; and the power of the Lord was with him to heal. And behold, men were bringing on a bed a man who was paralyzed, and they sought to bring him in and lay him before Jesus; but finding no way to bring him in, because of the crowd, they went up on the roof and let him down with his bed through the tiles into the midst before Jesus. And when he saw their faith he said: "Man, your sins are forgiven you." And the scribes and the Pharisees began to question, saying: "Who is this that speaks blasphemies? Who can forgive sins but God only?" When Jesus perceived their questionings, he answered them: "Why do you question in your hearts? Which is easier, to say: 'Your sins are forgiven you' or to say: 'Rise and walk'? But that you may know that the Son of Man has authority on earth to forgive sins"—he said to the man who was paralyzed: "I say to you, rise, take up your bed and go home." And immediately he rose before them, took up that on which he lay, and went home glorifying God. And amazement seized them all, and they glorified God and were filled with awe, saying: "We have seen strange things today."

- The patient is lowered through the roof, a helpless paralytic, dependent completely on faith-filled friends.

- Forgiveness gives us the energy and dynamism to rise, take up our bed, and walk. With it comes life, and more abundantly than before.

Tuesday 12th December   Matthew 18:12–14

Jesus said to his disciples: "What do you think? If a man has a hundred sheep, and one of them has gone astray, does he not leave the ninety-nine on the hills and go in search of the one that went astray? And if he finds it, truly I say to you, he rejoices over it more than over the ninety-nine that never went astray. So it is not the will of my father who is in heaven that one of these little ones should perish."

- What Jesus proposes is paradoxical, not simple. Is this what happens in business? Can a teacher of 30 pupils ignore the 29 and spend all their energies on the one who is not coping?
- Jesus touches many of us: when we feel inadequate, unworthy, not making the grade, on the edge of or outside the church, wandering without motivation. How am I touched by this?

Wednesday 13th December · Matthew 11:28–30

Jesus said, "Come to me, all you that are weary and are carrying heavy burdens, and I will give you rest. Take my yoke upon you, and learn from me; for I am gentle and humble in heart, and you will find rest for your souls. For my yoke is easy, and my burden is light."

- Let us sit a while with this precious and familiar text. Do I hear Jesus speak these words to me?
- How do I respond now?

Thursday 14th December · Isaiah 41:17–20

When the poor and needy seek water, and there is none, and their tongue is parched with thirst, I the Lord will answer them, I the God of Israel will not forsake them. I will open rivers on the bare heights, and fountains in the midst of the valleys; I will make the wilderness a pool of water, and the dry land springs of water. I will put in the wilderness the cedar, the acacia, the myrtle, and the olive; I will set in the desert the cypress, the plane and the pine together, so that all may see and know, all may consider and understand, that the hand of the LORD has done this, the Holy One of Israel has created it.

- This is a barren, parched and lifeless desert where God's people starve and thirst. God's gift is its transformation.
- Where do I see people thirsting for life? How do I bring that to the Lord?

Friday 15th December · Matthew 11:16–19

Jesus spoke to the crowds, "But to what will I compare this generation? It is like children sitting in the marketplaces and calling to one another, 'We played the flute for you, and you did not dance; we wailed, and you did not mourn.' For John came neither eating nor drinking, and they say, 'He has a demon'; the Son of Man came eating and drinking, and they say, 'Look, a glutton and a drunkard, a friend of tax collectors and sinners!' Yet wisdom is vindicated by her deeds."

- Can I hear the frustration of Jesus in this scene? (Do I need to slow down and really listen to him?) It seems as if his life, which is meant to reveal the very essence of God, is being misunderstood and misrepresented.
- What about me? Do I misunderstand or misrepresent? Do I minimize or play down the significance of Jesus?
- Can I catch the frustration and urgency of God, desiring to be heard? By me.

Saturday 16th December   Matthew 17:10–13

And the disciples asked him, "Why, then, do the scribes say that Elijah must come first?" He replied, "Elijah is indeed coming and will restore all things; but I tell you that Elijah has already come, and they did not recognize him, but they did to him whatever they pleased. So also the Son of Man is about to suffer at their hands." Then the disciples understood that he was speaking to them about John the Baptist.

- God's messengers—Elijah, John the Baptist, or even the Son of Man—tend to be rejected and even eliminated. This is a bitter truth to face in the midst of our Advent journey.
- Advent still calls us to a fulfillment promised and guaranteed by God. In my prayer today, can I hold together both the promise and the shadow?
- It is good to talk to the Lord about these things.

december 17–23

Something to think and pray about each day this week:

Mary's Yes

No scene of prayer is more familiar to us than the Annunciation, recalled every time the Angelus bell rings. Mary is listening, attentive but not passive. When the angel tells her that she is to conceive, she voices her problem: "I am a virgin." She listens on, then accepts her destiny: "I am the handmaid of the Lord." What happens next is astonishing.

She has just learned that she is to be the mother of God, the celebrity of all celebrities. Does she bask in it, in the warm sense of being chosen, in the anticipation of marvelous things to come? No, she puts on her cloak and sandals and walks to Judea. Because she has been told that her cousin is expecting a child, she hurries unbidden to help Elizabeth through her pregnancy. She will be Elizabeth's handmaid as well as the Lord's.

The Presence of God
What is present to me is what has a hold on my becoming.
I reflect on the presence of God always there in love,
amidst the many things that have a hold on me.
I pause and pray that I may let God
affect my becoming in this precise moment.

Freedom
There are very few people
who realize what God would make of them
if they abandoned themselves into his hands,
and let themselves be formed by his grace. (St. Ignatius)
I ask for the grace to trust myself totally to God's love.

Consciousness
In the presence of my loving Creator,
I look honestly at my feelings over the last day,
the highs, the lows and the level ground.
Can I see where the Lord has been present?

The Word
God speaks to each one of us individually. I need to listen to hear what he is saying to me. Read the text a few times, then listen. (Please turn to your scripture on the following pages. Inspiration points are there should you need them. When you are ready, return here to continue.)

Conversation
What is stirring in me as I pray?
Am I consoled, troubled, left cold?
I imagine Jesus himself standing or sitting at my side,
and share my feelings with him.

Conclusion
Glory be to the Father, and to the Son, and to the Holy Spirit,
As it was in the beginning, is now and ever shall be,
World without end. Amen

Sunday 17th December, Third Sunday of Advent
Luke 3:10–18

And the crowds asked John, "What then should we do?" In reply he said to them, "Whoever has two coats must share with anyone who has none; and whoever has food must do likewise." Even tax collectors came to be baptized, and they asked him, "Teacher, what should we do?" He said to them, "Collect no more than the amount prescribed for you." Soldiers also asked him, "And we, what should we do?" He said to them, "Do not extort money from anyone by threats or false accusation, and be satisfied with your wages." As the people were filled with expectation, and all were questioning in their hearts concerning John, whether he might be the Messiah, John answered all of them by saying, "I baptize you with water; but one who is more powerful than I is coming; I am not worthy to untie the thong of his sandals. He will baptize you with the Holy Spirit and fire. His winnowing fork is in his hand, to clear his threshing floor and to gather the wheat into his granary; but the chaff he will burn with unquenchable fire." So, with many other exhortations, he proclaimed the good news to the people.

- Part of the process of preparing for the coming of Jesus is to stand among the crowd and listen to John the Baptist.
- What do I make of him? How do his words move me?
- Do I look forward to the coming of the one who will "baptize with the Holy Spirit and fire"?
- I can bring my responses and reactions to the Lord.

Monday 18th December
Matthew 1:18–24

Now the birth of Jesus the Messiah took place in this way. When his mother Mary had been engaged to Joseph, but before they lived together, she was found to be with child from the Holy Spirit. Her husband Joseph, being a righteous man and unwilling to expose her to public disgrace, planned to dismiss her quietly. But just when he had resolved to do this, an angel of the Lord appeared to him in a dream and said, "Joseph, son of David, do not be afraid to take Mary as your wife, for the child conceived in her is from the Holy Spirit. She will bear a son, and you are to name him Jesus, for he will save his people from their sins." All this took place to fulfill what had been spoken by the Lord through the prophet: "Look, the virgin shall conceive and bear a son, and they shall name him Emmanuel," which means, "God is with us." When Joseph awoke from sleep, he did as the angel of the Lord commanded him; he took her as his wife.

- When God breaks in to human affairs it causes surprises and not a little initial upset.
- What must Joseph's first reaction have been? How could he have known what mysteries were afoot? Can I follow in imagination the steps he must have gone through before humbly accommodating himself to God's plans?
- What does this reality of God's "breaking in" say to me?

Tuesday 19th December   Judges 13:2–7, 24–25

There was a certain man of Zorah, of the tribe of the Danites, whose name was Manoah. His wife was barren, having borne no children. And the angel of the Lord appeared to the woman and said to her, "Although you are barren, having borne no children, you shall conceive and bear a son. Now be careful not to drink wine or strong drink, or to eat anything unclean, for you shall conceive and bear a son. No razor is to come on his head, for the boy shall be a nazirite to God from birth. It is he who shall begin to deliver Israel from the hand of the Philistines." Then the woman came and told her husband, "A man of God came to me, and his appearance was like that of an angel of God, most awe-inspiring; I did not ask him where he came from, and he did not tell me his name; but he said to me, 'You shall conceive and bear a son. So then drink no wine or strong drink, and eat nothing unclean, for the boy shall be a nazirite to God from birth to the day of his death.'" The woman bore a son, and named him Samson. The boy grew, and the Lord blessed him. The spirit of the Lord began to stir him in Mahaneh-dan, between Zorah and Eshtaol.

- Again we see the God of all creation in this story of God's power and creativity, overcoming our human limitations.

- How did the wife of Manoah feel, a woman stereotyped as barren? After years of "failure" how must she have viewed her son Samson?

- Are there areas of "barrenness" in my life where I might be open to being surprised?

Wednesday 20th December   Isaiah 7:10–14

Again the LORD spoke to Ahaz, saying, "Ask a sign of the LORD your God; let it be deep as Sheol or high as heaven." But Ahaz said, "I will not ask, and I will not put the LORD to the test." Then Isaiah said: "Hear then, O house of David! Is it too little for you to weary mortals, that you weary my God also? Therefore the LORD himself will give you a sign. Look, the young woman is with child and shall bear a son, and shall name him Emmanuel."

- As the birth of the Son of God comes near, it is good to remember the prophecy in Isaiah: "the young woman is with child . . ."
- Can I sit for a while with the thought that God planned from the beginning to take on flesh and share our lot, my lot? Emmanuel.

Thursday 21st December   Luke 1:39–45

In those days Mary set out and went with haste to a Judean town in the hill country, where she entered the house of Zechariah and greeted Elizabeth. When Elizabeth heard Mary's greeting, the child leaped in her womb. And Elizabeth was filled with the Holy Spirit and exclaimed with a loud cry, "Blessed are you among women, and blessed is the fruit of your womb. And why has this happened to me, that the mother of my Lord comes to me? For as soon as I heard the sound of your greeting, the child in my womb leaped for joy. And blessed is she who believed that there would be a fulfillment of what was spoken to her by the Lord."

- It is good to spend time gazing at this scene. Two women come together, both of them specially blessed and both called separately to cooperate in the unexpected designs of God.
- Together, they begin to understand. Mary's simple greeting brings forth Elizabeth's prophetic response. Giving hospitality to Jesus draws us into the hospitality of God.
- In life, do I always appreciate that my own faith story is one to share with others, in testimony and celebration?

Friday 22nd December   Luke 1:46–56

And Mary said, "My soul magnifies the Lord, and my spirit rejoices in God my Savior, for he has looked with favor on the lowliness of his servant. Surely, from now on all generations will call me blessed; for the Mighty One has done great things for me, and holy is his name. His mercy is for those who fear him from generation to generation. He has shown strength with his arm; he has scattered the proud in the thoughts of their hearts. He has brought down the powerful from their thrones, and lifted up the lowly; he has filled the hungry with good things, and sent the rich away empty. He has helped his servant Israel, in remembrance of his mercy, according to the promise he made to our ancestors, to Abraham and to his descendants forever." And Mary remained with Elizabeth about three months and then returned to her home.

- Mary's Magnificat is a prayer to savor. It echoes the song of Hannah in I Samuel 2:1, and the Beatitudes. It places us at the cusp of the Old and New Testaments, charged with the longing of the Old, and looking towards the fulfillment of the New.

- In the whole history of salvation, this is the moment of unalloyed joy. Can I slowly pray over her words and ask for the grace to share in her joy and sense of expectation?

Saturday 23rd December   Luke 1:57–66

Now the time came for Elizabeth to give birth, and she bore a son. Her neighbors and relatives heard that the Lord had shown his great mercy to her, and they rejoiced with her. On the eighth day they came to circumcise the child, and they were going to name him Zechariah after his father. But his mother said, "No; he is to be called John." They said to her, "None of your relatives has this name." Then they began motioning to his father to find out what name he wanted to give him. He asked for a writing tablet and wrote, "His name is John." And all of them were amazed. Immediately his mouth was opened and his tongue freed, and he began to speak, praising God. Fear came over all their neighbors, and all these things were talked about throughout the entire hill country of Judea. All who heard them pondered them and said, "What then will this child become?" For, indeed, the hand of the Lord was with him.

- "He is to be called John." He is in God's favor. Each one of us has received a name, and is known by a name. As a parent, we may also have given a name to our own child and wondered "What then will this child become?"
- God favors me, and knows me by my name. Can I give thanks for those who named me, for the hopes that others have for me, for each person who knows my name?

Something to think and pray about each day this week:

Mary's moment

For Mary there are rapid, fleeting moments when she realizes at once that Jesus is her son, her very own baby, and that he is God. She looks at him and thinks: "This God is my baby. This divine flesh is my flesh. He is made from me. He has my eyes, and the curve of his mouth is the curve of mine. He is like me. He is God and he is like me."

No other woman has been lucky enough to have a God for herself alone, a tiny little God whom she can take in her arms and cover with kisses, a warm-bodied God who smiles and breathes, a God that she can touch, who is alive. And it is in these moments that I would paint Mary, if I was a painter, and I would try to capture the air of radiant tenderness and timidity with which she lifts her finger to touch the sweet skin of her baby-God, whose warm weight she feels on her knees, and who smiles.

The Presence of God
God is with me, but more, God is within me.
Let me dwell for a moment on God's life-giving presence
in my body, in my mind, in my heart,
as I sit here, right now.

Freedom
A thick and shapeless tree-trunk would never believe
that it could become a statue, admired as a miracle of sculpture,
and would never submit itself to the chisel of the sculptor,
who sees by her genius what she can make of it. (St. Ignatius)
I ask for the grace to let myself be shaped by my loving Creator.

Consciousness
Knowing that God loves me unconditionally,
I can afford to be honest about how I am.
How has the last day been, and how do I feel now?
I share my feelings openly with the Lord.

The Word
I read the Word of God slowly, a few times over, and I listen to
what God is saying to me. (Please turn to your scripture on the
following pages. Inspiration points are there should you need
them. When you are ready, return here to continue.)

Conversation
Do I notice myself reacting as I pray with the Word of God?
Do I feel challenged, comforted, angry?
Imagining Jesus sitting or standing by me,
I speak out my feelings, as one trusted friend to another.

Conclusion
Glory be to the Father, and to the Son, and to the Holy Spirit,
As it was in the beginning, is now and ever shall be,
World without end. Amen

32

Sunday 24th December, Fourth Sunday of Advent
Luke 1:39–45

In those days Mary set out and went with haste to a Judean town in the hill country, where she entered the house of Zechariah and greeted Elizabeth. When Elizabeth heard Mary's greeting, the child leaped in her womb. And Elizabeth was filled with the Holy Spirit and exclaimed with a loud cry, "Blessed are you among women, and blessed is the fruit of your womb. And why has this happened to me, that the mother of my Lord comes to me? For as soon as I heard the sound of your greeting, the child in my womb leaped for joy. And blessed is she who believed that there would be a fulfillment of what was spoken to her by the Lord."

- Again, we see two women, chosen and set apart to cooperate in God's plan of salvation.
- Just like any pregnant woman they don't know how it will all work out. Yet, there is great joy and confidence in this scene. Where does that joy come from?

Monday 25th December, Feast of the Nativity of the Lord
Luke 2:6–14

While they were in Bethlehem, the time came for Mary to deliver her child. And she gave birth to her firstborn son and wrapped him in bands of cloth, and laid him in a manger, because there was no place for them in the inn. In that region there were shepherds living in the fields, keeping watch over their flock by night. Then an angel of the Lord stood before them, and the glory of the Lord shone around them, and they were terrified. But the angel said to them, "Do not be afraid; for see—I am bringing you good news of great joy for all the people: to you is born this day in the city of David a Savior, who is the Messiah, the Lord. This will be a sign for you: you will find a child wrapped in bands of cloth and lying in a manger." And

suddenly there was with the angel a multitude of the heavenly host, praising God and saying, "Glory to God in the highest heaven, and on earth peace among those whom he favors!"

- "And she gave birth to her first-born son." A normal, everyday event with ordinary people gathered together—but this birth in Bethlehem was one to shake the world. This baby is the Son of God, the Savior of the world.
- What is God doing here, among us? How do I care for this child in the manger?

Tuesday 26th December, St. Stephen the first martyr
Acts 6:8–10, 7:54–59

Stephen, full of grace and power, did great wonders and signs among the people. Then some of those who belonged to the synagogue of the Freedmen (as it was called), Cyrenians, Alexandrians, and others of those from Cilicia and Asia, stood up and argued with Stephen. But they could not withstand the wisdom and the Spirit with which he spoke. When they heard these things, they became enraged and ground their teeth at Stephen. But filled with the Holy Spirit, he gazed into heaven and saw the glory of God and Jesus standing at the right hand of God. "Look," he said, "I see the heavens opened and the Son of Man standing at the right hand of God!" But they covered their ears, and with a loud shout all rushed together against him. Then they dragged him out of the city and began to stone him; and the witnesses laid their coats at the feet of a young man named Saul. While they were stoning Stephen, he prayed, "Lord Jesus, receive my spirit." Then he knelt down and cried out in a loud voice, "Lord, do not hold this sin against them." When he had said this, he died.

- On the very day after Christmas we are invited to ponder the first martyrdom of a follower of Jesus.

- What does this event say about the meaning of Christmas? Is this the world that the Incarnate God is born into?
- How is Jesus present in the broken parts of my world?

Wednesday 27th December, St. John, Apostle and Evangelist
John 20:2–8

So Mary Magdalene ran and went to Simon Peter and the other disciple, the one whom Jesus loved, and said to them, "They have taken the Lord out of the tomb, and we do not know where they have laid him." Then Peter and the other disciple set out and went toward the tomb. The two were running together, but the other disciple outran Peter and reached the tomb first. He bent down to look in and saw the linen wrappings lying there, but he did not go in. Then Simon Peter came, following him, and went into the tomb. He saw the linen wrappings lying there, and the cloth that had been on Jesus' head, not lying with the linen wrappings but rolled up in a place by itself. Then the other disciple, who reached the tomb first, also went in, and he saw and believed.

- As we celebrate the feast of Jesus' birth, we acknowledge that Jesus' resurrection changes life. John saw and believed. I have not seen, but I live by that faith. Lord, for me as for John.
- The disciples "saw and believed"; can I allow myself to be drawn into the same response of faith?

Thursday 28th December, Feast of the Holy Innocents
Matthew 2:13–18

Now after the wise men had left, an angel of the Lord appeared to Joseph in a dream and said, "Get up, take the child and his mother, and flee to Egypt, and remain there until I tell you; for Herod is about to search for the child, to destroy him." Then Joseph got up, took the child and his mother by night, and went to Egypt, and remained there until the death of

Herod. This was to fulfill what had been spoken by the Lord through the prophet, "Out of Egypt I have called my son." When Herod saw that he had been tricked by the wise men, he was infuriated, and he sent and killed all the children in and around Bethlehem who were two years old or under, according to the time that he had learned from the wise men. Then was fulfilled what had been spoken through the prophet Jeremiah: "A voice was heard in Ramah, wailing and loud lamentation, Rachel weeping for her children; she refused to be consoled, because they are no more."

- The new-born Savior is intimately linked with the weakest and most vulnerable; God is biased towards the voiceless.
- But even the deaths of innocents at the hands of tyrants have a place in God's saving plan; each is precious in God's sight.
- Who are the voiceless innocents around me? How is the Christ related to them? How do I think of them?

Friday 29th December   Luke 2:25–32

Now there was a man in Jerusalem whose name was Simeon; this man was righteous and devout, looking forward to the consolation of Israel, and the Holy Spirit rested on him. It had been revealed to him by the Holy Spirit that he would not see death before he had seen the Lord's Messiah. Guided by the Spirit, Simeon came into the temple; and when the parents brought in the child Jesus, to do for him what was customary under the law, Simeon took him in his arms and praised God, saying, "Master, now you are dismissing your servant in peace, according to your word; for my eyes have seen your salvation, which you have prepared in the presence of all peoples, a light for revelation to the Gentiles and for glory to your people Israel."

- All his life, Simeon had been waiting and hoping. Now the Incarnate God lives! Now, filled with the Spirit, he utters his song of praise we call the Nunc Dimittis.
- What did Simeon see in this ordinary family's child? How did he see it? Do I see it?
- Can I join with Simeon in his song?

Saturday 30th December   Luke 2:36–40

There was also a prophet, Anna the daughter of Phanuel, of the tribe of Asher. She was of a great age, having lived with her husband seven years after her marriage, then as a widow to the age of eighty-four. She never left the temple but worshiped there with fasting and prayer night and day. At that moment she came, and began to praise God and to speak about the child to all who were looking for the redemption of Jerusalem. When they had finished everything required by the law of the Lord, they returned to Galilee, to their own town of Nazareth. The child grew and became strong, filled with wisdom; and the favor of God was upon him.

- Anna, a prophet in the Old Testament tradition like Simeon, recognizes that salvation has come in this child. Anna speaks up.
- What did Anna see in this ordinary family's child? How did she see it? Do I see it?

december 31 – january 6

Something to think and pray about each day this week:

Family living

Like every family, Jesus, Mary and Joseph were bonded by an unsentimental attachment that was strong enough to cope with the tensions of people living together. When Mary and Joseph lose 12-year-old Jesus in Jerusalem, and then hear him talking about "my father's business," we realize that there were tensions even here. Family life does not mean the absence of argument, but the ability to survive it.

The Presence of God
As I sit here, the beating of my heart,
the ebb and flow of my breathing, the movements of my mind
are all signs of God's ongoing creation of me.
I pause for a moment, and become aware
of this presence of God within me.

Freedom
I ask for the grace
to let go of my own concerns
and be open to what God is asking of me,
to let myself be guided and formed by my loving Creator.

Consciousness
In the presence of my loving Creator,
I look honestly at my feelings over the last day,
the highs, the lows and the level ground.
Can I see where the Lord has been present?

The Word
I take my time to read the Word of God, slowly, a few times,
allowing myself to dwell on anything that strikes me. (Please
turn to your scripture on the following pages. Inspiration points
are there should you need them. When you are ready, return
here to continue.)

Conversation
Remembering that I am still in God's presence,
I imagine Jesus himself standing or sitting beside me,
and say whatever is on my mind, whatever is in my heart,
speaking as one friend to another.

Conclusion
Glory be to the Father, and to the Son, and to the Holy Spirit,
As it was in the beginning, is now and ever shall be,
World without end. Amen

Sunday 31st December, Holy Family Luke 2:41–52

Now every year his parents went to Jerusalem for the festival of the Passover. And when he was twelve years old, they went up as usual for the festival. When the festival was ended and they started to return, the boy Jesus stayed behind in Jerusalem, but his parents did not know it. Assuming that he was in the group of travelers, they went a day's journey. Then they started to look for him among their relatives and friends. When they did not find him, they returned to Jerusalem to search for him. After three days they found him in the temple, sitting among the teachers, listening to them and asking them questions. And all who heard him were amazed at his understanding and his answers. When his parents saw him they were astonished; and his mother said to him, "Child, why have you treated us like this? Look, your father and I have been searching for you in great anxiety." He said to them, "Why were you searching for me? Did you not know that I must be in my Father's house?" But they did not understand what he said to them. Then he went down with them and came to Nazareth, and was obedient to them. His mother treasured all these things in her heart. And Jesus increased in wisdom and in years, and in divine and human favor.

- It would be good to spend some time watching events unfold in this scene and the tension and confusion that transpires.
- At the heart of the misunderstanding was the special relationship that the boy Jesus had with the One he called his Father. Even at the end Mary and Joseph couldn't fully grasp it all.
- How am I moved by this scene? Frustrated? Angered? Touched? Hopeful?

Monday 1st January, Solemnity of Mary, Mother of God
Luke 2:16–21

So they went with haste and found Mary and Joseph, and the child lying in the manger. When they saw this, they made known what had been told them about this child; and all who heard it were amazed at what the shepherds told them. But Mary treasured all these words and pondered them in her heart. The shepherds returned, glorifying and praising God for all they had heard and seen, as it had been told them. After eight days had passed, it was time to circumcise the child; and he was called Jesus, the name given by the angel before he was conceived in the womb.

- We start this year, as we start our life, under the protection of a mother. Mary is mother of God—it took the Christian church three hundred years to become clear about this—and our mother too.
- Do I speak often with my mother Mary? About her son? About myself?

Tuesday 2nd January
John 1:19–28

This is the testimony given by John when the Jews sent priests and Levites from Jerusalem to ask him, "Who are you?" He confessed and did not deny it, but confessed, "I am not the Messiah." And they asked him, "What then? Are you Elijah?" He said, "I am not." "Are you the prophet?" He answered, "No." Then they said to him, "Who are you? Let us have an answer for those who sent us. What do you say about yourself?" He said, "I am the voice of one crying out in the wilderness, 'Make straight the way of the Lord,'" as the prophet Isaiah said. Now they had been sent from the Pharisees. They asked him, "Why then are you baptizing if you are neither the Messiah, nor Elijah, nor the prophet?" John answered them, "I baptize with water. Among you stands one whom you do not know, the one who is coming after me; I am not worthy to untie

42

the thong of his sandal." This took place in Bethany across the Jordan where John was baptizing.

- John the Baptist has appeared on the scene. Can I imagine myself as one of those sent by the Pharisees to find out who he is and what is going on?
- What do I find?

Wednesday 3rd January   1 John 2:29–3:6

If you know that God is righteous, you may be sure that every-one who does right if born of him. See what love the Father has given us, that we should be called children of God; and so we are. The reason why the world does not know us is that it did not know him. Beloved, we are God's children now; it does not yet appear what we shall be, but we know that when he appears we shall be like him, for we shall see him as he is. And everyone who thus hopes in him purifies himself as he is pure. Every one who commits sit is guilty of lawlessness; sin is lawlessness. You know that he appeared to take away sins, and in him there is no sin. No one who abides in him sins; no one who sins has either seen him or known him.

- Moses was clear that no one can see God and live, so John is writing about a change in us, a new life. In that new life "we shall see God as he is." We shall be lifted into the likeness of God, a state which we cannot imagine, one which fulfills all our desires.
- Can I ask the Lord to work with me to keep that vision of my destiny always before me?

Thursday 4th January   John 1:35–42

The next day John again was standing with two of his disci-ples, and as he watched Jesus walk by, he exclaimed, "Look, here is the Lamb of God!" The two disciples heard him say this, and they followed Jesus. When Jesus turned and saw them fol-lowing, he said to them, "What are you looking for?" They said to him, "Rabbi" (which translated means Teacher), "where are you staying?" He said to them, "Come and see." They came and saw where he was staying, and they remained with him that day. It was about four o'clock in the afternoon. One of the two who heard John speak and followed him was Andrew, Simon Peter's brother. He first found his brother Simon and said to him, "We have found the Messiah" (which is translated Anointed). He brought Simon to Jesus, who looked at him and said, "You are Simon son of John. You are to be called Cephas" (which is translated Peter).

- John the Baptist, who had an immense following in Jerusalem, does something remarkable here. He points his followers towards Jesus, the Lamb of God. They walk away from John and follow Jesus, with John's blessing.
- John was not the light, but came to bear witness to the light. How do I point the way towards Jesus? Or does my ego block the way?

Friday 5th January   1 John 3:11–21

"Very truly, I tell you, we speak of what we know and testify to what we have seen; yet you do not receive our testimony. If I have told you about earthly things and you do not believe, how can you believe if I tell you about heavenly things? No one has ascended into heaven except the one who descended from heaven, the Son of Man. And just as Moses lifted up the serpent in the wilderness, so must the Son of Man be lifted up, that whoever believes in him may have eternal life. "For God so loved the world that he gave his only Son, so that everyone who believes in him may not perish but may have eternal life. "Indeed, God did not send the Son into the world to condemn the world, but in order that the world might be saved through him. Those who believe in him are not condemned; but those who do not believe are condemned already, because they have not believed in the name of the only Son of God. And this is the judgment, that the light has come into the world, and people loved darkness rather than light because their deeds were evil. For all who do evil hate the light and do not come to the light, so that their deeds may not be exposed. But those who do what is true come to the light, so that it may be clearly seen that their deeds have been done in God."

- In St. John's letters there are precious nuggets, simple truths that stay with us. If any one has the world's goods and sees his brother in need, yet closes his heart against him, how does God's love abide in him? Let us not love in word or speech, but in deed and truth.
- Can I be choosey about my love language? It is my behavior that reveals my heart.

Saturday 6th January, The Epiphany of the Lord
Matthew 2:1–12

In the time of King Herod, after Jesus was born in Bethlehem of Judea, wise men from the East came to Jerusalem, asking, "Where is the child who has been born king of the Jews? For we observed his star at its rising, and have come to pay him homage." When King Herod heard this, he was frightened, and all Jerusalem with him; and calling together all the chief priests and scribes of the people, he inquired of them where the Messiah was to be born. They told him, "In Bethlehem of Judea; for so it has been written by the prophet: 'And you, Bethlehem, in the land of Judah, are by no means least among the rulers of Judah; for from you shall come a ruler who is to shepherd my people Israel.'" Then Herod secretly called for the wise men and learned from them the exact time when the star had appeared. Then he sent them to Bethlehem, saying, "Go and search diligently for the child; and when you have found him, bring me word so that I may also go and pay him homage." When they had heard the king, they set out; and there, ahead of them, went the star that they had seen at its rising, until it stopped over the place where the child was. When they saw that the star had stopped, they were overwhelmed with joy. On entering the house, they saw the child with Mary his mother; and they knelt down and paid him homage. Then, opening their treasure chests, they offered him gifts of gold, frankincense, and myrrh. And having been warned in a dream not to return to Herod, they left for their own country by another road.

- Epiphany means the showing of God to all nations. The Magi follow a star. They are not deterred by the evil scheming of Herod; like many good people they seem hardly to perceive his wickedness, but make good use of the information he offers. They bring gifts; the gold of Gaspar, the myrrh of Melchior, the frankincense of Balthasar. And in the Christian tradition they symbolize all nations, and every race.

  There were three kings, and O what a sight!
  One was yellow and one was white,
  And one was black as Epiphany night
  On Christmas day in the morning.

- Can I keep my eyes on your star Lord, to sustain my hope in a world that is sometimes indifferent or evil? Sacred Space is a new epiphany, showing you to the nations.

Something to think and pray about each day this week:

Longing for the light

John the Baptist said of Jesus: "He must increase and I must decrease." The church's calendar reflects the northern hemisphere: From the date of Christ's birthday the days gradually lengthen, whereas from John the Baptist's feast on 24th June they start to shorten. Of course, the opposite applies in the Antipodes.

At this time of the year, people of northern lands long for light through the dark winter. These mornings as the sky brightens the nearby hills or water, it is more than just daylight; it is the return of the sun, lengthening the days, promising spring and summer. It is a grace.

When we read at the start of the Fourth Gospel, "We saw his glory," there is a hint of the shekinah, the glory of the Lord within the cloud that covered Sinai (Exodus 24:16). No one could see that light and live. But when Jesus came, we saw God's glory in the face of Jesus.

Many of those who have come close to death remember reaching across the bridge towards God's presence, and seeing it as a warm light that gave not merely brightness but joy. Lord, may we see your glory.

The Presence of God
I pause for a moment
and reflect on God's life-giving presence
in every part of my body, in everything around me,
in the whole of my life.

Freedom
I ask for the grace to believe
in what I could be and do
if I only allowed God, my loving Creator,
to continue to create me, guide me and shape me.

Consciousness
Knowing that God loves me unconditionally,
I look honestly over the last day, its events and my feelings.
Do I have something to be grateful for? Then I give thanks.
Is there something I am sorry for? Then I ask forgiveness.

The Word
God speaks to each one of us individually. I need to listen to
hear what he is saying to me. Read the text a few times, then listen. (Please turn to your scripture on the following pages. Inspiration points are there should you need them. When you are
ready, return here to continue.)

Conversation
How has God's Word moved me? Has it left me cold?
Has it consoled me or moved me to act in a new way?
I imagine Jesus standing or sitting beside me,
I turn and share my feelings with him.

Conclusion
Glory be to the Father, and to the Son, and to the Holy Spirit,
As it was in the beginning, is now and ever shall be,
World without end. Amen

Sunday 7th January, The Baptism of the Lord
Luke 3:15–16, 21–22

As the people were filled with expectation, and all were questioning in their hearts concerning John, whether he might be the Messiah, John answered all of them by saying, "I baptize you with water; but one who is more powerful than I is coming; I am not worthy to untie the thong of his sandals. He will baptize you with the Holy Spirit and fire." Now when all the people were baptized, and when Jesus also had been baptized and was praying, the heaven was opened, and the Holy Spirit descended upon him in bodily form like a dove. And a voice came from heaven, "You are my Son, the Beloved; with you I am well pleased."

• Let me spend some time looking at this scene. As he stands in, or near the river after baptism by John, something extraordinary happens to Jesus.
• Here is a little glimpse of the inner life of the Trinity.
• How do I feel as I observe this scene? Do I feel drawn towards these Persons? Am I standing to the side, hesitant and distant? What is the Lord saying to me?

Monday 8th January
Mark 1:14–20

Now after John was arrested, Jesus came to Galilee, proclaiming the good news of God, and saying, "The time is fulfilled, and the kingdom of God has come near; repent, and believe in the good news." As Jesus passed along the Sea of Galilee, he saw Simon and his brother Andrew casting a net into the sea—for they were fishermen. And Jesus said to them, "Follow me and I will make you fish for people." And immediately they left their nets and followed him. As he went a little farther, he saw James son of Zebedee and his brother John, who were in their boat mending the nets. Immediately he called them; and they left their father Zebedee in the boat with the hired men, and followed him.

- "They were fishermen." Fishing was a major industry in Galilee. Simon and Andrew owned nets and employed others; they left behind a thriving and secure business to follow Jesus. They had no special training to draw on; the compelling person and call of Jesus were all they needed.
- The Lord says to me: "Follow me." Can I see Jesus as the human face of God, and look to no other leader with confidence? Show me your spirit, Lord, as I turn to you in prayer.

Tuesday 9th January   Hebrews 2:5–12

Now God did not subject the coming world, about which we are speaking, to angels. But someone has testified somewhere, "What are human beings that you are mindful of them, or mortals, that you care for them? You have made them for a little while lower than the angels; you have crowned them with glory and honor, subjecting all things under their feet." Now in subjecting all things to them, God left nothing outside their control. As it is, we do not yet see everything in subjection to them, but we do see Jesus, who for a little while was made lower than the angels, now crowned with glory and honor because of the suffering of death, so that by the grace of God he might taste death for everyone. It was fitting that God, for whom and through whom all things exist, in bringing many children to glory, should make the pioneer of their salvation perfect through sufferings. For the one who sanctifies and those who are sanctified all have one Father. For this reason Jesus is not ashamed to call them brothers and sisters, saying, "I will proclaim your name to my brothers and sisters, in the midst of the congregation I will praise you."

- "He might taste death for everyone." Jesus faced the same battles with evil as faced throughout history. God was to make the pioneer of our salvation perfect through suffering. If you had not suffered and died, Lord, I could not believe in your humanity.

• I know you now as my brother, who would submit to learning this taste of salt at the bottom of our mouths when the whole world abandons us.

Wednesday 10th January   Mark 1:29–35

As soon as they left the synagogue, they entered the house of Simon and Andrew, with James and John. Now Simon's mother-in-law was in bed with a fever, and they told him about her at once. He came and took her by the hand and lifted her up. Then the fever left her, and she began to serve them. That evening, at sundown, they brought to him all who were sick or possessed with demons. And the whole city was gathered around the door. And he cured many who were sick with various diseases, and cast out many demons; and he would not permit the demons to speak, because they knew him. In the morning, while it was still very dark, Jesus got up and went out to a deserted place, and there he prayed.

• It is intriguing to think of Peter as married, giving a home to his wife's mother, and probably (according to an early tradition), the father of children. The story gives us a fresh perspective on the first leader of the church.

• "Jesus went out to a deserted place, and there he prayed." Can I have the same taste for prayer, for recovering my strength by turning to God?

Thursday 11th January   Mark 1:40–45

A leper came to Jesus and, kneeling, he begged him, "If you choose, you can make me clean." Moved with pity, Jesus stretched out his hand and touched him, and said to him, "I do choose. Be made clean!" Immediately the leprosy left him, and he was made clean. After sternly warning him he sent him away at once, saying to him, "See that you say nothing to anyone; but go, show yourself to the priest, and offer for your cleansing what Moses commanded, as a testimony to them." But he went out and began to proclaim it freely, and to spread the word, so that Jesus could no longer go into a town openly, but stayed out in the country; and people came to him from every quarter.

- Leprosy in the Bible was not precisely what we mean by the term, but was a general name for any repulsive, scaly, skin disease. Jesus' action, stretching out to touch the man, shows a deep, gut-wrenching compassion.
- Can I learn your touch, Lord? Can you touch the ugly bits of me that I do not like to look at. "If you will, you can make me clean."

Friday 12th January   Mark 2:1–5

When Jesus returned to Capernaum after some days, it was reported that he was at home. So many gathered around that there was no longer room for them, not even in front of the door; and he was speaking the word to them. Then some people came, bringing to him a paralyzed man, carried by four of them. And when they could not bring him to Jesus because of the crowd, they removed the roof above him; and after having dug through it, they let down the mat on which the paralytic lay. When Jesus saw their faith, he said to the paralytic, "Son, your sins are forgiven."

- Those in the crowd who looked up and saw the paralytic lowered through the roof by his friends, saw a man they believed was suffering for his personal sins. Jesus, fatherly response was to their strong and public faith—"Son, your sins were forgiven."
- Can I ask for help to identify and name my own anguish, my inner paralysis, my physical limitations, and put it before the Lord? Lord, I sometimes don't notice the paralysis within me. Teach me to walk tall.

Saturday 13th January   **Hebrews 4:12–16**

Indeed, the word of God is living and active, sharper than any two-edged sword, piercing until it divides soul from spirit, joints from marrow; it is able to judge the thoughts and intentions of the heart. And before him no creature is hidden, but all are naked and laid bare to the eyes of the one to whom we must render an account. Since, then, we have a great high priest who has passed through the heavens, Jesus, the Son of God, let us hold fast to our confession. For we do not have a high priest who is unable to sympathize with our weaknesses, but we have one who in every respect has been tested as we are, yet without sin. Let us therefore approach the throne of grace with boldness, so that we may receive mercy and find grace to help in time of need.

- "The word of God is living and active . . .; it is able to judge the thoughts and intentions of the heart." Much of what we say and what we hear in the day does not bear a second thought. It is cast aside but the Scriptures are different. God's word is meaty and powerful, pushing us to look at ourselves.
- Sow freely, Lord God, the seed of your word over the world. May it fall in good soil in us, and may it be heard wherever people live.

Something to think and pray about each day this week:

A people on the way
In these early weeks of the year the scripture readings open our minds to see that God's saving plan is universal: "The Lamb of God who takes away the sins of the world. That my salvation may reach to the ends of the earth."

Heavenly father, we are your church, a people on the way. We have a history, a long past of darkness and of light. Give us now, we pray you, a new future, and call us away from the certainties, the riches of this world in which we shelter, safely captive. Rather make us poor and insecure, displaced and free, so that we may once more hear your Gospel and follow your son.

Help us, Lord, to reach out to one another, and to remember that Christ is our peace, and that he has broken down the barriers that divide us.

The Presence of God
The world is charged with the grandeur of God (Gerard Manley Hopkins).
I dwell for a moment on the presence of God
around me, in every part of my body,
and deep within my being.

Freedom
"In these days, God taught me
as a schoolteacher teaches a pupil" (St. Ignatius).
I remind myself that there are things God has to teach me yet,
and ask for the grace to hear them and let them change me.

Consciousness
How do I find myself today?
Where am I with God? With others?
Do I have something to be grateful for? Then I give thanks.
Is there something I am sorry for? Then I ask forgiveness.

The Word
I read the Word of God slowly, a few times over, and I listen to what God is saying to me. (Please turn to your scripture on the following pages. Inspiration points are there should you need them. When you are ready, return here to continue.)

Conversation
What feelings are rising in me
as I pry and reflect on God's Word?
I imagine Jesus himself sitting or standing near me
and open my heart to him.

Conclusion
Glory be to the Father, and to the Son, and to the Holy Spirit,
As it was in the beginning, is now and ever shall be,
World without end. Amen

Sunday 14th January, Second Sunday in Ordinary Time
John 2:1–11

On the third day there was a wedding in Cana of Galilee, and the mother of Jesus was there. Jesus and his disciples had also been invited to the wedding. When the wine gave out, the mother of Jesus said to him, "They have no wine." And Jesus said to her, "Woman, what concern is that to you and to me? My hour has not yet come." His mother said to the servants, "Do whatever he tells you." Now standing there were six stone water jars for the Jewish rites of purification, each holding twenty or thirty gallons. Jesus said to them, "Fill the jars with water." And they filled them up to the brim. He said to them, "Now draw some out, and take it to the chief steward." So they took it. When the steward tasted the water that had become wine, and did not know where it came from (though the servants who had drawn the water knew), the steward called the bridegroom and said to him, "Everyone serves the good wine first, and then the inferior wine after the guests have become drunk. But you have kept the good wine until now." Jesus did this, the first of his signs, in Cana of Galilee, and revealed his glory.

- The Gospel writer tells us that this was the first of Jesus' "signs." He means that in this story we have clear pointers to the presence of God in Jesus.
- What happened? What did Jesus do? What are the qualities of this God/man?
- How does he move me?

Monday 15th January   Hebrews 5:1–10

Every high priest chosen from among mortals is put in charge of things pertaining to God on their behalf, to offer gifts and sacrifices for sins. He is able to deal gently with the ignorant and wayward, since he himself is subject to weakness; and because of this he must offer sacrifice for his own sins as well as for those of the people. And one does not presume to take this honor, but takes it only when called by God, just as Aaron was. So also Christ did not glorify himself in becoming a high priest, but was appointed by the one who said to him, "You are my Son, today I have begotten you"; as he says also in another place, "You are a priest forever, according to the order of Melchizedek." In the days of his flesh, Jesus offered up prayers and supplications, with loud cries and tears, to the one who was able to save him from death, and he was heard because of his reverent submission. Although he was a Son, he learned obedience through what he suffered; and having been made perfect, he became the source of eternal salvation for all who obey him, having been designated by God a high priest according to the order of Melchizedek.

- "Although he was a Son, he learned obedience by what he suffered." This is not a popular view. We don't like to be lectured on obedience. But it is the lot we were born for—in families, in business, in social structures, and in the laws of nature.
- Jesus in his humanity accepted not merely the authority of his parents, but suffering and death, the ultimate obedience. How does obedience affect me? How am I am coping with it?

Tuesday 16th January   Mark 2:23–28

One sabbath Jesus was going through the grainfields; and as they made their way his disciples began to pluck heads of grain. The Pharisees said to him, "Look, why are they doing what is not lawful on the sabbath?" And he said to them, "Have you never read what David did when he and his companions were hungry and in need of food? He entered the house of God, when Abiathar was high priest, and ate the bread of the Presence, which it is not lawful for any but the priests to eat, and he gave some to his companions." Then he said to them, "The sabbath was made for humankind, and not humankind for the sabbath; so the Son of Man is lord even of the sabbath."

- "The Sabbath was made for humankind." Whenever blind authoritarianism confronts common sense, this word of Jesus holds us. It is not easy to apply, and the Pharisees thought it revolutionary. They had extended the two great commandments—"love God, and love your neighbor"—into 612 regulations, a spider's web of constraints that stunted the spirit.
- You do not call me to a soft or uncontrolled existence, but to the law of love, which should suffuse my life. How am I responding?

Wednesday 17th January   Hebrews 7:1–3, 15–17

You remember that "King Melchizedek of Salem, priest of the Most High God, met Abraham as he was returning from defeating the kings and blessed him"; and to him Abraham apportioned "one-tenth of everything." His name, in the first place, means "king of righteousness"; next he is also king of Salem, that is, "king of peace." Without father, without mother, without genealogy, having neither beginning of days nor end of life, but resembling the Son of God, he remains a priest forever. It is even more obvious when another priest arises, resembling Melchizedek, one who has become a priest, not through a legal requirement concerning physical descent, but through the power of an indestructible life. For it is attested of him, "You are a priest forever, according to the order of Melchizedek."

- "A priest forever." Today's text prompts us to pray for the thousands who were ordained "a priest forever," but who for some reason have given up their ministry.
- Priesthood remains with them as an unforgotten but unfulfilled potential, perhaps a source of suffering. How do I regard those who have left their ministry?

Thursday 18th January   Mark 3:7–12

Jesus departed with his disciples to the sea, and a great multitude from Galilee followed him; hearing all that he was doing, they came to him in great numbers from Judea, Jerusalem, Idumea, beyond the Jordan, and the region around Tyre and Sidon. He told his disciples to have a boat ready for him because of the crowd, so that they would not crush him; for he had cured many, so that all who had diseases pressed upon him to touch him. Whenever the unclean spirits saw him, they fell down before him and shouted, "You are the Son of God!" But he sternly ordered them not to make him known.

- "He ordered them not to make him known." Since the prevailing idea of the Messiah was nationalistic and warlike, Jesus avoided giving a false and dangerous impression of his mission. This is often called "the Messianic secret."
- The unclean spirits recognized him as the Son of God, and so do I. The secret is out; I can spread the word.

Friday 19th January   Hebrews 8:6–13

But Jesus has now obtained a more excellent ministry, and to that degree he is the mediator of a better covenant, which has been enacted through better promises. For if that first covenant had been faultless, there would have been no need to look for a second one. God finds fault with them when he says: "The days are surely coming, says the Lord, when I will establish a new covenant with the house of Israel and with the house of Judah; not like the covenant that I made with their ancestors, on the day when I took them by the hand to lead them out of the land of Egypt; for they did not continue in my covenant, and so I had no concern for them, says the Lord. This is the covenant that I will make with the house of Israel after those days, says the Lord: I will put my laws in their minds, and write them on their hearts, and I will be their God, and they shall be my people. And they shall not teach one another or say to each other, 'Know the Lord,' for they shall all know me, from the least of them to the greatest. For I will be merciful toward their iniquities, and I will remember their sins no more." In speaking of "a new covenant," he has made the first one obsolete. And what is obsolete and growing old will soon disappear.

- "I will put my laws into their minds, and write them on their hearts, and I will be their God and they shall be my people." Conscience, God's voice in my heart and mind, is my first guide on how to behave, but it is easily shouted down.
- Many voices, including my passions and prejudices, conspire to distort my judgment. I need to stay alert to your voice, Lord. Lead me to quiet and to prayer every day,

Saturday 20th January   **Mark 3:20–21**

Then Jesus went home; and the crowd came together again, so that they could not even eat. When his family heard it, they went out to restrain him, for people were saying, "He has gone out of his mind."

- They said: "He is out of his mind." There was a melee round Jesus that embarrassed his relatives. They felt he was making a show of them, and wanted to take control of him.
- Have there been times in my life when I was causing myself, my family or friends embarrassment, disapproval or concern? How uncomfortable did I feel? Was I confused or even infuriated? Even then, you have been there with me Lord.

Something to think and pray about each day this week:

People of light
"The people who walked in darkness have seen a great light." We are challenged to lift our minds beyond the buildings, bureaucracies and hierarchies that we have created in the Lord's name. Open our eyes to a vision of you as the savior of all people.

We pray for all whose work it is to preach the gospel and to lead in prayer. May they never force you on people, or wrongly use your name. Help us to remember, Father, that we were sent only to spread your grace in all humility, because we have been accepted by you, and always need forgiveness.

The Presence of God

As I sit here, God is present,
breathing life into me and into everything around me.
For a few moments, I sit silently,
and become aware of God's loving presence.

Freedom

If God were trying to tell me something, would I know?
If God were reassuring me or challenging me, would I notice?
I ask for the grace to be free of my own preoccupations
and open to what God may be saying to me.

Consciousness

In God's loving presence I unwind the past day,
starting from now and looking back, moment by moment.
I gather in all the goodness and light, in gratitude.
I attend to the shadows and what they say to me,
seeking healing, courage, forgiveness.

The Word

I take my time to read the Word of God, slowly, a few times, allowing myself to dwell on anything that strikes me. (Please turn to your scripture on the following pages. Inspiration points are there should you need them. When you are ready, return here to continue.)

Conversation

What is stirring in me as I pray?
Am I consoled, troubled, left cold?
I imagine Jesus himself standing or sitting at my side,
and share my feelings with him.

Conclusion

Glory be to the Father, and to the Son, and to the Holy Spirit,
As it was in the beginning, is now and ever shall be,
World without end. Amen

Sunday 21st January, Third Sunday in Ordinary Time
Luke 4:14–21

Then Jesus, filled with the power of the Spirit, returned to Galilee, and a report about him spread through all the surrounding country. He began to teach in their synagogues and was praised by everyone. When he came to Nazareth, where he had been brought up, he went to the synagogue on the sabbath day, as was his custom. He stood up to read, and the scroll of the prophet Isaiah was given to him. He unrolled the scroll and found the place where it was written: "The Spirit of the Lord is upon me, because he has anointed me to bring good news to the poor. He has sent me to proclaim release to the captives and recovery of sight to the blind, to let the oppressed go free, to proclaim the year of the Lord's favor." And he rolled up the scroll, gave it back to the attendant, and sat down. The eyes of all in the synagogue were fixed on him. Then he began to say to them, "Today this scripture has been fulfilled in your hearing."

- Using my imagination, I can take my place in the synagogue. (Am I sitting near the front or the back or, perhaps, on the balcony?)
- I see Jesus stand up and go to the front, all eyes following him . . . What do I see? What do I hear?
- How do I feel? Threatened? Challenged? Consoled?
- Can I now open my heart to the Lord.

Monday 22nd January
Mark 3:22–30

And the scribes who came down from Jerusalem said, "He has Beelzebul, and by the ruler of the demons he casts out demons." And he called them to him, and spoke to them in parables, "How can Satan cast out Satan? If a kingdom is divided against itself, that kingdom cannot stand. And if a house is divided against itself, that house will not be able to stand. And if Satan has risen up against himself and is divided, he cannot stand, but his end has come. But no one can enter a strong man's house and plunder his property without first tying up the strong man; then indeed the house can be plundered. "Truly I tell you, people will be forgiven for their sins and whatever blasphemies they utter; but whoever blasphemes against the Holy Spirit can never have forgiveness, but is guilty of an eternal sin"—for they had said, "He has an unclean spirit."

- It was a blasphemy in bad faith, a gross sin, to do what the scribes did: attribute the work of the Holy Spirit (i.e. Jesus' healing miracles) to the power of Satan.
- But Jesus is remarkable: "All sins will be forgiven, all blasphemies." Even when our hearts condemn us, when we feel deep-dyed in guilt for actions that shame us, God does not condemn us. He always sees us as his children.

Tuesday 23rd January   Mark 3:31–35

Then the mother and brothers of Jesus came; and standing outside, they sent to him and called him. A crowd was sitting around him; and they said to him, "Your mother and your brothers and sisters are outside, asking for you." And he replied, "Who are my mother and my brothers?" And looking at those who sat around him, he said, "Here are my mother and my brothers! Whoever does the will of God is my brother and sister and mother."

- Jesus tells us that his own mother has an even more important relationship than the physical—it is their spiritual relationship founded on doing God's will.
- Do I find it hard to know what God's will is for me; do I avoid the question? Is this a solo task or can I use my community for support here?

Wednesday 24th January   Mark 4:1–12

Again he began to teach beside the sea. Such a very large crowd gathered around him that he got into a boat on the sea and sat there, while the whole crowd was beside the sea on the land. He began to teach them many things in parables, and in his teaching he said to them: "Listen! A sower went out to sow. And as he sowed, some seed fell on the path, and the birds came and ate it up. Other seed fell on rocky ground, where it did not have much soil, and it sprang up quickly, since it had no depth of soil. And when the sun rose, it was scorched; and since it had no root, it withered away. Other seed fell among thorns, and the thorns grew up and choked it, and it yielded no grain. Other seed fell into good soil and brought forth grain, growing up and increasing and yielding thirty and sixty and a hundred-fold." And he said, "Let anyone with ears to hear listen!" When he was alone, those who were around him along with the twelve asked him about the parables. And he said to them, "To you has been given the secret of the kingdom of God, but for those outside, everything comes in parables; in order that 'they may indeed look, but not perceive, and may indeed listen, but not understand; so that they may not turn again and be forgiven.'"

- If your word is like a seed, Lord, then it is an organism, with a life of its own. How do I receive the word? Do I give it roots and depth so that it can survive hardships; do I protect it from the thorns of busy-ness and indifference?
- Do I allow your word ever more space in my life, pushing back my limits so it may bear fruit?

Thursday 25th January, Conversion of St. Paul
Acts 22:3–16

Paul said: "I am a Jew, born in Tarsus in Cilicia, but brought up in this city at the feet of Gamaliel, educated strictly according to our ancestral law, being zealous for God, just as all of you are today. I persecuted this Way up to the point of death by binding both men and women and putting them in prison, as the high priest and the whole council of elders can testify about me. From them I also received letters to the brothers in

Damascus, and I went there in order to bind those who were there and to bring them back to Jerusalem for punishment. While I was on my way and approaching Damascus, about noon a great light from heaven suddenly shone about me. I fell to the ground and heard a voice saying to me, 'Saul, Saul, why are you persecuting me?' I answered, 'Who are you, Lord?' Then he said to me, 'I am Jesus of Nazareth whom you are persecuting.' Now those who were with me saw the light but did not hear the voice of the one who was speaking to me. I asked, 'What am I to do, Lord?' The Lord said to me, 'Get up and go to Damascus; there you will be told everything that has been assigned to you to do.' Since I could not see because of the brightness of that light, those who were with me took my hand and led me to Damascus. A certain Ananias, who was a devout man according to the law and well spoken of by all the Jews living there, came to me; and standing beside me, he said, 'Brother Saul, regain your sight!' In that very hour I regained my sight and saw him. Then he said, 'The God of our ancestors has chosen you to know his will, to see the Righteous One and to hear his own voice; for you will be his witness to all the world of what you have seen and heard. And now why do you delay? Get up, be baptized, and have your sins washed away, calling on his name.'"

- Paul's conversion is full of drama, a radical movement towards the Way he persecuted. Now he is beyond fear, he is who he is in God's eyes—nothing more, nothing less. Now he has no need to impress others with his fervor for the Law.
- In Christ I don't need my false self. Does my baptism mean I have "died" as Paul did? Or do I yearn for an easier way?

Friday 26th January   Mark 4:26–34

Jesus said to the crowd, "The kingdom of God is as if someone would scatter seed on the ground, and would sleep and rise night and day, and the seed would sprout and grow, he does not know how. The earth produces of itself, first the stalk, then the head, then the full grain in the head. But when the grain is ripe, at once he goes in with his sickle, because the harvest has come." He also said, "With what can we compare the kingdom of God, or what parable will we use for it? It is like a mustard seed, which, when sown upon the ground, is the smallest of all the seeds on earth; yet when it is sown it grows up and becomes the greatest of all shrubs, and puts forth large branches, so that the birds of the air can make nests in its shade." With many such parables he spoke the word to them, as they were able to hear it; he did not speak to them except in parables, but he explained everything in private to his disciples.

- Jesus thinks and speaks in parables, using everyday images from the world around him. He reaches especially for symbols of life and growth. From a tiny seed grows a mighty tree. From Mary, the twelve apostles and the holy women has grown a church of every color and culture.
- We are not uniform or cloned—all sorts of birds can make nests in our shade—but united in our recognition of Jesus as the revelation and Son of God.

Saturday 27th January　　　　**Hebrews 11:1–2, 8–12, 17–19**

Now faith is the assurance of things hoped for, the conviction of things not seen. Indeed, by faith our ancestors received approval. By faith Abraham obeyed when he was called to set out for a place that he was to receive as an inheritance; and he set out, not knowing where he was going. By faith he stayed for a time in the land he had been promised, as in a foreign land, living in tents, as did Isaac and Jacob, who were heirs with him of the same promise. For he looked forward to the city that has foundations, whose architect and builder is God. By faith he received power of procreation, even though he was too old— and Sarah herself was barren—because he considered him faithful who had promised. Therefore from one person, and this one as good as dead, descendants were born, "as many as the stars of heaven and as the innumerable grains of sand by the seashore." By faith Abraham, when put to the test, offered up Isaac. He who had received the promises was ready to offer up his only son, of whom he had been told, "It is through Isaac that descendants shall be named for you." He considered the fact that God is able even to raise someone from the dead—and figuratively speaking, he did receive him back.

- Can I tap into the spirit of Abraham, sojourning in the land of promise, and looking forward to the city which has foundations, whose builder and maker is God.
- How strong is my desire for a better city, a better country, designed and made by God? How do faith and hope live in me?

Something to think and pray about each day this week:

Becoming little ones

When Jesus speaks about care for 'the little ones', he includes in their number his own followers. In many parts of the world the church is indeed a little presence, inconspicuous and barely noticed. In other places it has great power, wealth and status.

Jesus does not want his missionaries, including the bishops and Pope, to be overly concerned at being treated with honor and respect. They are, and must see themselves, as 'little ones'. Do I have misgivings about this? Do I feel the church should aim to be a strong presence and a power-broker, able to have its way in public matters? How does that square with Jesus' words about our being a leaven in the world, germinating quietly while remaining true to our own flavor, like salt that keeps its savor?

This is not a simple matter. We want to profess the Lord before people, and make our voice heard. But when we strive for a public voice the way advertisers do, we risk compromising the word, and adapting to values other than Christ's. Guide me, Lord, in this difficult balance between being the light of the world and the unseen leaven.

The Presence of God
As I sit here with my book, God is here.
Around me, in my sensations, in my thoughts and deep within me.
I pause for a moment, and become aware
of God's life-giving presence.

Freedom
I need to close out the noise, to rise above the noise;
The noise that interrupts, that separates,
The noise that isolates.
I need to listen to God again.

Consciousness
I exist in a web of relationships—links to nature, people, God.
I trace out these links, giving thanks for the life that flows
through them.
Some links are twisted or broken: I may feel regret, anger, disappointment.
I pray for the gift of acceptance and forgiveness.

The Word
God speaks to each one of us individually. I need to listen to
what he is saying to me. (Please turn to your scripture on the following
pages. Inspiration points are there should you need
them. When you are ready, return here to continue.)

Conversation
Do I notice myself reacting as I pray with the Word of God?
Do I feel challenged, comforted, angry?
Imagining Jesus sitting or standing by me,
I speak out my feelings, as one trusted friend to another.

Conclusion
Glory be to the Father, and to the Son, and to the Holy Spirit,
As it was in the beginning, is now and ever shall be,
World without end. Amen

Sunday 28th January, Fourth Sunday in Ordinary Time
Luke 4:21–30

Then Jesus began to say to the crowd in the synagogue, "Today this scripture has been fulfilled in your hearing." All spoke well of him and were amazed at the gracious words that came from his mouth. They said, "Is not this Joseph's son?" He said to them, "Doubtless you will quote to me this proverb, 'Doctor, cure yourself!' And you will say, 'Do here also in your hometown the things that we have heard you did at Capernaum.'" And he said, "Truly I tell you, no prophet is accepted in the prophet's hometown. But the truth is, there were many widows in Israel in the time of Elijah, when the heaven was shut up three years and six months, and there was a severe famine over all the land; yet Elijah was sent to none of them except to a widow at Zarephath in Sidon. There were also many lepers in Israel in the time of the prophet Elisha, and none of them was cleansed except Naaman the Syrian." When they heard this, all in the synagogue were filled with rage. They got up, drove him out of the town, and led him to the brow of the hill on which their town was built, so that they might hurl him off the cliff. But he passed through the midst of them and went on his way.

- We are in the synagogue in Jesus' home town. He makes a huge impression on his local congregation—a fresh young rabbi. Then he challenges them in a way that questions narrow parochial attitudes . . .
- Warmth and welcome turns quickly to resentment and rejection.
- Is there something here for me to learn from?

Monday 29th January   Mark 5:1–13

Jesus and his disciples came to the other side of the sea, to the country of the Gerasenes. And when he had stepped out of the boat, immediately a man out of the tombs with an unclean spirit met him. He lived among the tombs; and no one could restrain him any more, even with a chain; for he had often been restrained with shackles and chains, but the chains he wrenched apart, and the shackles he broke in pieces; and no one had the strength to subdue him. Night and day among the tombs and on the mountains he was always howling and bruising himself with stones. When he saw Jesus from a distance, he ran and bowed down before him; and he shouted at the top of his voice, "What have you to do with me, Jesus, Son of the Most High God? I adjure you by God, do not torment me." For he had said to him, "Come out of the man, you unclean spirit!" Then Jesus asked him, "What is your name?" He replied, "My name is Legion; for we are many." He begged him earnestly not to send them out of the country. Now there on the hillside a great herd of swine was feeding; and the unclean spirits begged him, "Send us into the swine; let us enter them." So he gave them permission. And the unclean spirits came out and entered the swine; and the herd, numbering about two thousand, rushed down the steep bank into the sea, and were drowned in the sea.

- There is drama in this exorcism. It pits the demon, who torments the possessed man, against the calm, universal power of Jesus.
- Do I ask Jesus to leave my neighborhood, to quit my life? What subtle ways do I employ? Can I change my ways?

Tuesday 30th January   Hebrews 12:1–4

Therefore, since we are surrounded by so great a cloud of witnesses, let us also lay aside every weight and the sin that clings so closely, and let us run with perseverance the race that is set before us, looking to Jesus the pioneer and perfecter of our faith, who for the sake of the joy that was set before him endured the cross, disregarding its shame, and has taken his seat at the right hand of the throne of God. Consider him who endured such hostility against himself from sinners, so that you may not grow weary or lose heart. In your struggle against sin you have not yet resisted to the point of shedding your blood.

- Nothing is more human that illness and death; for each of us, life and death are surrounded by profound emotions.
- Can I ask for the grace to persevere when I seem to lose heart?

Wednesday 31st January, St. John Bosco   Matthew 18:1–5

At that time the disciples came to Jesus and asked, "Who is the greatest in the kingdom of heaven?" He called a child, whom he put among them, and said, "Truly I tell you, unless you change and become like children, you will never enter the kingdom of heaven. Whoever becomes humble like this child is the greatest in the kingdom of heaven. Whoever welcomes one such child in my name welcomes me."

- Jesus challenges his listeners and disciples to be more aware of their society, by placing the humble, defenseless child above wealth, power and conventional "greatness."
- It is also a challenge to me. Why would I want to have child-like humility? Can I talk to the Lord about this?

Thursday 1st February, St. Brigid   Mark 5:25–34

Now there was a woman who had been suffering from hemorrhages for twelve years. She had endured much under many physicians, and had spent all that she had; and she was no better, but rather grew worse. She had heard about Jesus, and came up behind him in the crowd and touched his cloak, for she said, "If I but touch his clothes, I will be made well." Immediately her hemorrhage stopped; and she felt in her body that she was healed of her disease. Immediately aware that power had gone forth from him, Jesus turned about in the crowd and said, "Who touched my clothes?" And his disciples said to him, "You see the crowd pressing in on you; how can you say, 'Who touched me?'" He looked all around to see who had done it. But the woman, knowing what had happened to her, came in fear and trembling, fell down before him, and told him the whole truth. He said to her, "Daughter, your faith has made you well; go in peace, and be healed of your disease."

- Jesus heals a woman of faith who reaches out through the crowd to touch him. Her gesture is simple, his response powerful.
- Are there things about me that I would like to change? Would I like to start again? With Jesus?

Friday 2nd February, The Presentation of the Lord
Luke 2:22–32

When the time came for their purification according to the law of Moses, they brought him up to Jerusalem to present him to the Lord (as it is written in the law of the Lord, "Every firstborn male shall be designated as holy to the Lord"), and they offered a sacrifice according to what is stated in the law of the Lord, "a pair of turtledoves or two young pigeons." Now there was a man in Jerusalem whose name was Simeon; this man was righteous and devout, looking forward to the consolation of Israel, and the Holy Spirit rested on him. It had been revealed to him by the Holy Spirit that he would not see death before he had seen the Lord's Messiah. Guided by the Spirit, Simeon came into the temple; and when the parents brought in the child Jesus, to do for him what was customary under the law, Simeon took him in his arms and praised God, saying, "Master, now you are dismissing your servant in peace, according to your word; for my eyes have seen your salvation, which you have prepared in the presence of all peoples, a light for revelation to the Gentiles and for glory to your people Israel."

- The Purification is the feast of the Lord coming to his temple, a feast that links the Old Testament, and God's promises to the Jews, with the fulfillment of those promises in Jesus. He comes as a baby in his mother's arms.

- Jesus shares my humanity in every way. Can I share in his saving work with our brothers and sisters?

Saturday 3rd February   Mark 6:30–34

The apostles gathered around Jesus, and told him all that they had done and taught. He said to them, "Come away to a deserted place all by yourselves and rest a while." For many were coming and going, and they had no leisure even to eat. And they went away in the boat to a deserted place by themselves. Now many saw them going and recognized them, and they hurried there on foot from all the towns and arrived ahead of them. As he went ashore, he saw a great crowd; and he had compassion for them, because they were like sheep without a shepherd; and he began to teach them many things.

- To his disciples, exhausted by all the unscripted coming and going of the crowds, Jesus said "Come away by yourselves to a lonely place, and rest a while."
- The Christian practice of retreating to a lonely place, where we can drop our public mask, reflect on our life, and rest stems from Jesus. I do it in a small way whenever I come to Sacred Space and devote some time to just God and me.

february 4–10

Something to think and pray about each day this week:

Courage

You tell me, Lord, that there is no need to be afraid. What is it that I fear? Sickness and death in those I love, the anger and hate of powerful people, or a catastrophe like a tsunami or an earthquake. You tell me that every hair on my head is numbered, that your Providence sustains me. You are urging me not to waste my energy on anxieties I can do nothing about. Nelson Mandela wrote: "Once you have rid yourself of the fear of the oppressor, his prisons, his police, his army, there is nothing they can do to you. You are free." I envy the courage of such a man. Perhaps I can grow towards it.

The Presence of God

I pause for a moment, aware that God is here.
I think of how everything around me,
the air I breathe, my whole body,
is tingling with the presence of God.

Freedom

I will ask God's help,
to be free from my own preoccupations,
to be open to God in this time of prayer,
to come to love and serve him more.

Consciousness

How am I really feeling? Light-hearted? Heavy-hearted?
I may be very much at peace, happy to be here.
Equally, I may be frustrated, worried or angry.
I acknowledge how I really am. It is the real me that the Lord loves.

The Word

I read the Word of God slowly, a few times over, and I listen to
what God is saying to me. (Please turn to your scripture on the
following pages. Inspiration points are there should you need
them. When you are ready, return here to continue.)

Conversation

Remembering that I am still in God's presence,
I imagine Jesus himself standing or sitting beside me,
and say whatever is on my mind, whatever is in my heart,
speaking as one friend to another.

Conclusion

Glory be to the Father, and to the Son, and to the Holy Spirit,
As it was in the beginning, is now and ever shall be,
World without end. Amen

Sunday 4th February, Fifth Sunday in Ordinary Time
Luke 5:3–11

Jesus got into one of the boats, the one belonging to Simon, and asked him to put out a little way from the shore. Then he sat down and taught the crowds from the boat. When he had finished speaking, he said to Simon, "Put out into the deep water and let down your nets for a catch." Simon answered, "Master, we have worked all night long but have caught nothing. Yet if you say so, I will let down the nets." When they had done this, they caught so many fish that their nets were beginning to break. So they signaled their partners in the other boat to come and help them. And they came and filled both boats, so that they began to sink. But when Simon Peter saw it, he fell down at Jesus' knees, saying, "Go away from me, Lord, for I am a sinful man!" For he and all who were with him were amazed at the catch of fish that they had taken; and so also were James and John, sons of Zebedee, who were partners with Simon. Then Jesus said to Simon, "Do not be afraid; from now on you will be catching people." When they had brought their boats to shore, they left everything and followed him.

- Can I imagine this scene? Perhaps I'm in one of the boats, or on the shore looking on. I might even be Simon Peter.
- What's the reaction when the carpenter's son tells Simon and his friends how to fish? What happens next?
- How does everyone react?
- Who is this man Jesus? How do I react to him?

Monday 5th February   Genesis 1:1–19

In the beginning when God created the heavens and the earth, the earth was a formless void and darkness covered the face of the deep, while a wind from God swept over the face of the waters. Then God said, "Let there be light"; and there was light. And God saw that the light was good; and God separated the light from the darkness. God called the light Day, and the darkness he called Night. And there was evening and there was morning, the first day. And God said, "Let there be a dome in the midst of the waters, and let it separate the waters from the waters." So God made the dome and separated the waters that were under the dome from the waters that were above the dome. And it was so. God called the dome Sky. And there was evening and there was morning, the second day. And God said, "Let the waters under the sky be gathered together into one place, and let the dry land appear." And it was so. God called the dry land Earth, and the waters that were gathered together he called Seas. And God saw that it was good. Then God said, "Let the earth put forth vegetation: plants yielding seed, and fruit trees of every kind on earth that bear fruit with the seed in it." And it was so. The earth brought forth vegetation: plants yielding seed of every kind, and trees of every kind bearing fruit with the seed in it. And God saw that it was good. And there was evening and there was morning, the third day. And God said, "Let there be lights in the dome of the sky to separate the day from the night; and let them be for signs and for seasons and for days and years, and let them be lights in the dome of the sky to give light upon the earth." And it was so. God made the two great lights—the greater light to rule the day and the lesser light to rule the night—and the stars. God set them in the dome of the sky to give light upon the earth, to rule over the day and over the night, and to separate the light from the darkness. And God saw that it was good. And there was evening and there was morning, the fourth day.

- "God saw that it was good." I thank you, Lord, for the wonders of creation. Every tree, every cloud, every river speaks to me of you. In Gerard Manley Hopkins' words:
    The world is charged with the grandeur of God.
    It will flame out like shining from shook foil.

Tuesday 6th February   **Genesis 1:20–2:4**

And God said, "Let the waters bring forth swarms of living creatures, and let birds fly above the earth across the dome of the sky." So God created the great sea monsters and every living creature that moves, of every kind, with which the waters swarm, and every winged bird of every kind. And God saw that it was good. God blessed them, saying, "Be fruitful and multiply and fill the waters in the seas, and let birds multiply on the earth." And there was evening and there was morning, the fifth day. And God said, "Let the earth bring forth living creatures of every kind: cattle and creeping things and wild animals of the earth of every kind." And it was so. God made the wild animals of the earth of every kind, and the cattle of every kind, and everything that creeps upon the ground of every kind. And God saw that it was good. Then God said, "Let us make humankind in our image, according to our likeness; and let them have dominion over the fish of the sea, and over the birds of the air, and over the cattle, and over all the wild animals of the earth, and over every creeping thing that creeps upon the earth." So God created humankind in his image, in the image of God he created them; male and female he created them. God blessed them, and God said to them, "Be fruitful and multiply, and fill the earth and subdue it; and have dominion over the fish of the sea and over the birds of the air and over every living thing that moves upon the earth." God said, "See, I have given you every plant yielding seed that is upon the face of all the earth, and every tree with seed in its fruit; you shall have them for food. And to every beast of the earth, and to every bird of the air, and to everything that creeps on the earth, everything that has the breath of life, I have given every green plant for food." And it was so. God saw everything that he had made, and indeed, it was very good. And there was evening and there was morning, the sixth day. Thus the heavens and the earth were finished, and all their multitude. And on the seventh day God finished the work that he had done, and he rested on the seventh day from all the work that he had done. These are the generations of the heavens and the earth when they were created.

- Lord, you made us stewards of this precious planet. We have not always been good stewards; in fact, we are often ignorant and destructive stewards.
- Can I learn now to respect this planet, to hand it down intact to future generations? Can I moderate my appetites and demands for more and more material goods that deplete this planet?

Wednesday 7th February   **Mark 7:14–23**

Then he called the crowd again and said to them, "Listen to me, all of you, and understand: there is nothing outside a person that by going in can defile, but the things that come out are what defile." When he had left the crowd and entered the house, his disciples asked him about the parable. He said to them, "Then do you also fail to understand? Do you not see that whatever goes into a person from outside cannot defile, since it enters, not the heart but the stomach, and goes out into the sewer?" (Thus he declared all foods clean.) And he said, "It is what comes out of a person that defiles. For it is from within, from the human heart, that evil intentions come: fornication, theft, murder, adultery, avarice, wickedness, deceit, licentiousness, envy, slander, pride, folly. All these evil things come from within, and they defile a person."

- If I can remember just one time when I did or said something I felt ashamed of afterwards—something harmful, lewd or deceitful—then I already know what Jesus is talking about.
- Perhaps I can ask myself, "What comes out of me?" and notice, over the next day or so, what does.

Thursday 8th February   **Mark 7:24–30**

From there Jesus set out and went away to the region of Tyre. He entered a house and did not want anyone to know he was there. Yet he could not escape notice, but a woman whose little daughter had an unclean spirit immediately heard about him, and she came and bowed down at his feet. Now the woman was a Gentile, of Syrophoenician origin. She begged him to cast the demon out of her daughter. He said to her, "Let the children be fed first, for it is not fair to take the children's food and throw it to the dogs." But she answered him, "Sir, even the dogs under the table eat the children's crumbs." Then he said to her, "For saying that, you may go—the demon has left your daughter." So she went home, found the child lying on the bed, and the demon gone.

- Against all social conventions, Jesus speaks to this gentile woman and she answers back, to which he responds positively. Jesus breaks down this barrier for the sake of the child's need for healing.
- Do I build walls to keep others away? Do I see walls that others build, and leave them intact? What walls keep Jesus away from me? It is the real me that he loves and wants to talk to.

Friday 9th February   Mark 7:31–37

Then Jesus returned from the region of Tyre, and went by way of Sidon towards the Sea of Galilee, in the region of the Decapolis. They brought to him a deaf man who had an impediment in his speech; and they begged him to lay his hand on him. He took him aside in private, away from the crowd, and put his fingers into his ears, and he spat and touched his tongue. Then looking up to heaven, he sighed and said to him, "Ephphatha," that is, "Be opened." And immediately his ears were opened, his tongue was released, and he spoke plainly. Then Jesus ordered them to tell no one; but the more he ordered them, the more zealously they proclaimed it. They were astounded beyond measure, saying, "He has done everything well; he even makes the deaf to hear and the mute to speak."

- The stories of Jesus healing for the mute and blind have meaning beyond their physical infirmity. Notice all the mentions of spitting, the tongue, the ears, and touching, and understand that Jesus is talking about our human senses.
- Jesus repeatedly urges us to use our senses, to be sensitive to what is around us, to have eyes to see and ears to hear.
- Are there things around me that I ignore, that I block out of my senses, that I am "closed" to? Can I imagine Jesus speaking those words, "Be opened," to me?

Saturday 10th February   Mark 8:1–8

In those days when there was again a great crowd without anything to eat, Jesus called his disciples and said to them, "I have compassion for the crowd, because they have been with me now for three days and have nothing to eat. If I send them away hungry to their homes, they will faint on the way—and some of them have come from a great distance." His disciples replied, "How can one feed these people with bread here in the desert?" He asked them, "How many loaves do you have?" They said, "Seven." Then he ordered the crowd to sit down on the ground; and he took the seven loaves, and after giving thanks he broke them and gave them to his disciples to distribute; and they distributed them to the crowd. They had also a few small fish; and after blessing them, he ordered that these too should be distributed. They ate and were filled; and they took up the broken pieces left over, seven baskets full.

- Jesus is in touch with the actual needs of these people, and responds to them. His compassion is deeply felt.

- The disciples are rational about this; it is not possible. But Jesus is determined to find a way.

- How do I react to this story? disbelief? uncertainty? wonder? Can I talk to Jesus about this?

Something to think and pray about each day this week:

Equality in Jesus

"You are, all of you, children of God in Christ Jesus. There are no more distinctions between Jew and Greek, slave and free, male and female, but all of you are one in Christ Jesus." St. Paul is saying something revolutionary here.

The Jews put women in an inferior position. Her religious obligations were on the same level as those of a slave. She did not have to pray the Shema, the morning and evening prayer of men, because like a slave she was not the mistress of her own time—her husband might need his supper when she was praying.

St. Paul's message—abolish these distinctions!—was lost in the following centuries, as men shaped the liturgy of the church, and spoke as though all children were "sons," all listeners were "brothers," all worshippers were "men." We are starting to put things right, but we have a long way to go before we regain the attitude of Jesus.

In our prayer we may spot remnants of old prejudices. Men may retain unspoken assumptions of being better; women may feel long-standing resentments. Our prayer shows us where we are in God's sight: all equal on a level field, "one in Christ Jesus."

The Presence of God

For a few moments, I think of God's veiled presence in things:
in the elements, giving them existence;
in plants, giving them life; in animals, giving them sensation;
and finally, in me, giving me all this and more,
making me a temple, a dwelling-place of the Spirit.

Freedom

God is not foreign to my freedom.
Instead the Spirit breathes life into my most intimate desires,
gently nudging me towards all that is good.
I ask for the grace to let myself be enfolded by the Spirit.

Consciousness

Knowing that God loves me unconditionally,
I can afford to be honest about how I am.
How has the last day been, and how do I feel now?
I share my feelings openly with the Lord.

The Word

I take my time to read the Word of God, slowly, a few times,
allowing myself to dwell on anything that strikes me. (Please
turn to your scripture on the following pages. Inspiration points
are there should you need them. When you are ready, return
here to continue.)

Conversation

How has God's Word moved me? Has it left me cold?
Has it consoled me or moved me to act in a new way?
I imagine Jesus standing or sitting beside me,
I turn and share my feelings with him.

Conclusion

Glory be to the Father, and to the Son, and to the Holy Spirit,
As it was in the beginning, is now and ever shall be,
World without end. Amen

Sunday 11th February, Sixth Sunday in Ordinary Time
Luke 6:17, 20–26

Jesus came down with them and stood on a level place, with a great crowd of his disciples and a great multitude of people from all Judea, Jerusalem, and the coast of Tyre and Sidon. Then he looked up at his disciples and said: "Blessed are you who are poor, for yours is the kingdom of God. "Blessed are you who are hungry now, for you will be filled. "Blessed are you who weep now, for you will laugh. "Blessed are you when people hate you, and when they exclude you, revile you, and defame you on account of the Son of Man. Rejoice in that day and leap for joy, for surely your reward is great in heaven; for that is what their ancestors did to the prophets. "But woe to you who are rich, for you have received your consolation. "Woe to you who are full now, for you will be hungry. "Woe to you who are laughing now, for you will mourn and weep. "Woe to you when all speak well of you, for that is what their ancestors did to the false prophets."

- What can Jesus possibly mean when he says I am blessed specifically when I am deprived of all that gives me comfort?
- How does this talk of poverty, hunger, rejection move me? Does it make me feel uncomfortable, alienated or consoled in some way?
- Can I trust in God for every eventuality?

Monday 12th February   Mark 8:11–13

The Pharisees came and began to argue with Jesus, asking him for a sign from heaven, to test him. And he sighed deeply in his spirit and said, "Why does this generation ask for a sign? Truly I tell you, no sign will be given to this generation." And he left them, and getting into the boat again, he went across to the other side.

- The Pharisees were asking for a sign when in fact the Sign was standing in front of them.

- Does my generation, my cultural group look for signs? If they saw one, would they recognize it?
- And me? What sign do I crave?

Tuesday 13th February   Mark 8:14–21

Now the disciples had forgotten to bring any bread; and they had only one loaf with them in the boat. And he cautioned them, saying, "Watch out—beware of the yeast of the Pharisees and the yeast of Herod." They said to one another, "It is because we have no bread." And becoming aware of it, Jesus said to them, "Why are you talking about having no bread? Do you still not perceive or understand? Are your hearts hardened? Do you have eyes, and fail to see? Do you have ears, and fail to hear? And do you not remember? When I broke the five loaves for the five thousand, how many baskets full of broken pieces did you collect?" They said to him, "Twelve." "And the seven for the four thousand, how many baskets full of broken pieces did you collect?" And they said to him, "Seven." Then he said to them, "Do you not yet understand?"

- "It is because we have no bread." The apostles argued among themselves and their lack of understanding is evident. Jesus' exasperation with them demonstrates his basic humanity.
- How often do I remain preoccupied with my own interests and concerns? Do I recognize that I am always a beginner in the following of Jesus?

Wednesday 14th February, Sts. Cyril and Methodius

Matthew 25:31–46

Jesus said to the disciples, "When the Son of Man comes in his glory, and all the angels with him, then he will sit on the throne of his glory. All the nations will be gathered before him, and he will separate people one from another as a shepherd separates the sheep from the goats, and he will put the sheep at his right hand and the goats at the left. Then the king will say to those at his right hand, 'Come, you that are blessed by my Father, inherit the kingdom prepared for you from the foundation of the world; for I was hungry and you gave me food, I was thirsty and you gave me something to drink, I was a stranger and you welcomed me, I was naked and you gave me clothing, I was sick and you took care of me, I was in prison and you visited me.' Then the righteous will answer him, 'Lord, when was it that we saw you hungry and gave you food, or thirsty and gave you something to drink? And when was it that we saw you a stranger and welcomed you, or naked and gave you clothing? And when was it that we saw you sick or in prison and visited you?' And the king will answer them, 'Truly I tell you, just as you did it to one of the least of these who are members of my family, you did it to me.' Then he will say to those at his left hand, 'You that are accursed, depart from me into the eternal fire prepared for the devil and his angels; for I was hungry and you gave me no food, I was thirsty and you gave me nothing to drink, I was a stranger and you did not welcome me, naked and you did not give me clothing, sick and in prison and you did not visit me.' Then they also will answer, 'Lord, when was it that we saw you hungry or thirsty or a stranger or naked or sick or in prison, and did not take care of you?' Then he will answer them, 'Truly I tell you, just as you did not do it to one of the least of these, you did not do it to me.' And these will go away into eternal punishment, but the righteous into eternal life."

- This message is so simple. The Lord will judge me on my love and service of others.
- The Lord is there in the poor, the sick, the prisoners, the strangers. May I recognize his face.

Thursday 15th February   **Mark 8:22–25**

They came to Bethsaida. Some people brought a blind man to Jesus and begged him to touch him. He took the blind man by the hand and led him out of the village; and when he had put saliva on his eyes and laid his hands on him, he asked him, "Can you see anything?" And the man looked up and said, "I can see people, but they look like trees, walking." Then Jesus laid his hands on his eyes again; and he looked intently and his sight was restored, and he saw everything clearly.

- Do I know what it is like to be blind? Can I imagine what I would be missing in my life, what adjustments I would need to make?
- How do I want to respond to Jesus when he asks me, "Can you see anything?"
- What is it like when my sight is restored?
- Are there things I fail to see, or refuse to face in my life? Can I ask the Lord for the grace to see them?

Friday 16th February   **Mark 8:34–9:1**

Jesus called the crowd with his disciples, and said to them, "If any want to become my followers, let them deny themselves and take up their cross and follow me. For those who want to save their life will lose it, and those who lose their life for my sake, and for the sake of the gospel, will save it. For what will it profit them to gain the whole world and forfeit their life? Indeed, what can they give in return for their life? Those who are ashamed of me and of my words in this adulterous and sinful generation, of them the Son of Man will also be ashamed when he comes in the glory of his Father with the holy angels." And he said to them, "Truly I tell you, there are some standing here who will not taste death until they see that the kingdom of God has come with power."

- To the apostles and his followers, Jesus' words were hard to swallow. They had thought he would be king, but instead he offers them an invitation: to deny oneself, to carry one's cross, and to follow him.

- If I want to live for myself, I can choose that; nobody is going to stop me.
- If I choose living for others, a decision I'll need to renew again and again, then my relationships take on a new quality. It is then that I am fully alive.

Saturday 17th February   **Mark 9:2–8**

Six days later, Jesus took with him Peter and James and John, and led them up a high mountain apart, by themselves. And he was transfigured before them, and his clothes became dazzling white, such as no one on earth could bleach them. And there appeared to them Elijah with Moses, who were talking with Jesus. Then Peter said to Jesus, "Rabbi, it is good for us to be here; let us make three dwellings, one for you, one for Moses, and one for Elijah." He did not know what to say, for they were terrified. Then a cloud overshadowed them, and from the cloud there came a voice, "This is my Son, the Beloved; listen to him!" Suddenly when they looked around, they saw no one with them any more, but only Jesus.

- Imagine yourself to be present. What is it like for Peter, James or John?
- The same apostles were with Jesus in his agony at Gethsemane, where they slept while he prayed and struggled.
- How did they understand these two events they witnessed? Do I have a deeper understanding of this Son: Son of God and Son of Man?

february 18–24

Something to think and pray about each day this week:

Getting started

We are starting Lent this week, a somber time. You did not come, O God, to judge us, but to seek what is lost, to set free those who are imprisoned in guilt and fear, and to save us when our hearts accuse us.

Take us as we are here with all that sinful past of the world. You are greater than our heart, and greater than all our guilt—you are the creator of a new future and a God of Love for ever and ever.

The Presence of God
I pause for a moment
and think of the love and the grace that God showers on me,
creating me in his image and likeness, making me his temple.

Freedom
Everything has the potential to draw forth from me a fuller love
and life.
Yet my desires are often fixed, caught, on illusions of fulfillment.
I ask that God, through my freedom, may orchestrate
my desires in a vibrant loving melody rich in harmony.

Consciousness
In the presence of my loving Creator,
I look honestly at my feelings over the last day,
the highs, the lows and the level ground.
Can I see where the Lord has been present?

The Word
God speaks to each one of us individually. I need to listen to
what he is saying to me. (Please turn to your scripture on the following pages. Inspiration points are there should you need
them. When you are ready, return here to continue.)

Conversation
What feelings are rising in me
as I pray and reflect on God's Word?
I imagine Jesus himself sitting or standing beside me,
and open my heart to him.

Conclusion
Glory be to the Father, and to the Son, and to the Holy Spirit,
As it was in the beginning, is now and ever shall be,
World without end. Amen

Sunday 18th February, Seventh Sunday in Ordinary Time
Luke 6:27–29, 36–38

Jesus said to the disciples, "But I say to you that listen, Love your enemies, do good to those who hate you, bless those who curse you, pray for those who abuse you. If anyone strikes you on the cheek, offer the other also; and from anyone who takes away your coat do not withhold even your shirt. Be merciful, just as your Father is merciful. Do not judge, and you will not be judged; do not condemn, and you will not be condemned. Forgive, and you will be forgiven; give, and it will be given to you. A good measure, pressed down, shaken together, running over, will be put into your lap; for the measure you give will be the measure you get back."

- When I read Jesus' words, what is my first response? Does their familiarity leave me tranquil? Do they seem simply excessive? Do I need to say to the Lord, "this is more than I can manage!"?
- Perhaps the key is, "Be merciful as your Father is merciful." Only in so far as I experience the mercy and love of God can I move in the direction of the life that Jesus is calling me to.
- How is God trying to show me this mercy and love?

Monday 19th February   James 3:13–18

Who is wise and understanding among you? Show by your good life that your works are done with gentleness born of wisdom. But if you have bitter envy and selfish ambition in your hearts, do not be boastful and false to the truth. Such wisdom does not come down from above, but is earthly, unspiritual, devilish. For where there is envy and selfish ambition, there will also be disorder and wickedness of every kind. But the wisdom from above is first pure, then peaceable, gentle, willing to yield, full of mercy and good fruits, without a trace of partiality or hypocrisy. And a harvest of righteousness is sown in peace for those who make peace.

- The words James uses give a strong contrast between "wisdom from above" and the qualities of people who are street smart.
- Do I recognize the wisdom and truth in these words? How do they apply to me?

Tuesday 20th February   Mark 9:30–37

They went on from there and passed through Galilee. He did not want anyone to know it; for he was teaching his disciples, saying to them, "The Son of Man is to be betrayed into human hands, and they will kill him, and three days after being killed, he will rise again." But they did not understand what he was saying and were afraid to ask him. Then they came to Capernaum; and when he was in the house he asked them, "What were you arguing about on the way?" But they were silent, for on the way they had argued with one another who was the greatest. He sat down, called the twelve, and said to them, "Whoever wants to be first must be last of all and servant of all." Then he took a little child and put it among them; and taking it in his arms, he said to them, "Whoever welcomes one such child in my name welcomes me, and whoever welcomes me welcomes not me but the one who sent me."

- Yet again, Mark shows us that the disciples just don't get it. They hear the words Jesus says but do not understand.
- Jesus takes the child in his arms to challenge the disciples about what is really important: service without hope of reward. Can I let him challenge me?

Wednesday 21st February, Ash Wednesday   Joel 2:12–14

Yet even now, says the Lord, return to me with all your heart, with fasting, with weeping, and with mourning; rend your hearts and not your clothing. Return to the Lord, your God, for he is gracious and merciful, slow to anger, and abounding in steadfast love, and relents from punishing. Who knows whether he will not turn and relent, and leave a blessing behind him, a grain offering and a drink offering for the Lord, your God?

- "Return to me with all your heart . . . rend your hearts and not your clothing." The Lord asks not for a list of good deeds but for a profound revolution within us.
- Perhaps I can start from Joel's description of the Lord's character—graciousness, mercy, slowness to anger, steadfastness, love. . . .

Thursday 22nd February, The See of St. Peter
Matthew 16:13–19

Now when Jesus came into the district of Caesarea Philippi, he asked his disciples, "Who do people say that the Son of Man is?" And they said, "Some say John the Baptist, but others Elijah, and still others Jeremiah or one of the prophets." He said to them, "But who do you say that I am?" Simon Peter answered, "You are the Messiah, the Son of the living God." And Jesus answered him, "Blessed are you, Simon son of Jonah! For flesh and blood has not revealed this to you, but my Father in heaven. And I tell you, you are Peter, and on this rock I will build my church, and the gates of Hades will not prevail against it. I will give you the keys of the kingdom of heaven, and whatever you bind on earth will be bound in heaven, and whatever you loose on earth will be loosed in heaven."

- Peter shows a deeper insight into Jesus than others: He is a prophet, yes, and also the Messiah—but much more too, as Peter recognizes that Jesus has an intimate relationship with God.
- Can I stand alongside Peter? Can I imagine his response to Jesus' answer: "Blessed are you, Simon."?
- On what paths will this God-given insight take him? Or me?

Friday 23rd February   Isaiah 58:5–9

Is such the fast that I choose, a day to humble oneself? Is it to bow down the head like a bulrush, and to lie in sackcloth and ashes? Will you call this a fast, a day acceptable to the Lord? Is not this the fast that I choose: to loose the bonds of injustice, to undo the thongs of the yoke, to let the oppressed go free, and to break every yoke? Is it not to share your bread with the hungry, and bring the homeless poor into your house; when you see the naked, to cover them, and not to hide yourself from your own kin? Then your light shall break forth like the dawn, and your healing shall spring up quickly; your vindicator shall go before you, the glory of the Lord shall be your rear guard. Then you shall call, and the Lord will answer; you shall cry for help, and he will say, Here I am.

• "Is not this the fast that I choose," says the Lord, ". . . to share your bread with the hungry, and bring the homeless poor into your house? . . . Then you shall call and the Lord will answer."

Saturday 24th February   Luke 5:27–32

After this he went out and saw a tax collector named Levi, sitting at the tax booth; and he said to him, "Follow me." And he got up, left everything, and followed him. Then Levi gave a great banquet for him in his house; and there was a large crowd of tax collectors and others sitting at the table with them. The Pharisees and their scribes were complaining to his disciples, saying, "Why do you eat and drink with tax collectors and sinners?" Jesus answered, "Those who are well have no need of a physician, but those who are sick; I have come to call not the righteous but sinners to repentance."

• Levi's response frees him, to leave everything and follow.
• Jesus provokes us, as he provokes the religious leaders. Does this letting-go, this repentance, bring joy into my life?

february 25 – march 3

Something to think and pray about each day this week:

Temptations

Father, you are not happy with us when we make each other unhappy. You cannot bear it when we kill and destroy each other. Break, we pray you, the cycle of evil that holds us captive, and let sin die in us, as the sin of the world died in Jesus your son, and death was killed. He lives for us today and every day.

The Presence of God

I reflect for a moment on God's presence around me and in me.
Creator of the universe, the sun and the moon, the earth,
every molecule, every atom, everything that is:
God is in every beat of my heart. God is with me, now.

Freedom

If God were trying to tell me something, would I know?
If God were reassuring me or challenging me, would I notice?
I ask for the grace to be free of my own preoccupations
and open to what God may be saying to me.

Consciousness

How do I find myself today?
Where am I with God? With others?
Do I have something to be grateful for? Then I give thanks.
Is there something I am sorry for? Then I ask forgiveness.

The Word

I read the Word of God slowly, a few times over, and I listen to
what God is saying to me. (Please turn to your scripture on the
following pages. Inspiration points are there should you need
them. When you are ready, return here to continue.)

Conversation

What is stirring in me as I pray?
Am I consoled, troubled, left cold?
I imagine Jesus himself standing or sitting at my side,
and share my feelings with him.

Conclusion

Glory be to the Father, and to the Son, and to the Holy Spirit,
As it was in the beginning, is now and ever shall be,
World without end. Amen   •

Sunday 25th February, First Sunday of Lent   Luke 4:1–13

Jesus, full of the Holy Spirit, returned from the Jordan and was led by the Spirit in the wilderness, where for forty days he was tempted by the devil. He ate nothing at all during those days, and when they were over, he was famished. The devil said to him, "If you are the Son of God, command this stone to become a loaf of bread." Jesus answered him, "It is written, 'One does not live by bread alone.'" Then the devil led him up and showed him in an instant all the kingdoms of the world. And the devil said to him, "To you I will give their glory and all this authority; for it has been given over to me, and I give it to anyone I please. If you, then, will worship me, it will all be yours." Jesus answered him, "It is written, 'Worship the Lord your God, and serve only him.'" Then the devil took him to Jerusalem, and placed him on the pinnacle of the temple, saying to him, "If you are the Son of God, throw yourself down from here, for it is written, 'He will command his angels concerning you, to protect you,' and 'On their hands they will bear you up, so that you will not dash your foot against a stone.'" Jesus answered him, "It is said, 'Do not put the Lord your God to the test.'" When the devil had finished every test, he departed from him until an opportune time.

- How do the temptations of Jesus speak to my life? Do the devil's false promises and manipulations ring a bell with me?
- How am I tempted to dominate and use the material gifts of the world around me?
- Does the realization of temptation in my life weigh me down?

Monday 26th February   Matthew 25:31–40

"When the Son of Man comes in his glory, and all the angels with him, then he will sit on the throne of his glory. All the nations will be gathered before him, and he will separate people one from another as a shepherd separates the sheep from the goats, and he will put the sheep at his right hand and the goats at the left. Then the king will say to those at his right hand, 'Come, you that are blessed by my Father, inherit the kingdom prepared for you from the foundation of the world; for I was hungry and you gave me food, I was thirsty and you gave me something to drink, I was a stranger and you welcomed me, I was naked and you gave me clothing, I was sick and you took care of me, I was in prison and you visited me. 'Then the righteous will answer him, 'Lord, when was it that we saw you hungry and gave you food, or thirsty and gave you something to drink? And when was it that we saw you a stranger and welcomed you, or naked and gave you clothing? And when was it that we saw you sick or in prison and visited you?' And the king will answer them, 'Truly I tell you, just as you did it to one of the least of these who are members of my family, you did it to me.'"

- This message is so simple, Lord. You will judge me on my love and service of others. You are there in the poor, the sick, the prisoners, the strangers. May I recognize your face.

Tuesday 27th February   Matthew 6:7–15

"When you are praying, do not heap up empty phrases as the Gentiles do; for they think that they will be heard because of their many words. Do not be like them, for your Father knows what you need before you ask him. "Pray then in this way: Our Father in heaven, hallowed be your name. Your kingdom come. Your will be done, on earth as it is in heaven. Give us this day our daily bread. And forgive us our debts, as we also have forgiven our debtors. And do not bring us to the time of trial, but rescue us from the evil one. For if you forgive others their trespasses, your heavenly Father will also forgive you; but if you do not forgive others, neither will your Father forgive your trespasses."

- Father, as I turn to you in prayer, you already know what I need. I do not change you by asking; I change myself.
- I may call God 'Abba'—my daddy. And I shall be forgiven as I forgive others. Can I be true to that relationship?

Wednesday 28th February
Psalm 50(51):1–3, 10–11, 16–17

Have mercy on me, O God, according to your steadfast love according to your abundant mercy blot out my transgressions. Wash me thoroughly from my iniquity, and cleanse me from my sin. For I know my transgressions, and my sin is ever before me. Create in me a clean heart, O God, and put a new and right spirit within me. Do not cast me away from your presence, and do not take your holy spirit from me. For you have no delight in sacrifice if I were to give a burnt offering, you would not be pleased. The sacrifice acceptable to God is a contrite spirit a humbled and contrite heart, O God, you will not spurn.

- "Wash me thoroughly . . . cleanse me. . . . Create in me a clean heart, O God." There is a good deal of scrubbing to do Lord. I need to keep a habitual sense of my weakness, to save me from arrogance.
- I have confidence that you will keep me close to your presence, and teach me to live in the Spirit. With a humbled heart.

Thursday 1st March   Matthew 7:7–11

Jesus said to the crowds, "Ask, and it will be given you; search, and you will find; knock, and the door will be opened for you. For everyone who asks receives, and everyone who searches finds, and for everyone who knocks, the door will be opened. Is there anyone among you who, if your child asks for bread, will give a stone? Or if the child asks for a fish, will give a snake? If you then, who are evil, know how to give good gifts to your children, how much more will your Father in heaven give good things to those who ask him!"

- "Ask . . . search . . . knock." Three aspects of prayer, each one giving us confidence of gaining a hearing. Jesus' teaching is demanding, but our Father is willing to give us the capacity if we but ask.
- With the confidence of the child, we can demand, "Give us this day our daily bread." Each day, we are invited to ask, to demand.

Friday 2nd March   **Matthew 5:20–26**

Jesus said to his disciples, "For I tell you, unless your righteousness exceeds that of the scribes and Pharisees, you will never enter the kingdom of heaven. You have heard that it was said to those of ancient times, 'You shall not murder'; and 'whoever murders shall be liable to judgment.' But I say to you that if you are angry with a brother or sister, you will be liable to judgment; and if you insult a brother or sister, you will be liable to the council; and if you say, 'You fool,' you will be liable to the hell of fire. So when you are offering your gift at the altar, if you remember that your brother or sister has something against you, leave your gift there before the altar and go; first be reconciled to your brother or sister, and then come and offer your gift. Come to terms quickly with your accuser while you are on the way to court with him, or your accuser may hand you over to the judge, and the judge to the guard, and you will be thrown into prison. Truly I tell you, you will never get out until you have paid the last penny."

- Jesus takes the law of Moses and makes it deeper, more interior. The root of the act of killing is in the angry hatred in the killer's heart. Tackle the evil at its source.
- It is not just a question of my anger or my guilt. Rather, if there is a rift, I must recognize it and work to heal it..Reconciliation with brother and sister is supremely important.
- Am I afraid this is too hard for me? Can I ask the Lord about it?

Saturday 3rd March   **Matthew 5:43–48**

Jesus said to the disciples, "You have heard that it was said, 'You shall love your neighbor and hate your enemy.' But I say to you, Love your enemies and pray for those who persecute you, so that you may be children of your Father in heaven; for he makes his sun rise on the evil and on the good, and sends rain on the righteous and on the unrighteous. For if you love those who love you, what reward do you have? Do not even the tax collectors do the same? And if you greet only your brothers and sisters, what more are you doing than others? Do not even the Gentiles do the same? Be perfect, therefore, as your heavenly Father is perfect."

- Lord, you teach us that the children of God are to go beyond the accepted standards. Our call is to act as the Creator acts towards all people, even towards our enemies.
- Is this is hopeless idealism or a wise strategy for overcoming the persecutor? Teach me to change aggression into a strategy for winning through the wisdom of love.

march 4–10

Something to think and pray about each day this week:

Transfiguration

When Peter saw Jesus transfigured on Tabor, he wanted to put up tents on the top of the mountain and settle down there. It was a peak experience, and he wanted it to go on for ever. But Jesus brought them down from the mountain, back to the level everyday routine.

I know, Lord, that we cannot live for ever on a charismatic high. I am lucky if from time to time you lift me out of myself. But for most of the time I have to be content with the routine of survival, living on faith, which is a mixture of light and darkness.

The Presence of God
For a few moments, I think of God's veiled presence in things:
in the elements, giving them existence;
in plants, giving them life; in animals, giving them sensation;
and finally, in me, giving me all this and more,
making me a temple, a dwelling-place of the Spirit.

Freedom
God is not foreign to my freedom.
Instead the Spirit breathes life into my most intimate desires,
gently nudging me towards all that is good.
I ask for the grace to let myself be enfolded by the Spirit.

Consciousness
Knowing that God loves me unconditionally,
I can afford to be honest about how I am.
How has the last day been, and how do I feel now?
I share my feelings openly with the Lord.

The Word
I take my time to read the Word of God, slowly, a few times,
allowing myself to dwell on anything that strikes me. (Please
turn to your scripture on the following pages. Inspiration points
are there should you need them. When you are ready, return
here to continue.)

Conversation
How has God's Word moved me? Has it left me cold?
Has it consoled me or moved me to act in a new way?
I imagine Jesus standing or sitting beside me,
I turn and share my feelings with him.

Conclusion
Glory be to the Father, and to the Son, and to the Holy Spirit,
As it was in the beginning, is now and ever shall be,
World without end. Amen

Sunday 4th March, Second Sunday of Lent   Luke 9:28b–36

Now about eight days after these sayings Jesus took with him Peter and John and James, and went up on the mountain to pray. And while he was praying, the appearance of his face changed, and his clothes became dazzling white. Suddenly they saw two men, Moses and Elijah, talking to him. They appeared in glory and were speaking of his departure, which he was about to accomplish at Jerusalem. Now Peter and his companions were weighed down with sleep; but since they had stayed awake, they saw his glory and the two men who stood with him. Just as they were leaving him, Peter said to Jesus, "Master, it is good for us to be here; let us make three dwellings, one for you, one for Moses, and one for Elijah"—not knowing what he said. While he was saying this, a cloud came and overshadowed them; and they were terrified as they entered the cloud. Then from the cloud came a voice that said, "This is my Son, my Chosen; listen to him!" When the voice had spoken, Jesus was found alone. And they kept silent and in those days told no one any of the things they had seen.

- In this moment of "transfiguration" God the Father affirms Jesus for who he really is: "This is my Son, my Chosen." This must have been profoundly consoling. But, Jesus' being who he really was inevitably involved him going forward to do what he had to do.
- Can I allow the Father to affirm me for who I really am? Is there consolation for me?
- Does being who I really am hold any terrors for me?

Monday 5th March   **Luke 6:36–38**

Be merciful, just as your Father is merciful. "Do not judge, and you will not be judged; do not condemn, and you will not be condemned. Forgive, and you will be forgiven; give, and it will be given to you. A good measure, pressed down, shaken together, running over, will be put into your lap; for the measure you give will be the measure you get back."

- "The measure you give will be the measure you get back." God aims to be extravagantly generous with each of us; the limitations come from me.
- How do I place limits of God's generosity?
- Why do I do that? Am I fearful of what might happen to my life?

Tuesday 6th March   Matthew 23:8–12

Jesus said to the crowds and to his disciples, "You are not to be called rabbi, for you have one teacher, and you are all students. And call no one your father on earth, for you have one Father—the one in heaven. Nor are you to be called instructors, for you have one instructor, the Messiah. The greatest among you will be your servant. All who exalt themselves will be humbled, and all who humble themselves will be exalted."

- Jesus, you made yourself a baby, a child, a carpenter, my servant, a sufferer, and a victim of injustice. I know that when you teach me the Beatitudes, and tell me to love others, you speak from your human experience as well as being the Word of God.
- You know what you are asking. As St. Peter exclaimed: "Lord, to whom should we go? You have the message of eternal life." May I always know you as my master.

Wednesday 7th March   Matthew 20:17–23

While Jesus was going up to Jerusalem, he took the twelve disciples aside by themselves, and said to them on the way, "See, we are going up to Jerusalem, and the Son of Man will be handed over to the chief priests and scribes, and they will condemn him to death; then they will hand him over to the Gentiles to be mocked and flogged and crucified; and on the third day he will be raised. Then the mother of the sons of Zebedee came to him with her sons, and kneeling before him, she asked a favour of him. And he said to her, "What do you want?" She said to him, "Declare that these two sons of mine will sit, one at your right hand and one at your left, in your kingdom." But Jesus answered, "You do not know what you are asking. Are you able to drink the cup that I am about to drink?" They said to him, "We are able." He said to them, "You will indeed drink my cup, but to sit at my right hand and at my left, this is not mine to grant, but it is for those for whom it has been prepared by my Father."

- Is there a yearning within me for power and glory, for myself or close friend I look up to?
- Do I ever have a "magical" attitude to faith that would like to use God's power for my own ends?

Thursday 8th March   Jeremiah 17:5–8

Thus says the Lord: Cursed are those who trust in mere mortals and make mere flesh their strength, whose hearts turn away from the Lord. They shall be like a shrub in the desert, and shall not see when relief comes. They shall live in the parched places of the wilderness, in an uninhabited salt land. Blessed are those who trust in the Lord, whose trust is the Lord. They shall be like a tree planted by water, sending out its roots by the stream. It shall not fear when heat comes, and its leaves shall stay green; in the year of drought it is not anxious, and it does not cease to bear fruit.

- The one who trusts in the Lord is like a tree planted by water, "sending out its roots by the stream." I know, Lord, what dryness, desolation and sterility feel like.
- Let me pray with you.

Friday 9th March   Matthew 21:33–43, 45–46

Jesus said: "Listen to another parable. There was a landowner who planted a vineyard, put a fence around it, dug a wine press in it, and built a watchtower. Then he leased it to tenants and went to another country. When the harvest time had come, he sent his slaves to the tenants to collect his produce. But the tenants seized his slaves and beat one, killed another, and stoned another. Again he sent other slaves, more than the first; and they treated them in the same way. Finally he sent his son to them, saying, 'They will respect my son.' But when the tenants saw the son, they said to themselves, 'This is the heir; come, let us kill him and get his inheritance.' So they seized him, threw him out of the vineyard, and killed him. Now when the owner of the vineyard comes, what will he do to those tenants?" They said to him, "He will put those wretches to a miserable death, and lease the vineyard to other tenants who will give him the produce at the harvest time." Jesus said to them, "Have you never read in the scriptures: 'The stone that the builders rejected has become the cornerstone; this was the Lord's doing, and it is amazing in our eyes'? Therefore I tell you, the kingdom of God will be taken away from you and given to a people that produces the fruits of the kingdom. When the chief priests and the Pharisees heard his parables, they realized that he was speaking about them. They wanted to arrest him, but they feared the crowds, because they regarded him as a prophet."

- Lord, this parable is about the Jews, but also about me. I am the tenant of your vineyard. For me you have planted and protected a crop, and from me you expect some harvest.
- The fruit of my labors is for you, not for me. I may feel annoyed when you ask, but you are right to expect something of me.

Saturday 10th March   **Micah 7:14–15, 18–20**
Shepherd your people with your staff, the flock that belongs to you, which lives alone in a forest in the midst of a garden land; let them feed in Bashan and Gilead as in the days of old. As in the days when you came out of the land of Egypt, show us

marvelous things. Who is a God like you, pardoning iniquity and passing over the transgression of the remnant of your possession? He does not retain his anger forever, because he delights in showing clemency. He will again have compassion upon us; he will tread our iniquities under foot. You will cast all our sins into the depths of the sea. You will show faithfulness to Jacob and unswerving loyalty to Abraham, as you have sworn to our ancestors from the days of old.

- "He does not retain his anger for ever, because he delights in steadfast love." The parable of the Prodigal Son shows me how steadfast that love is.
- Can I accept that you pardon me Lord, do not retain anger against me, and that you even take delight in me? Let me talk with you about this.

march 11–17

Something to think and pray about each day this week:

Spreading the Word

If there is a hierarchy in heaven based on the churches named after you, Patrick must be at the top. He is our antidote to racism—a Welsh boy educated in France and missioned by Italians, who became the loved apostle of Ireland, and the toast of Irish people everywhere on 17th March. He is our antidote to conservatism—a slave who ran away from his owners and returned to Ireland to face down kings and chieftains. He was a visionary who followed his dreams, and loved the high mountains like Slemish and Croagh Patrick. Above all he was a religious man who turned to God during his leisured hours as a swineherd.

All through his Confessions you sense his overflowing gratitude for the privilege of knowing Almighty God and Jesus Christ his son as he wrote: "In the light of our faith in the Trinity, regardless of danger, I must make known the gift of God and everlasting consolation, without fear and frankly. I must spread everywhere the name of God so that after my decease I may leave a bequest to those whom I have baptized in the Lord; so many thousands of people."

The Presence of God
I pause for a moment
and think of the love and the grace that God showers on me,
creating me in his image and likeness, making me his temple.

Freedom
Everything has the potential to draw forth from me a fuller love
and life.
Yet my desires are often fixed, caught, on illusions of fulfillment.
I ask that God, through my freedom, may orchestrate
my desires in a vibrant loving melody rich in harmony.

Consciousness
In the presence of my loving Creator,
I look honestly at my feelings over the last day,
the highs, the lows and the level ground.
Can I see where the Lord has been present?

The Word
God speaks to each one of us individually. I need to listen to
what he is saying to me. (Please turn to your scripture on the following pages. Inspiration points are there should you need
them. When you are ready, return here to continue.)

Conversation
What feelings are rising in me
as I pray and reflect on God's Word?
I imagine Jesus himself sitting or standing beside me,
and open my heart to him.

Conclusion
Glory be to the Father, and to the Son, and to the Holy Spirit,
As it was in the beginning, is now and ever shall be,
World without end. Amen

Sunday 11th March, Third Sunday of Lent   Luke 13:1–9

At that very time there were some present who told him about the Galileans whose blood Pilate had mingled with their sacrifices. He asked them, "Do you think that because these Galileans suffered in this way they were worse sinners than all other Galileans? No, I tell you; but unless you repent, you will all perish as they did. Or those eighteen who were killed when the tower of Siloam fell on them—do you think that they were worse offenders than all the others living in Jerusalem? No, I tell you; but unless you repent, you will all perish just as they did." Then he told this parable: "A man had a fig tree planted in his vineyard; and he came looking for fruit on it and found none. So he said to the gardener, 'See here! For three years I have come looking for fruit on this fig tree, and still I find none. Cut it down! Why should it be wasting the soil?' He replied, 'Sir, let it alone for one more year, until I dig around it and put manure on it. If it bears fruit next year, well and good; but if not, you can cut it down.'"

- Do I hear different voices of judgment in the passage? What do they spark in me?
- What about the gardener? What does he say?
- Is there a tendency towards harsh judgment in me—towards others or towards myself?
- Can I hear the voice of the gardener speaking within me?

Monday 12th March   Luke 4:24–30

And he said, "Truly I tell you, no prophet is accepted in the prophet's hometown. But the truth is, there were many widows in Israel in the time of Elijah, when the heaven was shut up three years and six months, and there was a severe famine over all the land; yet Elijah was sent to none of them except to a widow at Zarephath in Sidon. There were also many lepers in Israel in the time of the prophet Elisha, and none of them was cleansed except Naaman the Syrian." When they heard this, all in the synagogue were filled with rage. They got up, drove him out of the town, and led him to the brow of the hill on which their town was built, so that they might hurl him off the cliff. But he passed through the midst of them and went on his way.

- Jesus' story reminds us of the self-important Naaman who felt he had been slighted when Elisha did not attend upon the great man personally, but sent a messenger with a simple instruction.
- I am the same, Lord. Do I become angry or stand back when my expectations are not met? Even when I need you greatly? I want not just a cure, but to be the centre of attention.

Tuesday 13th March   Matthew 18:21–35

Then Peter came and said to him, "Lord, if another member of the church sins against me, how often should I forgive? As many as seven times?" Jesus said to him, "Not seven times, but, I tell you, seventy-seven times. "For this reason the kingdom of heaven may be compared to a king who wished to settle accounts with his slaves. When he began the reckoning, one who owed him ten thousand talents was brought to him; and, as he could not pay, his lord ordered him to be sold, together with his wife and children and all his possessions, and payment to be made. So the slave fell on his knees before him, saying, 'Have patience with me, and I will pay you everything.' And out of pity for him, the lord of that slave released him and forgave him the debt. But that same slave, as he went out, came upon one of his fellow slaves who owed him a hundred denarii; and seizing him by the throat, he said, 'Pay what you owe.' Then his fellow slave fell down and pleaded with him, 'Have patience with me, and I will pay you.' But he refused; then he went and threw him into prison until he would pay the debt. When his fellow slaves saw what had happened, they were greatly distressed, and they went and reported to their lord all that had taken place. Then

120

his lord summoned him and said to him, 'You wicked slave! I forgave you all that debt because you pleaded with me. Should you not have had mercy on your fellow slave, as I had mercy on you?' And in anger his lord handed him over to be tortured until he would pay his entire debt. So my heavenly Father will also do to every one of you, if you do not forgive your brother or sister from your heart."

- The servant is forgiven a huge debt he could not hope to repay—justice is completely overwhelmed by mercy. In that light, his refusal to his own debtor is even more monstrous and brutal.

- Lord, do I choose harsh justice for others when mercy could be extended? Will I find hypocrisy in my words, my attitudes, my actions? Can I look hard at this?

Wednesday 14th March · Matthew 5:17–19

Do not think that I have come to abolish the law or the prophets; I have come not to abolish but to fulfill. For truly I tell you, until heaven and earth pass away, not one letter, not one stroke of a letter, will pass from the law until all is accomplished. Therefore, whoever breaks one of the least of these commandments, and teaches others to do the same, will be called least in the kingdom of heaven; but whoever does them and teaches them will be called great in the kingdom of heaven.

- Jesus did not reject the Old Testament of the Jews, but brought it back to its essentials: love God and love your neighbor. Our life should be whole—people should be able to read our principles from our behavior.

- It is harder to live one sermon than to preach a dozen.

Thursday 15th March · Jeremiah 7:23–28

But this command I gave them, "Obey my voice, and I will be your God, and you shall be my people; and walk only in the way that I command you, so that it may be well with you." Yet they did not obey or incline their ear, but, in the stubbornness of their evil will, they walked in their own counsels, and looked backward rather than forward. From the day that your ancestors came out of the land of Egypt until this day, I have persistently sent all my servants the prophets to them, day after day; yet they did not listen to me, or pay attention, but they stiffened their necks. They did worse than their ancestors did. So you shall speak all these words to them, but they will not listen to you. You shall call to them, but they will not answer you. You shall say to them: This is the nation that did not obey the voice of the Lord their God, and did not accept discipline; truth has perished; it is cut off from their lips.

- "Obey my voice, and I will be your God, and you shall be my people." In the dialogue between God and humanity, there is the give-and-take of constant self-revelation and response; as with any relationship.

- Yet I often find it so hard, Lord, to respond positively. I look to my own ways, while you remain open and loving in the face of my persistent stubbornness. Open my heart to your love.

Friday 16th March   Mark 12:28–34

One of the scribes came near and heard them disputing with one another, and seeing that he answered them well, he asked him, "Which commandment is the first of all?" Jesus answered, "The first is, 'Hear, O Israel: the Lord our God, the Lord is one; you shall love the Lord your God with all your heart, and with all your soul, and with all your mind, and with all your strength.' The second is this, 'You shall love your neighbor as yourself.' There is no other commandment greater than these." Then the scribe said to him, "You are right, Teacher; you have truly said that 'he is one, and besides him there is no other'; and 'to love him with all the heart, and with all the understanding, and with all the strength,' and 'to love one's neighbor as oneself,'—this is much more important than all whole burnt offerings and sacrifices." When Jesus saw that he answered wisely, he said to him, "You are not far from the kingdom of God." After that no one dared to ask him any question.

- The scribe is not hostile but a sincere person, seeking the truth. He is deeply impressed with the answer Jesus gives him; Jesus is equally impressed with the scribe's understanding.

- How do I measure up here? Are my religious observances more important than my relationships with God and neighbor? Am I reconciled with others or in dispute? How far am I from the kingdom of God?

Saturday 17th March, St. Patrick   Isaiah 52:7–10

How beautiful upon the mountains are the feet of the messenger who announces peace, who brings good news, who announces salvation, who says to Zion, "Your God reigns." Listen! Your sentinels lift up their voices, together they sing for joy; for in plain sight they see the return of the Lord to Zion. Break forth together into singing, you ruins of Jerusalem; for the Lord has comforted his people, he has redeemed Jerusalem. The Lord has bared his holy arm before the eyes of all the nations; and all the ends of the earth shall see the salvation of our God.

- How important are the heroes in my life, the men and women whom I look up to, now or when I was younger?

- Do I think of Jesus as my hero? Do I have a particular hero among the people who brought the good news to me or to my ancestors? Can I ask for their support?

march 18–24

Something to think and pray about each day this week:

Faithful insecurity
Imagine walking unassisted in a darkened room. I move my hands around in front of my body, lest I bump into a wall, a piece of furniture and come to grief.

This is not dissimilar from what God calls us to on the journey of faith. It is not easy for us, as we want to have our pathways well signposted. We want to know where, how, why and when we are moving. Faith, though, is the security to be insecure. Our trust is in God, and not in our own charm, intelligence or insight, our status or power.

The Presence of God

I reflect for a moment on God's presence around me and in me.
Creator of the universe, the sun and the moon, the earth,
every molecule, every atom, everything that is:
God is in every beat of my heart. God is with me, now.

Freedom

A thick and shapeless tree trunk would never believe
that it could become a statue, admired as a miracle of sculpture,
and would never submit itself to the chisel of the sculptor,
who sees by her genius what she can make of it. (St. Ignatius)
I ask for the grace to let myself be shaped by my loving Creator.

Consciousness

Knowing that God loves me unconditionally,
I look honestly over the last day, its events and my feelings.
Do I have something to be grateful for? Then I give thanks.
Is there something I am sorry for? Then I ask forgiveness.

The Word

I read the Word of God slowly, a few times over, and I listen to
what God is saying to me. (Please turn to your scripture on the
following pages. Inspiration points are there should you need
them. When you are ready, return here to continue.)

Conversation

What is stirring in me as I pray?
Am I consoled, troubled, left cold?
I imagine Jesus himself standing or sitting at my side,
and share my feelings with him.

Conclusion

Glory be to the Father, and to the Son, and to the Holy Spirit,
As it was in the beginning, is now and ever shall be,
World without end. Amen

Sunday 18th March, Fourth Sunday of Lent

Luke 15:12–24

Then Jesus said, "There was a man who had two sons. The younger of them said to his father, 'Father, give me the share of the property that will belong to me.' So he divided his property between them. A few days later the younger son gathered all he had and traveled to a distant country, and there he squandered his property in dissolute living. When he had spent everything, a severe famine took place throughout that country, and he began to be in need. So he went and hired himself out to one of the citizens of that country, who sent him to his fields to feed the pigs. He would gladly have filled himself with the pods that the pigs were eating; and no one gave him anything. But when he came to himself he said, 'How many of my father's hired hands have bread enough and to spare, but here I am dying of hunger! I will get up and go to my father, and I will say to him, "Father, I have sinned against heaven and before you; I am no longer worthy to be called your son; treat me like one of your hired hands."' So he set off and went to his father. But while he was still far off, his father saw him and was filled with compassion; he ran and put his arms around him and kissed him. Then the son said to him, 'Father, I have sinned against heaven and before you; I am no longer worthy to be called your son.' But the father said to his slaves, 'Quickly, bring out a robe—the best one—and put it on him; put a ring on his finger and sandals on his feet. And get the fatted calf and kill it, and let us eat and celebrate; for this son of mine was dead and is alive again; he was lost and is found!' And they began to celebrate."

- When I do a quick scan of this story, where does my gaze lie? Is it on the abandonment, the dream gone sour, the degradation and squalor? Or, do I go straight to the picture of the father scanning the horizon, the compassion, the reconciliation and the forgiveness?

- My spontaneous inclination might tell me something about what I need to learn from this scripture.

- Where am I in my journey? Am I walking out the door? Am I in a foreign land? Or, am I on the way home?

Monday 19th March, St. Joseph   Matthew 1:18–25

Now the birth of Jesus the Messiah took place in this way. When his mother Mary had been engaged to Joseph, but before they lived together, she was found to be with child from the Holy Spirit. Her husband Joseph, being a righteous man and unwilling to expose her to public disgrace, planned to dismiss her quietly. But just when he had resolved to do this, an angel of the Lord appeared to him in a dream and said, "Joseph, son of David, do not be afraid to take Mary as your wife, for the child conceived in her is from the Holy Spirit. She will bear a son, and you are to name him Jesus, for he will save his people from their sins." All this took place to fulfill what had been spoken by the Lord through the prophet: "Look, the virgin shall conceive and bear a son, and they shall name him Emmanuel," which means, "God is with us." When Joseph awoke from sleep, he did as the angel of the Lord commanded him; he took her as his wife, but had no marital relations with her until she had borne a son; and he named him Jesus.

- How do we think about St. Joseph? Yes, he receives the news of the annunciation, and he is there with Mary during her pregnancy and the birth of Jesus. But he is also the man working to support his family for many years, providing guidance, education and example to the young Jesus.

- Can I imagine the everyday life of Joseph, with the young Jesus trailing behind him, copying his actions, listening carefully to what he said? What did Joseph observe in this growing boy? What glimpses of the future did he see?

Tuesday 20th March　　　　　　　　　　　**John 5:1–8**

After this there was a festival of the Jews, and Jesus went up to Jerusalem. Now in Jerusalem by the Sheep Gate there is a pool, called in Hebrew Beth-zatha, which has five porticoes. In these lay many invalids—blind, lame, and paralyzed. One man was there who had been ill for thirty-eight years. When Jesus saw him lying there and knew that he had been there a long time, he said to him, "Do you want to be made well?" The sick man answered him, "Sir, I have no one to put me into the pool when the water is stirred up; and while I am making my way, someone else steps down ahead of me." Jesus said to him, "Stand up, take your mat and walk."

- "Do you want to be made well?" It looks obvious to a healthy person but the question makes sense, because a cure would change his life completely.

- Lord, I do want to be healed, to change my life and take on all that you may ask of me.

Wednesday 21st March　　　　　　　　**Isaiah 49:13–15**

For the Lord has comforted his people, and will have compassion on his suffering ones. But Zion said, "The Lord has forsaken me, my Lord has forgotten me. "Can a woman forget her nursing child, or show no compassion for the child of her womb? Even these may forget, yet I will not forget you."

- Here is a reminder of the motherhood of God: "Can a woman forget her nursing child, or show no compassion for the child of her womb? Even these may forget, yet I will not forget you."

- My God, you tell me that for you I am unique, and that I have a place in your mind which nobody else can fill. You regard me with the delight and tenderness of a mother with her baby.

Thursday 22nd March   John 5:44–47

Jesus said to the Jews, "How can you believe when you accept glory from one another and do not seek the glory that comes from the one who alone is God? Do not think that I will accuse you before the Father; your accuser is Moses, on whom you have set your hope. If you believed Moses, you would believe me, for he wrote about me. But if you do not believe what he wrote, how will you believe what I say?"

- This reading reflects the nub of the struggle between God and his chosen people, the Jews. It says something to us too: our desire to seek human glory and admiration from others while refusing to see and accept the signs of God's presence.

- Lord, draw me out from my closed-in world, from my own cosy groups where I am sure of my world, and frightened of being opened up to the new, in your name.

Friday 23rd March   Wisdom 2:1, 12–15

For the godless reasoned unsoundly, saying to themselves, "Short and sorrowful is our life, and there is no remedy when a life comes to its end, and no one has been known to return from Hades. Let us lie in wait for the righteous man, because he is inconvenient to us and opposes our actions; he reproaches us for sins against the law, and accuses us of sins against our training. He professes to have knowledge of God, and calls himself a child of the Lord. He became to us a reproof of our thoughts; the very sight of him is a burden to us, because his manner of life is unlike that of others, and his ways are strange."

- "He became to us a reproof of our thoughts; the very sight of him is a burden to us." You touch me where it hurts, Lord, when you describe the jealousy we often feel for somebody whose life is different.

- Lord, make my heart more generous, so that I rejoice in the goodness of others.

Saturday 24th March, Annunciation of the Lord
Luke 1:26–32, 34–35, 38a

In the sixth month the angel Gabriel was sent by God to a town in Galilee called Nazareth, to a virgin whose name was Mary. And he came to her and said, "Greetings, favored one! The Lord is with you." But she was much perplexed by his words and pondered what sort of greeting this might be. The angel said to her, "Do not be afraid, Mary, for you have found favor with God. And now, you will conceive in your womb and bear a son, and you will name him Jesus. He will be great, and will be called the Son of the Most High, and the Lord God will give to him the throne of his ancestor David." Mary said to the angel, "How can this be, since I am a virgin?" The angel said to her, "The Holy Spirit will come upon you, and the power of the Most High will overshadow you; therefore the child to be born will be holy; he will be called Son of God." Then Mary said, "Here am I, the servant of the Lord; let it be with me according to your word."

- Can I take the time to think about these events, to imagine what Mary felt as she was given this awesome news.

- Mary has questions and voices them, but she says "Yes" to God's will for her. Can I learn from her example?

march 25–31

Something to think and pray about each day this week:

The place of prayer

Prayer is a spiritual place, a psychological place, a place where we go to get out of ourselves, a place created by and inhabited by our God. Whatever disciplines can help us to get to where God's reality can get at us, are those we should embrace.

Prayer isn't bending God's power in order to get things we want, or talking God into seeing things our way. It is whatever calls us to detach from our own self, from our own compulsions and addictions, from our own ego, from our own cozy space. We are all too trapped in our own places by virtue of the egocentricity of the human person. In prayer the Spirit entices us outside our narrow comfort zone.

No wonder we avoid prayer: We have to change places, to move to a sacred space.

The Presence of God
In the silence of my innermost being,
in the fragments of my yearned-for wholeness,
can I hear the whispers of God's presence?
Can I remember when I felt God's nearness?
When we walked together and I let myself be embraced by God's love.

Freedom
There are very few people
who realize what God would make of them
if they abandoned themselves into his hands,
and let themselves be formed by his grace. (St. Ignatius)
I ask for the grace to trust myself totally to God's love.

Consciousness
How do I find myself today?
Where am I with God? With others?
Do I have something to be grateful for? Then I give thanks.
Is there something I am sorry for? Then I ask forgiveness.

The Word
I take my time to read the Word of God, slowly, a few times, allowing myself to dwell on anything that strikes me. (Please turn to your scripture on the following pages. Inspiration points are there should you need them. When you are ready, return here to continue.)

Conversation
Do I notice myself reacting as I pray with the Word of God?
Do I feel challenged, comforted, angry?
Imagining Jesus sitting or standing by me,
I speak out my feelings, as one trusted friend to another.

Conclusion
Glory be to the Father, and to the Son, and to the Holy Spirit,
As it was in the beginning, is now and ever shall be,
World without end. Amen

Sunday 25th March, Fifth Sunday of Lent   John 8:2–11

Early in the morning Jesus came again to the temple. All the people came to him and he sat down and began to teach them. The scribes and the Pharisees brought a woman who had been caught in adultery; and making her stand before all of them, they said to him, "Teacher, this woman was caught in the very act of committing adultery. Now in the law Moses commanded us to stone such women. Now what do you say?" They said this to test him, so that they might have some charge to bring against him. Jesus bent down and wrote with his finger on the ground. When they kept on questioning him, he straightened up and said to them, "Let anyone among you who is without sin be the first to throw a stone at her." And once again he bent down and wrote on the ground. When they heard it, they went away, one by one, beginning with the elders; and Jesus was left alone with the woman standing before him. Jesus straightened up and said to her, "Woman, where are they? Has no one condemned you?" She said, "No one, sir." And Jesus said, "Neither do I condemn you. Go your way, and from now on do not sin again."

- I try to imagine this scene in the temple area with people coming and going. Suddenly there is a commotion. An angry crowd comes to Jesus, parading a solitary woman in front of him.

- What is happening? Do I identify with any of the characters in the scene? Which one?

- How does Jesus react? How does his reaction touch me?

Monday 26th March   Daniel 13:55–56, 60–62

Daniel said, "Indeed! Your lie recoils on you own head: the angel of God has already received from him your sentence and will cut you in half." He dismissed the man, ordered the other to be brought and said to him, "Son of Canaan, not of Huday, beauty has seduced you, lust has led your heart astray!"

Then the whole assembly shouted, blessing God, the Savior of those who trust in him. And they turned on the two elders whom Daniel had convicted of false evidence out of their own mouths. As the Law of Moses prescribes, they were given the same punishment as they had schemed to inflict on their neighbor. They were put to death. And thus, that day, an innocent life was saved.

- "Beauty has seduced you, lust has led your heart astray." Plenty of others—more men than women—have followed those old men in being led by lust into personal disaster.

- Incitement to lust is all around us. We can ask the Lord to guide us away from these temptations, and keep us centered on God.

Tuesday 27th March   Numbers 21:4–9

From Mount Hor they set out by the way to the Red Sea, to go around the land of Edom; but the people became impatient on the way. The people spoke against God and against Moses, "Why have you brought us up out of Egypt to die in the wilderness? For there is no food and no water, and we detest this miserable food." Then the Lord sent poisonous serpents among the people, and they bit the people, so that many Israelites died. The people came to Moses and said, "We have sinned by speaking against the Lord and against you; pray to the Lord to take away the serpents from us." So Moses prayed for the people. And the Lord said to Moses, "Make a poisonous serpent, and set it on a pole; and everyone who is bitten shall look at it and live." So Moses made a serpent of bronze, and put it upon a pole; and whenever a serpent bit someone, that person would look at the serpent of bronze and live.

- The Book of Numbers tells a story of people complaining, being punished, turning to God, and finding relief.

- Lord, you have often taught me like a strict parent. You lead me to more abundant life through pruning and pain.

Wednesday 28th March · · · · · · · · · · · · · · · · · · · John 8:31–32

Then Jesus said to the Jews who had believed in him, "If you continue in my word, you are truly my disciples; and you will know the truth, and the truth will make you free."

- "The truth will make you free." We are often confused by this word "free." It has a cost; we have to pay a price. Throughout history, men and women have stood up against abusive power, without fear for their lives, to win freedom.

- Have I experienced the freedom that comes from truth? Or have I felt trapped by my fear of the truth?

- Can I speak to the Lord about this?

Thursday 29th March · Genesis 17:3–8

Then Abram fell on his face; and God said to him, "As for me, this is my covenant with you: You shall be the ancestor of a multitude of nations. No longer shall your name be Abram, but your name shall be Abraham; for I have made you the ancestor of a multitude of nations. I will make you exceedingly fruitful; and I will make nations of you, and kings shall come from you. I will establish my covenant between me and you, and your offspring after you throughout their generations, for an everlasting covenant, to be God to you and to your offspring after you. And I will give to you, and to your offspring after you, the land where you are now an alien, all the land of Canaan, for a perpetual holding; and I will be their God."

- God made a "covenant" with Abram. It was a new start for the man and his descendants, and with it his new name—Abraham.

- How does God's covenant with Abraham embrace me?

Friday 30th March   **John 10:31–42**

The Jews took up stones again to stone him. Jesus replied, "I have shown you many good works from the Father. For which of these are you going to stone me?" The Jews answered, "It is not for a good work that we are going to stone you, but for blasphemy, because you, though only a human being, are making yourself God." Jesus answered, "Is it not written in your law, 'I said, you are gods'? If those to whom the word of God came were called 'gods'—and the scripture cannot be annulled—can you say that the one whom the Father has sanctified and sent into the world is blaspheming because I said, 'I am God's Son'? If I am not doing the works of my Father, then do not believe me. But if I do them, even though you do not believe me, believe the works, so that you may know and understand that the Father is in me and I am in the Father." Then they tried to arrest him again, but he escaped from their hands. He went away again across the Jordan to the place where John had been baptizing earlier, and he remained there. Many came to him, and they were saying, "John performed no sign, but everything that John said about this man was true." And many believed in him there.

- "If I am not doing the works of my Father, then do not believe me." Love is shown not so much in words as in deeds. We are bombarded with words, by advertisers, politicians, media and every sort of preacher.

- To each of these, as to myself, I say: If your works do not square with your words, then I will not believe you.

- How do I measure up?

Saturday 31st March   **Ezekiel 37:26–28**

I will make a covenant of peace with them; it shall be an everlasting covenant with them; and I will bless them and multiply them, and will set my sanctuary among them forever-more. My dwelling place shall be with them; and I will be their God, and they shall be my people. Then the nations shall know that I the Lord sanctify Israel, when my sanctuary is among them forevermore.

- "It shall be an everlasting covenant with them." Ezekiel records that God's loving plan is renewed with a people, even though they have abandoned and betrayed him.

- There is a plan for me, no matter what has happened.

- What does this say to me?

april 1–7

Something to think and pray about each day this week:

Prayer of the Cross
This is Holy Week. Through our life we struggle against suffering and evil. We strive for happiness by our nature. But there are times when we cannot beat evil, only endure it, as when we face a wasting sickness, or betrayal by a loved one. At those times our only recourse is to Jesus in his passion. Our prayer then is desolate, the fruit of faith, that is to say, of darkness. In that obscure faith the understanding must be left behind, in order to go to God by love. It is the prayer of Jesus in Gethsemane, a prayer so painful that he sweated blood. We do not look for this sort of cross, but when it comes, prayer centered on the crucifix may be the only thing that can save us from drink or dementia.

The Presence of God
God is with me, but more,
God is within me, giving me existence.
Let me dwell for a moment on God's life-giving presence
in my body, my mind, my heart
and in the whole of my life.

Freedom
I ask for the grace to believe in what I could be and do
if I only allowed God, my loving Creator,
to continue to create me, guide me and shape me.

Consciousness
I exist in a web of relationships—links to nature, people, God.
I trace out these links, giving thanks for the life that flows
through them.
Some links are twisted or broken: I may feel regret, anger,
disappointment.
I pray for the gift of acceptance and forgiveness.

The Word
I read the Word of God slowly, a few times over, and I listen to
what God is saying to me. (Please turn to your scripture on the
following pages. Inspiration points are there should you need
them. When you are ready, return here to continue.)

Conversation
How has God's Word moved me? Has it left me cold?
Has it consoled me or moved me to act in a new way?
I imagine Jesus standing or sitting beside me,
I turn and share my feelings with him.

Conclusion
Glory be to the Father, and to the Son, and to the Holy Spirit,
As it was in the beginning, is now and ever shall be,
World without end. Amen

Sunday 1st April, Palm Sunday of the Lord's Passion
Philippians 2:6–11

Let the same mind be in you that was in Christ Jesus, who, though he was in the form of God, did not regard equality with God as something to be exploited, but emptied himself, taking the form of a slave, being born in human likeness. And being found in human form, he humbled himself and became obedient to the point of death—even death on a cross. Therefore God also highly exalted him and gave him the name that is above every name, so that at the name of Jesus every knee should bend, in heaven and on earth and under the earth, and every tongue should confess that Jesus Christ is Lord, to the glory of God the Father.

- As Holy Week begins, I fix my eyes on Jesus. Simply mulling over the words of this beautiful early Christian hymn can help me appreciate the mystery of it.

Monday 2nd April
Isaiah 42:1–4

Here is my servant, whom I uphold, my chosen, in whom my soul delights; I have put my spirit upon him; he will bring forth justice to the nations. He will not cry or lift up his voice, or make it heard in the street; a bruised reed he will not break, and a dimly burning wick he will not quench; he will faithfully bring forth justice. He will not grow faint or be crushed until he has established justice in the earth; and the coastlands wait for his teaching.

- "He will not grow faint or be crushed until he has established justice in the earth; and the coastlands wait for his teaching."

- That is our mission too, Lord: not to succumb to pressure but by firm persistence, to establish justice on the earth, and to go forth with his teaching on our lips.

Tuesday 3rd April   **John 13:21–27, 31–33, 36–38**

After saying this Jesus was troubled in spirit, and declared, "Very truly, I tell you, one of you will betray me." The disciples looked at one another, uncertain of whom he was speaking. One of his disciples—the one whom Jesus loved—was reclining next to him; Simon Peter therefore motioned to him to ask Jesus of whom he was speaking. So while reclining next to Jesus, he asked him, "Lord, who is it?" Jesus answered, "It is the one to whom I give this piece of bread when I have dipped it in the dish." So when he had dipped the piece of bread, he gave it to Judas son of Simon Iscariot. After he received the piece of bread, Satan entered into him. Jesus said to him, "Do quickly what you are going to do." . . . When Judas had gone out, Jesus said, "Now the Son of Man has been glorified, and God has been glorified in him. If God has been glorified in him, God will also glorify him in himself and will glorify him at once. Little children, I am with you only a little longer. You will look for me; and as I said to the Jews so now I say to you, 'Where I am going, you cannot come.' Simon Peter said to him, "Lord, where are you going?" Jesus answered, "Where I am going, you cannot follow me now; but you will follow afterward." Peter said to him, "Lord, why can I not follow you now? I will lay down my life for you." Jesus answered, "Will you lay down your life for me? Very truly, I tell you, before the cock crows, you will have denied me three times."

- Two treacheries: Judas went out to grab his money, betray Jesus, and kill himself in despair. Peter despite his protests would deny his Lord; he faced his own appalling guilt, wept bitterly, and his failure was not the end of his mission, but the beginning.

- Success is what I do with my failures. Teach me to trust in your love, Lord, and to learn from my mistakes and treacheries.

Wednesday 4th April   Matthew 26:14–16

Then one of the twelve, who was called Judas Iscariot, went to the chief priests and said, "What will you give me if I betray him to you?" They paid him thirty pieces of silver. And from that moment he began to look for an opportunity to betray him.

- Judas' greatest mistake was not that he betrayed Jesus, but that he had no confidence in the Lord's mercy and in his own power to recover from that betrayal, as Peter did. Am I confident?

Thursday 5th April, Holy Thursday   John 13:12–16

After Jesus had washed their feet, had put on his robe, and had returned to the table, he said to them, "Do you know what I have done to you? You call me Teacher and Lord—and you are right, for that is what I am. So if I, your Lord and Teacher, have washed your feet, you also ought to wash one another's feet. For I have set you an example, that you also should do as I have done to you. Very truly, I tell you, servants are not greater than their master, nor are messengers greater than the one who sent them."

- John's gospel describes the Last Supper by describing how Jesus washed his friends' feet, an act of service integral to discipleship.

- On his knees like a servant, Jesus turned human status upside down. Do I understand what he had done?

Friday 6th April, Good Friday   Isaiah 53:1–5

Who has believed what we have heard? And to whom has the arm of the Lord been revealed? For he grew up before him like a young plant, and like a root out of dry ground; he had no form or majesty that we should look at him, nothing in his appearance that we should desire him. He was despised and rejected by others; a man of suffering and acquainted with infirmity; and as one from whom others hide their faces he was despised, and we held him of no account. Surely he has borne our infirmities and carried our diseases; yet we accounted him stricken, struck down by God, and afflicted. But he was wounded for our transgressions, crushed for our iniquities; upon him was the punishment that made us whole, and by his bruises we are healed.

- Now we are at the heart of Jesus' mission: to suffer appallingly and to die without faltering in his love for us. This is where the Gospel begins and ends.

- Love demands that we trust in a goodness and a life beyond our own. Lord, it is hard to contemplate. I shy away from the pain and injustice of this Cross. Your love draws me back.

Saturday 7th April, Holy Saturday   Romans 6:3–9

Do you not know that all of us who have been baptized into Christ Jesus were baptized into his death? Therefore we have been buried with him by baptism into death, so that, just as Christ was raised from the dead by the glory of the Father, so we too might walk in newness of life. For if we have been united with him in a death like his, we will certainly be united with him in a resurrection like his. We know that our old self was crucified with him so that the body of sin might be destroyed, and we might no longer be enslaved to sin. For whoever has died is freed from sin. But if we have died with Christ, we believe that we will also live with him. We know that Christ, being raised from the dead, will never die again; death no longer has dominion over him.

- Tonight we re-affirm our ancient faith: Christ has robbed death of its ultimate sting, and has invigorated this sweet, precious, precarious, once-only life that is slipping away from us with every hour and day and year.

- To be Christian means to be an optimist because we know that Jesus' death was not in vain; his leap of faith was not in vain; his trust in his Father was not in vain. God raised him up.

april 8–14

Something to think and pray about each day this week:

Risen into life

On the first Easter morning, the apostles and the holy women did not see a ghost of Jesus. They saw him in the flesh, but in a different flesh, as the oak tree is different from the acorn that was its origin. We touch on the mystery of a body, not just Jesus' body but our own, which will express us at our best, will not blunt our spirit with weariness and rebellion, but express it with ease and joy. This is a mystery beyond our imagination, but it is the centre of our faith. As we grow older, nothing in our faith makes more sense than the Passion and the Resurrection, the certainty that our body, like Jesus', must suffer and die, and the certainty that we, in our bodies, have a life beyond death.

The Presence of God

To be present is to arrive as one is and open up to the other.
At this instant, as I arrive here, God is present waiting for me.
God always arrives before me, desiring to connect with me
even more than my most intimate friend.
I take a moment and greet my loving God.

Freedom

"In these days, God taught me
as a schoolteacher teaches a pupil" (St. Ignatius).
I remind myself that there are things God has to teach me yet,
and ask for the grace to hear them and let them change me.

Consciousness

How am I really feeling? Light-hearted? Heavy-hearted?
I may be very much at peace, happy to be here.
Equally, I may be frustrated, worried or angry.
I acknowledge how I really am. It is the real me that the Lord loves.

The Word

I take my time to read the Word of God, slowly, a few times,
allowing myself to dwell on anything that strikes me. (Please
turn to your scripture on the following pages. Inspiration points
are there should you need them. When you are ready, return
here to continue.)

Conversation

What feelings are rising in me
as I pray and reflect on God's Word?
I imagine Jesus himself sitting or standing beside me,
and open my heart to him.

Conclusion

Glory be to the Father, and to the Son, and to the Holy Spirit,
As it was in the beginning, is now and ever shall be,
World without end. Amen

Sunday 8th April, Easter Sunday   John 20:1–9

Early on the first day of the week, while it was still dark, Mary Magdalene came to the tomb and saw that the stone had been removed from the tomb. So she ran and went to Simon Peter and the other disciple, the one whom Jesus loved, and said to them, "They have taken the Lord out of the tomb, and we do not know where they have laid him." Then Peter and the other disciple set out and went toward the tomb. The two were running together, but the other disciple outran Peter and reached the tomb first. He bent down to look in and saw the linen wrappings lying there, but he did not go in. Then Simon Peter came, following him, and went into the tomb. He saw the linen wrappings lying there, and the cloth that had been on Jesus' head, not lying with the linen wrappings but rolled up in a place by itself. Then the other disciple, who reached the tomb first, also went in, and he saw and believed; for as yet they did not understand the scripture, that he must rise from the dead.

- Can I imagine myself standing near to the tomb on the morning in question, before first light? I observe the comings and goings.

- How do the people look? First, the woman; can I see her face? What does she do next? Then two men. . . .

- What has happened here?

Monday 9th April   Matthew 28:8–10

So the women left the tomb quickly with fear and great joy, and ran to tell his disciples. Suddenly Jesus met them and said, "Greetings!" And they came to him, took hold of his feet, and worshiped him. Then Jesus said to them, "Do not be afraid; go and tell my brothers to go to Galilee; there they will see me."

- "Go and tell my brothers." There is healing and forgiveness; the same disciples had abandoned him, but are still his brothers.

- They must now gather together, overcome fear, and become the people of God, those who will tell the good news. There is work to be done.

Tuesday 10th April   **John 20:11–17**

A s Mary wept, she bent over to look into the tomb; and she saw two angels in white, sitting where the body of Jesus had been lying, one at the head and the other at the feet. They said to her, "Woman, why are you weeping?" She said to them, "They have taken away my Lord, and I do not know where they have laid him." When she had said this, she turned around and saw Jesus standing there, but she did not know that it was Jesus. Jesus said to her, "Woman, why are you weeping? Whom are you looking for?" Supposing him to be the gardener, she said to him, "Sir, if you have carried him away, tell me where you have laid him, and I will take him away." Jesus said to her, "Mary!" She turned and said to him in Hebrew, "Rabbouni!" (which means Teacher). Jesus said to her, "Do not hold on to me, because I have not yet ascended to the Father. But go to my brothers and say to them, 'I am ascending to my Father and your Father, to my God and your God.'"

- Jesus called her Mary. That was enough. You know my name and my body, Lord. You see my lived-in face, shaped by my history, showing the lines of love, excesses, suffering, humor, gentleness.

- Teach me to love my face and body. It will grow old and die with me, but that is not the end. My body is sacred, and Easter opens a window for it and me onto a mysterious but endless vista.

Wednesday 11th April   **Luke 24:13–27**

N ow on that same day two of them were going to a village called Emmaus, about seven miles from Jerusalem, and talking with each other about all these things that had happened. While they were talking and discussing, Jesus himself came near and went with them, but their eyes were kept from recognizing him. And he said to them, "What are you discussing with each other while you walk along?" They stood still, looking sad. Then one of them, whose name was Cleopas, answered him, "Are you the only stranger in Jerusalem who does not know the things that have taken place there in these days?" He asked them, "What things?" They replied, "The things about Jesus of Nazareth, who was a prophet mighty in deed and word before God and all the people, and how our chief priests and leaders handed him over to be condemned to death and crucified him. But we had hoped that he was the one to redeem Israel. Yes, and besides all this, it is now the third day since these things took place. Moreover, some women of our group astounded us. They were at the tomb early this morning, and when they did not find his body there, they came back and told us that they had indeed seen a vision of angels who said that he was alive. Some of those who were with us went to the tomb and found it just as the women had said; but they did not see him." Then he said to them, "Oh, how foolish you are, and how slow of heart to believe all that the prophets have declared! Was it not necessary that the Messiah should suffer these things and then enter into his glory?" Then beginning with Moses and all the prophets, he interpreted to them the things about himself in all the scriptures.

- Like Cleopas I walk with you, Lord, in all sorts of shapes; but I do not always recognize you.

- Open the scriptures to me, show me your face in those I walk with, put some warmth into my heart. Encourage me to be hospitable, to offer my food to the stranger I walk with.

Thursday 12th April · Luke 24:36–43

While they were talking about this, Jesus himself stood among them and said to them, "Peace be with you."

They were startled and terrified, and thought that they were seeing a ghost. He said to them, "Why are you frightened, and why
do doubts arise in your hearts? Look at my hands and my feet;
see that it is I myself. Touch me and see; for a ghost does not
have flesh and bones as you see that I have." And when he had
said this, he showed them his hands and his feet. While in their
joy they were disbelieving and still wondering, he said to them,
"Have you anything here to eat?" They gave him a piece of
broiled fish, and he took it and ate in their presence.

- There is so much fear, grief and doubt among this tentative,
  closed-in group; this is no vibrant early church community.

- "Peace be with you." This is the real Jesus with them, flesh and
  blood, hungry and thirsty. Can I stand with them, and take time
  to be in their presence?

Friday 13th April   **John 21:2–8**
Gathered there together were Simon Peter, Thomas called
the Twin, Nathanael of Cana in Galilee, the sons of
Zebedee, and two others of his disciples. Simon Peter said to
them, "I am going fishing." They said to him, "We will go with
you." They went out and got into the boat, but that night they
caught nothing. Just after daybreak, Jesus stood on the beach;
but the disciples did not know that it was Jesus. Jesus said to
them, "Children, you have no fish, have you?" They answered
him, "No." He said to them, "Cast the net to the right side of
the boat, and you will find some." So they cast it, and now they
were not able to haul it in because there were so many fish. That
disciple whom Jesus loved said to Peter, "It is the Lord!" When
Simon Peter heard that it was the Lord, he put on some clothes,
for he was naked, and jumped into the sea. But the other disciples came in the boat, dragging the net full of fish, for they were
not far from the land, only about a hundred yards off.

- It is dawn. Peter and his companions are weary from a wasted night fishing. Then, a stranger appears on the beach.

- "It is the Lord!" Recognition replaces ignorance, and their empty nets are filled.

- Can I recognize the Lord in those I meet, the strangers, the ordinary people in the street and workplace? You cross my path many times a day.

Saturday 14th April · Mark 16:9–15

Now after he rose early on the first day of the week, he appeared first to Mary Magdalene, from whom he had cast out seven demons. She went out and told those who had been with him, while they were mourning and weeping. But when they heard that he was alive and had been seen by her, they would not believe it. After this he appeared in another form to two of them, as they were walking into the country. And they went back and told the rest, but they did not believe them. Later he appeared to the eleven themselves as they were sitting at the table; and he upbraided them for their lack of faith and stubbornness, because they had not believed those who saw him after he had risen. And he said to them, "Go into all the world and proclaim the good news to the whole creation."

- What an extraordinary command to slow-witted and faint-hearted fishermen, to preach the gospel "to the whole creation."

- The best preaching is not found in words, but in the life lived in Christ. As the holy Brazilian bishop Helder Camara used to warn his catechists: "Watch how you live. Your lives may be the only gospel your sisters and brothers will ever read."

april 15–21

Something to think and pray about each day this week:

My Lord and my God

St. Thomas did us all a favor by his skepticism. He was missing from the group on Easter Sunday evening, and was miffed at the others' delighted report: "We have seen the Lord." We can imagine the tension in the group as he implied that the disciples had been imagining things. A week later they were all together when Jesus appeared to them. Before he addressed Thomas, Jesus wished "Peace" on the whole company.

Suddenly the tensions and irritations in the group appear silly and irrelevant. In the light of Jesus' love, quarrels make no sense. Jesus picks out Thomas and answers his question by guiding his hand into the wounds.

Lord, lift me out of the small annoyances that take up too much of my energy. I believe in your resurrection from the dead. I thank you for the peace that you bring, putting all our lives into perspective.

The Presence of God

What is present to me is what has a hold on my becoming.
I reflect on the presence of God always there in love,
amidst the many things that have a hold on me.
I pause and pray that I may let God
affect my becoming in this precise moment.

Freedom

If God were trying to tell me something, would I know?
If God were reassuring me or challenging me, would I notice?
I ask for the grace to be free of my own preoccupations
and open to what God may be saying to me.

Consciousness

Knowing that God loves me unconditionally,
I can afford to be honest about how I am.
How has the last day been, and how do I feel now?
I share my feelings openly with the Lord.

The Word

God speaks to each one of us individually. I need to listen to
what he is saying to me. (Please turn to your scripture on the following pages. Inspiration points are there should you need
them. When you are ready, return here to continue.)

Conversation

What is stirring in me as I pray?
Am I consoled, troubled, left cold?
I imagine Jesus himself standing or sitting at my side,
and share my feelings with him.

Conclusion

Glory be to the Father, and to the Son, and to the Holy Spirit,
As it was in the beginning, is now and ever shall be,
World without end. Amen

Sunday 15th April, Second Sunday of Easter
John 20:24–29

But Thomas (who was called the Twin), one of the twelve, was not with them when Jesus came. So the other disciples told him, "We have seen the Lord." But he said to them, "Unless I see the mark of the nails in his hands, and put my finger in the mark of the nails and my hand in his side, I will not believe." A week later his disciples were again in the house, and Thomas was with them. Although the doors were shut, Jesus came and stood among them and said, "Peace be with you." Then he said to Thomas, "Put your finger here and see my hands. Reach out your hand and put it in my side. Do not doubt but believe." Thomas answered him, "My Lord and my God!" Jesus said to him, "Have you believed because you have seen me? Blessed are those who have not seen and yet have come to believe."

- Can I imagine that I am Thomas and the others come and say: We have seen Jesus who died?

- What is my reaction?

- Can I move through the scene as it unfolds?

- Where does it bring me to?

Monday 16th April
John 3:1–8

Now there was a Pharisee named Nicodemus, a leader of the Jews. He came to Jesus by night and said to him, "Rabbi, we know that you are a teacher who has come from God; for no one can do these signs that you do apart from the presence of God." Jesus answered him, "Very truly, I tell you, no one can see the kingdom of God without being born from above." Nicodemus said to him, "How can anyone be born after having grown old? Can one enter a second time into the mother's womb and be born?" Jesus answered, "Very truly, I tell you, no one can enter the kingdom of God without being born of water and

Spirit. What is born of the flesh is flesh, and what is born of the Spirit is spirit. Do not be astonished that I said to you, 'You must be born from above.' The wind blows where it chooses, and you hear the sound of it, but you do not know where it comes from or where it goes. So it is with everyone who is born of the Spirit."

- The Holy Spirit moves us like the wind. When a sailor is helming a small boat, working with tiller and mainsail to take advantage of an unseen breeze, he has to be alert every moment to the slightest gust.

- Am I one "who is born of the spirit"? Am I gaining that poise, readiness to respond, and energy that is the opposite of inertia?

Tuesday 17th April   Acts 4:32–37

Now the whole group of those who believed were of one heart and soul, and no one claimed private ownership of any possessions, but everything they owned was held in common. With great power the apostles gave their testimony to the resurrection of the Lord Jesus, and great grace was upon them all. There was not a needy person among them, for as many as owned lands or houses sold them and brought the proceeds of what was sold. They laid it at the apostles' feet, and it was distributed to each as any had need. There was a Levite, a native of Cyprus, Joseph, to whom the apostles gave the name Barnabas (which means "son of encouragement"). He sold a field that belonged to him, then brought the money, and laid it at the apostles' feet.

- "The company of those who believed were of one heart and soul, and had everything in common." That has been the ideal of Christian communities through the ages: a sort of voluntary communism, born of love.

- This Jerusalem model remains as an example of easy trust and sharing, as a vision to inspire us in the communities we live in.

Wednesday 18th April   John 3:16–17

Jesus said to Nicodemus, "For God so loved the world that he gave his only Son, so that everyone who believes in him may not perish but may have eternal life. Indeed, God did not send the Son into the world to condemn the world, but in order that the world might be saved through him."

- "Everyone who believes in him . . . may have eternal life." If we trust and believe in him, we will have eternal life—the life of God given to us today.

- As we enter into relationship with Jesus and follow him, we receive the life that is in him. Have I started to recognize eternal life within me, seeing people as Jesus sees them?

Thursday 19th April   Acts 5:27–33

When they had brought the apostles, they had them stand before the council. The high priest questioned them, saying, "We gave you strict orders not to teach in this name, yet here you have filled Jerusalem with your teaching and you are determined to bring this man's blood on us." But Peter and the apostles answered, "We must obey God rather than any human authority. The God of our ancestors raised up Jesus, whom you had killed by hanging him on a tree. God exalted him at his right hand as Leader and Savior that he might give repentance to Israel and forgiveness of sins. And we are witnesses to these things, and so is the Holy Spirit whom God has given to those who obey him." When they heard this, they were enraged and wanted to kill them.

- "We must obey God rather than men." This was the response of the early martyrs, when called on to offer sacrifice to idols.

- Can I live a disarmed life? Can I be so secure in your love, Jesus, that I can let go, and be insecure in this world?

- Accept the flaws, the wounds I cannot accept, and take me close to you today.

Friday 20th April — Acts 5:34–42

But a Pharisee in the council named Gamaliel, a teacher of the law, respected by all the people, stood up and ordered the men to be put outside for a short time. Then he said to them, "Fellow Israelites, consider carefully what you propose to do to these men. For some time ago Theudas rose up, claiming to be somebody, and a number of men, about four hundred, joined him; but he was killed, and all who followed him were dispersed and disappeared. After him Judas the Galilean rose up at the time of the census and got people to follow him; he also perished, and all who followed him were scattered. So in the present case, I tell you, keep away from these men and let them alone; because if this plan or this undertaking is of human origin, it will fail; but if it is of God, you will not be able to overthrow them—in that case you may even be found fighting against God!" They were convinced by him, and when they had called in the apostles, they had them flogged. Then they ordered them not to speak in the name of Jesus, and let them go. As they left the council, they rejoiced that they were considered worthy to suffer dishonor for the sake of the name. And every day in the temple and at home they did not cease to teach and proclaim Jesus as the Messiah.

- "If this plan is of human origin, it will fail; but if it is of God you will not be able to overthrow them." Gamaliel's words are full of wisdom.

- The good news about Jesus, the Messiah, drew people from a pantheon of half-human gods to the unimaginable Trinity.

- With Gamaliel's words to encourage me, Lord, gather me back in with your followers when I stray.

Saturday 21st April   John 6:16–21

When evening came, his disciples went down to the sea, got into a boat, and started across the sea to Capernaum. It was now dark, and Jesus had not yet come to them. The sea became rough because a strong wind was blowing. When they had rowed about three or four miles, they saw Jesus walking on the sea and coming near the boat, and they were terrified. But he said to them, "It is I; do not be afraid." Then they wanted to take him into the boat, and immediately the boat reached the land toward which they were going.

- "It is I; do not be afraid." When things are bad, I become fearful, I feel I am liable to sink at any moment, I flail and panic. Let me put my hand in the hand of the man who walked on the water.

- Lord, you always calm me. Give me the courage to put one foot in front of another, to move forward and not go into hiding.

april 22–28

Something to think and pray about each day this week:

Breaking open

The encounter with Jesus on the walk to Emmaus (Luke 24:13–35) is a model for all our prayer. We start off, possibly in company (like Cleopas and his companion—or wife?), preoccupied with present worries: in Cleopas' case the events of Holy Week and the loss of Jesus. The Lord joins us and starts with our concerns: "What are these things that you talk about?" He asks, and he listens. Then he begins to open the word of God to them; he breaks open the Scriptures. He gives them the option of letting him go on or asking him to stay. Jesus is often not easy to spot or recognize. They only know him in the breaking of bread. When they recognize him, and think about his words and presence, it hits them with such force that they have to tell others about it.

The Presence of God
God is with me, but more, God is within me.
Let me dwell for a moment on God's life-giving presence
in my body, in my mind, in my heart,
as I sit here, right now.

Freedom
I need to close out the noise, to rise above the noise;
The noise that interrupts, that separates,
The noise that isolates.
I need to listen to God again.

Consciousness
In the presence of my loving Creator,
I look honestly at my feelings over the last day,
the highs, the lows and the level ground.
Can I see where the Lord has been present?

The Word
I read the Word of God slowly, a few times over, and I listen to
what God is saying to me. (Please turn to your scripture on the
following pages. Inspiration points are there should you need
them. When you are ready, return here to continue.)

Conversation
Do I notice myself reacting as I pray with the Word of God?
Do I feel challenged, comforted, angry?
Imagining Jesus sitting or standing by me,
I speak out my feelings, as one trusted friend to another.

Conclusion
Glory be to the Father, and to the Son, and to the Holy Spirit,
As it was in the beginning, is now and ever shall be,
World without end. Amen

Sunday 22nd April, Third Sunday of Easter
John 21:15–19

When they had finished breakfast, Jesus said to Simon Peter, "Simon son of John, do you love me more than these?" He said to him, "Yes, Lord; you know that I love you." Jesus said to him, "Feed my lambs." A second time he said to him, "Simon son of John, do you love me?" He said to him, "Yes, Lord; you know that I love you." Jesus said to him, "Tend my sheep." He said to him the third time, "Simon son of John, do you love me?" Peter felt hurt because he said to him the third time, "Do you love me?" And he said to him, "Lord, you know everything; you know that I love you." Jesus said to him, "Feed my sheep. Very truly, I tell you, when you were younger, you used to fasten your own belt and to go wherever you wished. But when you grow old, you will stretch out your hands, and someone else will fasten a belt around you and take you where you do not wish to go." (He said this to indicate the kind of death by which he would glorify God.) After this he said to him, "Follow me."

- Can I put myself under the gaze of Jesus and hear these questions?

- How does it feel?

- How do I react?

- Where is Jesus going with this?

- Am I prepared to be led?

Monday 23rd April
John 6:26–27

Jesus answered them, "Very truly, I tell you, you are looking for me, not because you saw signs, but because you ate your fill of the loaves. Do not work for the food that perishes, but for the food that endures for eternal life, which the Son of Man will give you.

- "Do not work for food that perishes." The crowd who gathered to Jesus had mixed motives. They cannot see beyond a filling meal. What must they do for this food they have to work for?

- I also have the same muddle of motives in me; not pure love, but selfishness, weariness, and the hope of relief from anxiety and guilt. Lead me gently, Lord.

Tuesday 24th April   John 6:35

Jesus said to the people: "I am the bread of life. No one who comes to me will ever hunger. No one who believes in me will ever thirst."

- This was something that the Jewish people well understood: The word of God, the Torah, was an incredible form of nourishment, bread for the heart and mind.

- Do I see the word of God as the revelation of the love of God for me, food for my life, source of wisdom and truth?

Wednesday 25th April, St. Mark the Evangelist
Mark 16:15–20

And Jesus said to the disciples, "Go into all the world and proclaim the good news to the whole creation. The one who believes and is baptized will be saved; but the one who does not believe will be condemned. And these signs will accompany those who believe: by using my name they will cast out demons; they will speak in new tongues; they will pick up snakes in their hands, and if they drink any deadly thing, it will not hurt them; they will lay their hands on the sick, and they will recover." So then the Lord Jesus, after he had spoken to them, was taken up into heaven and sat down at the right hand of God. And they went out and proclaimed the good news everywhere, while the Lord worked with them and confirmed the message by the signs that accompanied it.

- If I read this passage slowly I could, by turns, be challenged, frightened, amazed, distorted, inspired, consoled . . .

- Which reactions do I rest with spontaneously? Does that tell me something about myself?

- Both the first and the last sentence of the passage tell of "Good News." Can I situate my reactions within the context of this "Good News"?

Thursday 26th April   John 6:45

Jesus said to the people: "It is written in the prophets: They will all be taught by God; everyone who has listened to the Father and learned from him comes to me."

- "They will all be taught by God." When St. Francis of Assisi sent his friars out to preach, he told them: "You will spread the good news wherever you go. Sometimes you will use words."

- Let me think of one instance where I have learnt from God, without words, touched by an encounter, by pleasure or by the pain of everyday living. Let me sit with that for a while.

Friday 27th April   Acts 9:1–9

Meanwhile Saul, still breathing threats and murder against the disciples of the Lord, went to the high priest and asked him for letters to the synagogues at Damascus, so that if he found any who belonged to the Way, men or women, he might bring them bound to Jerusalem. Now as he was going along and approaching Damascus, suddenly a light from heaven flashed around him. He fell to the ground and heard a voice saying to him, "Saul, Saul, why do you persecute me?" He asked, "Who are you, Lord?" The reply came, "I am Jesus, whom you are persecuting. But get up and enter the city, and you will be told what you are to do." The men who were traveling with him stood speechless because they heard the voice but saw no one.

Saul got up from the ground, and though his eyes were open, he could see nothing; so they led him by the hand and brought him into Damascus. For three days he was without sight, and neither ate nor drank.

- It took a thunderbolt, an unsaddling, and sudden blindness, to bring a change of heart in Saul.

- What about my conversion, my turning? Am I gradually turning more towards God, or in some other direction?

Saturday 28th April John 6:60, 66–69

After hearing Jesus (promise his flesh to eat), many of his followers said: "This is intolerable language. How could anyone accept it?" After this, many of his disciples went away and followed him no more. Then Jesus said to the Twelve: "What about you, do you want to go away too?" Simon Peter answered: "Lord, to whom shall we go? You have the message of eternal life, and we believe, we have come to know that you are the Holy One of God."

- "This is intolerable language. How could anyone accept it?" Indeed your words are sometimes hard, Lord. At times I am tempted to join those disciples who walked away.

- But you, Lord, are my star, the north to which my compass points. Without your words I have no direction.

april 29 – may 5

Something to think and pray about each day this week:

Ready for prayer
Jesus prayed that we may have life and have it more abundantly. It starts in our bodies. As you settle in to pray, first quiet the whole of your body. Then focus your attention on the top of your head, and slowly move your focus down your whole body, relaxing each nerve and muscle as you become aware of them. Some parts in particular need attention: the muscles at the back of your neck, and your stomach area. Tension easily shows itself there. Let the muscles go soft and flabby. Send a little rolling wave of peace down to your stomach.

Now hear Jesus speak of the good things and good people that have been part of your life. When our body is relaxed, and our emotional palate is clean, we can taste the beauty of people and things. Slow me down, Lord, so that I may taste and relish the life around me.

The Presence of God

As I sit here, the beating of my heart,
the ebb and flow of my breathing, the movements of my mind
are all signs of God's ongoing creation of me.
I pause for a moment, and become aware
of this presence of God within me.

Freedom

I will ask God's help,
to be free from my own preoccupations,
to be open to God in this time of prayer,
to come to love and serve him more.

Consciousness

Knowing that God loves me unconditionally,
I look honestly over the last day, its events and my feelings.
Do I have something to be grateful for? Then I give thanks.
Is there something I am sorry for? Then I ask forgiveness.

The Word

I take my time to read the Word of God, slowly, a few times,
allowing myself to dwell on anything that strikes me. (Please
turn to your scripture on the following pages. Inspiration points
are there should you need them. When you are ready, return
here to continue.)

Conversation

Remembering that I am still in God's presence,
I imagine Jesus himself standing or sitting beside me,
and say whatever is on my mind, whatever is in my heart,
speaking as one friend to another.

Conclusion

Glory be to the Father, and to the Son, and to the Holy Spirit,
As it was in the beginning, is now and ever shall be,
World without end. Amen

Sunday 29th April, Fourth Sunday of Easter
John 10:27–30

Jesus said to the Jews, "My sheep hear my voice. I know them, and they follow me. I give them eternal life, and they will never perish. No one will snatch them out of my hand. What my Father has given me is greater than all else, and no one can snatch it out of the Father's hand. The Father and I are one."

- When Jesus speaks about "my sheep," what tone do I hear in his voice? Pride? Loyalty? Trust?

- What response do I have to being one of the "sheep"? Does it make me feel cared for? Or tied down?

- These images can't begin to explore the depth of the divine mystery.

Monday 30th April
John 10:1–6

Jesus said to the Pharisees, "Very truly, I tell you, anyone who does not enter the sheepfold by the gate but climbs in by another way is a thief and a bandit. The one who enters by the gate is the shepherd of the sheep. The gatekeeper opens the gate for him, and the sheep hear his voice. He calls his own sheep by name and leads them out. When he has brought out all his own, he goes ahead of them, and the sheep follow him because they know his voice. They will not follow a stranger, but they will run from him because they do not know the voice of strangers." Jesus used this figure of speech with them, but they did not understand what he was saying to them.

- Can I stay with the image of the shepherd who calls each sheep by its own name and who leads them along safe paths?

- Do I allow Jesus to call me by name? Do I feel confidence in the sound of his voice?

- How do I respond now? Can I increase my understanding of what Jesus is saying here?

Tuesday 1st May   Acts 11:26

The disciples went to Antioch. So it was that for an entire year they met with the church and taught a great many people, and it was in Antioch that the disciples were first called "Christians."

- Do I call myself a Christian?

- In Antioch the name "Christian" was given to the disciples. A disciple is one who learns from the master.

- Am I still learning? Am I perhaps able to teach others?

Wednesday 2nd May   John 12:44–45

Jesus said to the people: "Whoever believes in me believes not in me but in the one who sent me, and whoever sees me sees the one who sent me."

- "Whoever sees me sees him who sent me." The God we believe in is not visible, nor even imaginable to the most brilliant mind, since he is outside our categories of time and space. Yet Jesus says: See me and you see God.

- Lord, I look for you, I try to imagine your features and listen to the story of your dealings as a man. You are my way to the Father, and the knowledge of you is precious to me.

Thursday 3rd May, Sts. Philip and James   John 14:6–14

Jesus said to him, "I am the way, and the truth, and the life. No one comes to the Father except through me. If you know me, you will know my Father also. From now on you do know him and have seen him." Philip said to him, "Lord, show us the Father, and we will be satisfied." Jesus said to him, "Have I been with you all this time, Philip, and you still do not know me? Whoever has seen me has seen the Father. How can you say, 'Show us the Father'? Do you not believe that I am in the Father and the Father is in me? The words that I say to you I do not speak on my own; but the Father who dwells in me does his works. Believe me that I am in the Father and the Father is in me; but if you do not, then believe me because of the works themselves. Very truly, I tell you, the one who believes in me will also do the works that I do and, in fact, will do greater works than these, because I am going to the Father. I will do whatever you ask in my name, so that the Father may be glorified in the Son. If in my name you ask me for anything, I will do it."

- Can I allow these words, addressed to Philip, be spoken to me?

- Do these mysterious concepts about Jesus and his heavenly Father intrigue me, delight me, confuse me?

- The "one who believes in me" can, it seems, take part in the mystery too. Does this mean me? Am I open to that?

Friday 4th May   John 14:1–3

Jesus said to his disciples, "Do not let your hearts be troubled. Believe in God, believe also in me. In my Father's house there are many dwelling places. If it were not so, would I have told you that I go to prepare a place for you? And if I go and prepare a place for you, I will come again and will take you to myself, so that where I am, there you may be also."

- "In my Father's house there are many dwelling places." That matters a lot to me, Lord. So many of my friends would not feel at ease in heaven's guest bedroom. They just hope they can fit in somewhere.

- The suicides, the addicted, the thieves, the sexually deviant, the publicly pilloried, the "lepers" who are cast aside from society—all count on your mercy to find a place for them, no matter how dirty they feel.

- So do I count on your mercy. Any room will do as long as you are there.

Saturday 5th May   John 14:7–9a

Jesus said to his disciples, "If you know me, you will know my Father also. From now on you do know him and have seen him." Philip said to him, "Lord, show us the Father, and we will be satisfied." Jesus said to him, "Have I been with you all this time, Philip, and you still do not know me?

- "You still do not know me?" I know I am slow to grasp your message, Lord. You put all your energy into me, and sometimes I think I have the answers; until something happens that makes me realize I don't understand your ways.

- Like the disciples I want to take shortcuts, to get straight to the kingdom, and the Father. Slow me down, Lord, so I come to the Father through you, even when the gate is narrow and the path rough.

may 6–12

Something to think and pray about each day this week:

Taking stock

At the end of the week, give yourself time to review what has happened since last Sunday. Work backwards from where you are now and touch upon all areas of concern.

What things worried you? Have some of those worries already been resolved? What unfinished business is still causing an itch in your mind? Who are the people you remember meeting this week? Did some of them leave a nasty taste in your mouth? Do you need to be reconciled, or to ask forgiveness, or to forgive? You may remember other meetings as moments of blessing— when others left you feeling uplifted, or you stroked others with your attention and warmth. Have any of your worries grown out of proportion, bothering you more than they should?

Take time to put things back into perspective. Then thank the Lord for his presence in all the encounters of your life.

The Presence of God
I pause for a moment
and reflect on God's life-giving presence
in every part of my body, in everything around me,
in the whole of my life.

Freedom
God is not foreign to my freedom.
Instead the Spirit breathes life into my most intimate desires,
gently nudging me towards all that is good.
I ask for the grace to let myself be enfolded by the Spirit.

Consciousness
How do I find myself today?
Where am I with God? With others?
Do I have something to be grateful for? Then I give thanks.
Is there something I am sorry for? Then I ask forgiveness.

The Word
God speaks to each one of us individually. I need to listen to what he is saying to me. (Please turn to your scripture on the following pages. Inspiration points are there should you need them. When you are ready, return here to continue.)

Conversation
How has God's Word moved me? Has it left me cold?
Has it consoled me or moved me to act in a new way?
I imagine Jesus standing or sitting beside me,
I turn and share my feelings with him.

Conclusion
Glory be to the Father, and to the Son, and to the Holy Spirit,
As it was in the beginning, is now and ever shall be,
World without end. Amen

Sunday 6th May, Fifth Sunday of Easter
John 13:31–33, 34–35

When Judas had gone out, Jesus said to the apostles, "Now the Son of Man has been glorified, and God has been glorified in him. If God has been glorified in him, God will also glorify him in himself and will glorify him at once. Little children, I am with you only a little longer. I give you a new commandment, that you love one another. Just as I have loved you, you also should love one another. By this everyone will know that you are my disciples, if you have love for one another."

- The scene is set for something truly dramatic. The betrayer has just left and the end is very close.

- In these final precious moments what does Jesus want to say?

- Can I give these words the serious response that Jesus wants for them?

Monday 7th May
John 14:26

Jesus said to his disciples: "The Advocate, the Holy Spirit, whom the Father will send in my name, will teach you everything, and remind you of all that I have said to you."

- Patrick Kavanagh the poet used to say: "We only learn what we already know." Teachers may try to condition us from the outside with learning facts and formulas. But where do I get the convictions I live by, and those that I might die for? Where does reflecting on my own experience come into this?

- Lord, as I pray, send me your Holy Spirit to keep me in mind of you.

Tuesday 8th May
John 14:27–29

Jesus said to his disciples, "Peace I leave with you; my peace I give to you. I do not give to you as the world gives. Do not let your hearts be troubled, and do not let them be afraid. You heard me say to you, 'I am going away, and I am coming to you.' If you loved me, you would rejoice that I am going to the Father, because the Father is greater than I. And now I have told you this before it occurs, so that when it does occur, you may believe."

• Jesus offers us a peace that is different from the peace that the world gives. What makes it different? How do I know if I have it?

• Jesus, now reunited with the Father, guarantees our peace. Can I open my heart to this truth and be touched by it?

Wednesday 9th May   John 15:7
Jesus said to his disciples, "If you abide in me, and my words abide in you, ask for whatever you wish, and it will be done for you."

• Think of the music of that lovely hymn:
      Abide with me; fast falls the eventide;
      The darkness deepens; Lord, with me abide;
      When other helpers fail, and comforts flee,
      Help of the helpless, O, abide with me.

Thursday 10th May   Acts 15:7–9
Peter stood up and addressed the council at Jerusalem: "You know perfectly well that in the early days God made his choice among you; the gentiles were to learn the good news from me and so become believers. God, who can read everyone's heart, showed his approval of the Gentiles by giving the Holy Spirit to them as he did to us Jews; and he made no distinction between them and us, since he purified their hearts by faith."

• This was a moment of truth for the church. She firmly set her face against distinctions based on race or culture.

180

- Do I find myself making distinctions between "them" and "us"? It can come in many subtle forms, Lord; open my eyes to what is in my heart.

Friday 11th May   John 15:15

Jesus said to his disciples: "No longer do I call you servants, because a servant does not know his master's business; I call you friends, because I have made known to you everything I have learnt from my Father."

- "I call you friends." Jesus my friend, in your company I can relax, be silent or talk, grumble or boast, vent and complain or feel thankful and light-hearted.

- Lord, you know my heart, and you continue to make allowances. I do not have to pretend.

Saturday 12th May   John 15:19

Jesus said to his disciples: "If you belonged to the world, the world would love you as its own. Because you do not belong to the world, but I have chosen you out of the world—therefore the world hates you."

- Forgive me, Lord; there are times when I try to keep up with the prejudices and fripperies of fashion, or echo the cynicism and materialism around me.

- When the worldly love me, I need to look hard at myself. I need to remember that you, the most lovable of men, suffered great acclaim, followed by hatred and then execution. When people are giving me a hard time, it may well be that I am blessed.

may 13–19

Something to think and pray about each day this week:

Natural growth

In Ireland, if there is one week of the year we would not want to miss, it is this week, starting with Mayday. Flowers and bushes are in blossom, the trees glow with a miraculous light green, the birds are nesting and singing, the trout are on the Mayfly, there is warmth in the sun, and summer is still ahead of us. Hopkins sings, in "The May Magnificat":

> Cluster of bugle blue eggs thin
> Forms and warms the life within;
>> And bird and blossom swell
>> In sod or sheath or shell.
> All things rising, all things sizing
> Mary sees, sympathising
>> With that world of good,
>> Nature's motherhood.

For each of us there is a special time when we find God in nature: We look out more than in. There are days when we feel: "If only time would stop, and leave the world like this!" Lord, thank you for this annual miracle of beautiful new life.

The Presence of God

The world is charged with the grandeur of God (Gerard Manley Hopkins).
I dwell for a moment on the presence of God
around me, in every part of my body,
and deep within my being.

Freedom

Everything has the potential to draw forth from me a fuller love and life.
Yet my desires are often fixed, caught, on illusions of fulfillment.
I ask that God, through my freedom, may orchestrate
my desires in a vibrant loving melody rich in harmony.

Consciousness

In God's loving presence I unwind the past day,
starting from now and looking back, moment by moment.
I gather in all the goodness and light, in gratitude.
I attend to the shadows and what they say to me,
seeking healing, courage, forgiveness.

The Word

I read the Word of God slowly, a few times over, and I listen to what God is saying to me. (Please turn to your scripture on the following pages. Inspiration points are there should you need them. When you are ready, return here to continue.)

Conversation

What feelings are rising in me
as I pray and reflect on God's Word?
I imagine Jesus himself sitting or standing beside me,
and open my heart to him.

Conclusion

Glory be to the Father, and to the Son, and to the Holy Spirit,
As it was in the beginning, is now and ever shall be,
World without end. Amen

Sunday 13th May, Sixth Sunday of Easter John 14:23–29

Jesus answered him, "Those who love me will keep my word, and my Father will love them, and we will come to them and make our home with them. Whoever does not love me does not keep my words; and the word that you hear is not mine, but is from the Father who sent me. I have said these things to you while I am still with you. But the Advocate, the Holy Spirit, whom the Father will send in my name, will teach you everything, and remind you of all that I have said to you. Peace I leave with you; my peace I give to you. I do not give to you as the world gives. Do not let your hearts be troubled, and do not let them be afraid. You heard me say to you, 'I am going away, and I am coming to you.' If you loved me, you would rejoice that I am going to the Father, because the Father is greater than I. And now I have told you this before it occurs, so that when it does occur, you may believe."

- The promise is that Jesus and his Father will come to me and make their home with me. How does that idea sit with me? Have I experienced their promise or am I confused about what they want?

- Do I feel the need of the promised Holy Spirit, who will teach me everything?

- Am I prepared to wait and listen?

Monday 14th May John 15:26–16:4

Jesus said to his disciples, "When the Advocate comes, whom I will send to you from the Father, the Spirit of truth who comes from the Father, he will testify on my behalf. You also are to testify because you have been with me from the beginning. I have said these things to you to keep you from stumbling. They will put you out of the synagogues. Indeed, an hour is coming when those who kill you will think that by doing so they are offering worship to God. And they will do this because they have not known the Father or me. But I have said these things to you so that when their hour comes you may remember that I told you about them. I did not say these things to you from the beginning, because I was with you."

- The Holy Spirit, the Advocate, is sent by Jesus and comes from the Father; the full expression of God among and within us. The presence of the Advocate strengthens us to become more like the Jesus who is no longer with us.

- How am I open to the Spirit, my Advocate?

Tuesday 15th May   Acts 16:22–28

The crowd joined in attacking Paul and Silas, and the magistrates had them stripped of their clothing and ordered them to be beaten with rods. After they had given them a severe flogging, they threw them into prison and ordered the jailer to keep them securely. Following these instructions, he put them in the innermost cell and fastened their feet in the stocks. About midnight Paul and Silas were praying and singing hymns to God, and the prisoners were listening to them. Suddenly there was an earthquake, so violent that the foundations of the prison were shaken; and immediately all the doors were opened and everyone's chains were unfastened. When the jailer woke up and saw the prison doors wide open, he drew his sword and was about to kill himself, since he supposed that the prisoners had escaped. But Paul shouted in a loud voice, "Do not harm yourself, for we are all here."

- Paul's fetters were unfastened but he stayed behind bars with the prisoners. In God's presence, the physical chains did not disturb him.

- Can I look deeper, to the interior bonds that warp my judgment and limit my freedom of choice: my dislikes, jealousies, and uncontrolled appetites?

Wednesday 16th May   Acts 17:15, 22–25

Those who conducted Paul brought him as far as Athens; and after receiving instructions to have Silas and Timothy join him as soon as possible, they left him. Then Paul stood in front of the Areopagus and said, "Athenians, I see how extremely religious you are in every way. For as I went through the city and looked carefully at the objects of your worship, I found among them an altar with the inscription, 'To an unknown god.' What therefore you worship as unknown, this I proclaim to you. The God who made the world and everything in it, he who is Lord of heaven and earth, does not live in shrines made by human hands, nor is he served by human hands, as though he needed anything, since he himself gives to all mortals life and breath and all things."

- "To an unknown God." I do not know you, Lord, but I seek you. I have glimpses of you in the face of Christ. I feel close to you in sacred places, in the sacraments and in prayer.

- Can I know the Lord outside of my church or devotional time, in the people to whom God gives "life and breath"?

Thursday 17th May   Acts 18:1–3

After this Paul left Athens and went to Corinth. There he found a Jew named Aquila, a native of Pontus, who had recently come from Italy with his wife Priscilla, because Claudius had ordered all Jews to leave Rome. Paul went to see them, and, because he was of the same trade, he stayed with them, and they worked together—by trade they were tentmakers.

- Paul's preaching and prayer were not a barrier to him earning his keep. God's work does not require idleness.

- Work is part of our human calling. Even when work is drudgery, and I am weary or bored, I know it puts me in close contact with the great mass of the human race, and my own humanity.

Friday 18th May   John 16:20–23

Very truly, I tell you, you will weep and mourn, but the world will rejoice; you will have pain, but your pain will turn into joy. When a woman is in labor, she has pain, because her hour has come. But when her child is born, she no longer remembers the anguish because of the joy of having brought a human being into the world. So you have pain now; but I will see you again, and your hearts will rejoice, and no one will take your joy from you. On that day you will ask nothing of me. Very truly, I tell you, if you ask anything of the Father in my name, he will give it to you.

- Discipleship is confronting indeed. Jesus uses the image of a mother in childbirth to show us that we are called to a new "aloneness" in the spiritual life. But with that purification of faith comes a new transformation in God.

- Can I talk to the Lord about any pain I face? Can I, as my mother did, face acute pain, continue on each day, and look forward to the joy promised to us through salvation?

Saturday 19th May   John 16:23–27

Jesus said to his disciples, "On that day you will ask nothing of me. Very truly, I tell you, if you ask anything of the Father in my name, he will give it to you. Until now you have not asked for anything in my name. Ask and you will receive, so that your joy may be complete. I have said these things to you in figures of speech. The hour is coming when I will no longer speak to you in figures, but will tell you plainly of the Father. On that day you will ask in my name. I do not say to you that I will ask the Father on your behalf; for the Father himself loves you, because you have loved me and have believed that I came from God."

- "The Father himself loves you." This is where I fit into the inner dynamic of the Blessed Trinity; taken into oneness with our brother. As Jesus is joined to the Father through the Holy Spirit, so too are we, because Jesus is our brother.

- Can I take some time to sit with my reflections on this?

Something to think and pray about each day this week:

Absence and presence

Those who have visited the Holy Land will remember moments of nostalgia—"if only I could have walked these fields and streets when Jesus was here." After the Ascension, Peter, Andrew and the rest of the Twelve must have felt this more acutely, remembering his presence. The period between the Ascension and Pentecost prepares them and us not just for his absence, but for his continuing presence to us through the Holy Spirit: "I will not leave you orphans."

In Romans 8:15–16, St. Paul explains: "This is not the spirit of slaves bringing fear into your lives again, but the spirit of children, and it makes us cry out Abba, Father. The Holy Spirit and our spirit bear united witness that we are children of God."

The Presence of God
As I sit here, God is present,
breathing life into me and into everything around me.
For a few moments, I sit silently,
and become aware of God's loving presence.

Freedom
There are very few people
who realize what God would make of them
if they abandoned themselves into his hands,
and let themselves be formed by his grace. (St. Ignatius)
I ask for the grace to trust myself totally to God's love.

Consciousness
I exist in a web of relationships—links to nature, people, God.
I trace out these links, giving thanks for the life that flows
through them.
Some links are twisted or broken: I may feel regret, anger,
disappointment.
I pray for the gift of acceptance and forgiveness.

The Word
I take my time to read the Word of God, slowly, a few times, allowing
myself to dwell on anything that strikes me. (Please turn to your scripture on the following pages. Inspiration points are there should you
need them. When you are ready, return here to continue.)

Conversation
What is stirring in me as I pray?
Am I consoled, troubled, left cold?
I imagine Jesus himself standing or sitting at my side,
and share my feelings with him.

Conclusion
Glory be to the Father, and to the Son, and to the Holy Spirit,
As it was in the beginning, is now and ever shall be,
World without end. Amen

Sunday 20th May, Ascension of the Lord — Acts 1:6–11

So when they had come together, they asked him, "Lord, is this the time when you will restore the kingdom to Israel?" He replied, "It is not for you to know the times or periods that the Father has set by his own authority. But you will receive power when the Holy Spirit has come upon you; and you will be my witnesses in Jerusalem, in all Judea and Samaria, and to the ends of the earth." When he had said this, as they were watching, he was lifted up, and a cloud took him out of their sight. While he was going and they were gazing up toward heaven, suddenly two men in white robes stood by them. They said, "Men of Galilee, why do you stand looking up toward heaven? This Jesus, who has been taken up from you into heaven, will come in the same way as you saw him go into heaven."

- Because of Jesus' Ascension to the Father, humankind now has a place in heaven. We will no longer be out of place there. One of our own' sits at God's right hand.

- If I have difficulty appreciating this I can look at the disciples in the scene. Even at the end they seem not to understand.

Monday 21st May — Acts 19:1–2, 6–8

While Apollos was in Corinth, Paul passed through the interior regions and came to Ephesus, where he found some disciples. He said to them, "Did you receive the Holy Spirit when you became believers?" They replied, "No, we have not even heard that there is a Holy Spirit." When Paul had laid his hands on them, the Holy Spirit came upon them, and they spoke in tongues and prophesied—altogether there were about twelve of them. He entered the synagogue and for three months spoke out boldly, and argued persuasively about the kingdom of God.

- "We have not even heard that there is a Holy Spirit." Let me focus on the Paraclete, our Advocate before the Father.

- How intimate is the Holy Spirit to my existence: not as a separate God, but rather that by which we—and Jesus—are wrapped into the Godhead.

Tuesday 22nd May   John 17:1–3

After Jesus had spoken these words, he looked up to heaven and said, "Father, the hour has come; glorify your Son so that the Son may glorify you, since you have given him authority over all people, to give eternal life to all whom you have given him. And this is eternal life, that they may know you, the only true God, and Jesus Christ whom you have sent."

- All is complete. Jesus contemplates God's glory and prays that we all may live it—that glory which all creation sings and reveals.

- Lord, quiet my mind, relax my body, and guide me in this silence to contemplate your beautiful plan of salvation.

Wednesday 23rd May   Acts 20:32–35

Paul said to the elders of the church of Ephesus: "Now I commend you to God and to the message of his grace, a message that is able to build you up and to give you the inheritance among all who are sanctified. I coveted no one's silver or gold or clothing. You know for yourselves that I worked with my own hands to support myself and my companions. In all this I have given you an example that by such work we must support the weak, remembering the words of the Lord Jesus, for he himself said, 'It is more blessed to give than to receive.'"

- Paul emphasizes that he works hard to support himself; prayer and preaching are part of the fabric of our daily lives.

- Do I think of prayer and work as separate parts of my life? Can I speak to the Lord about linking my prayer and my daily tasks closer together?

Thursday 24th May   Acts 23:6–8

When Paul noticed that some in the Sanhedrin were Sadducees and others were Pharisees, he called out in the council, "Brothers, I am a Pharisee, a son of Pharisees. I am on trial concerning the hope of the resurrection of the dead." When he said this, a dissension began between the Pharisees and the Sadducees, and the assembly was divided. (The Sadducees say that there is no resurrection, or angel, or spirit; but the Pharisees acknowledge all three.)

- Paul used his wits, playing on the theological divisions between the ruling factions, Pharisees and Sadducees; he grasped the opportunity to divert anger from himself. To be a Christian does not mean that you are passive or a fool.

- Give me the grace, Lord, to use my wits and all my skills, in your service.

Friday 25th May   John 21:15–17

When they had finished breakfast, Jesus said to Simon Peter, "Simon son of John, do you love me more than these?" He said to him, "Yes, Lord; you know that I love you." Jesus said to him, "Feed my lambs." A second time he said to him, "Simon son of John, do you love me?" He said to him, "Yes, Lord; you know that I love you." Jesus said to him, "Tend my sheep." He said to him the third time, "Simon son of John, do you love me?" Peter felt hurt because he said to him the third time, "Do you love me?" And he said to him, "Lord, you know everything; you know that I love you." Jesus said to him, "Feed my sheep."

- "You know that I love you." Peter's response is almost plaintive; gone is the confident Peter who went on to deny his Lord. He is profoundly aware of his failings.

- Lord, I want to answer like Peter: "Lord, you know everything; you know that I love you." Maybe my life does not match my intentions, but then, neither did Peter's. Teach me to grow in your love.

Saturday 26th May   John 21:20–24

Peter turned and saw the disciple whom Jesus loved following them; he was the one who had reclined next to Jesus at the supper and had said, "Lord, who is it that is going to betray you?" When Peter saw him, he said to Jesus, "Lord, what about him?" Jesus said to him, "If it is my will that he remain until I come, what is that to you? Follow me!" So the rumor spread in the community that this disciple would not die. Yet Jesus did not say to him that he would not die, but, "If it is my will that he remain until I come, what is that to you?" This is the disciple who is testifying to these things and has written them, and we know that his testimony is true.

- "Lord, what about him?" Peter was confirmed as the leader, the shepherd of the community, but knew that Jesus loved John, the beloved disciple, in a special way.

- Peter's role as shepherd was to lead all people to Jesus, so that we all become "beloved disciples".

- Can I hear Jesus say to me, "Follow me"?

may 27 – june 2

Something to think and pray about each day this week:

Spirit of conviction
That mighty wind and tongues of fire at Pentecost were outward signs of the change the Holy Spirit brought about in the disciples. They were the same women and men as before, but they suddenly had the courage of their convictions. They were suddenly able to draw on their memories of Jesus. The Holy Spirit does not transform our personalities, or fill us with new information. Rather the Spirit enables us to be ourselves, and to reflect on what we have experienced from the Lord. We are made courageous and confident, or as they say now, self-esteem is lifted.

Come Holy Spirit, fill the hearts of your faithful, and kindle in them the fire of your love.

The Presence of God

As I sit here with my book, God is here.
Around me, in my sensations, in my thoughts and deep within me.
I pause for a moment, and become aware
of God's life-giving presence.

Freedom

A thick and shapeless tree-trunk would never believe
that it could become a statue, admired as a miracle of sculpture,
and would never submit itself to the chisel of the sculptor,
who sees by her genius what she can make of it. (St. Ignatius)
I ask for the grace to let myself be shaped by my loving Creator.

Consciousness

How am I really feeling? Light-hearted? Heavy-hearted?
I may be very much at peace, happy to be here.
Equally, I may be frustrated, worried or angry.
I acknowledge how I really am. It is the real me that the Lord loves.

The Word

God speaks to each one of us individually. I need to listen to
what he is saying to me. (Please turn to your scripture on the following pages. Inspiration points are there should you need
them. When you are ready, return here to continue.)

Conversation

Do I notice myself reacting as I pray with the Word of God?
Do I feel challenged, comforted, angry?
Imagining Jesus sitting or standing by me,
I speak out my feelings, as one trusted friend to another.

Conclusion

Glory be to the Father, and to the Son, and to the Holy Spirit,
As it was in the beginning, is now and ever shall be,
World without end. Amen

Sunday 27th May, Pentecost

Acts 2:1–4

When the day of Pentecost had come, they were all together in one place. And suddenly from heaven there came a sound like the rush of a violent wind, and it filled the entire house where they were sitting. Divided tongues, as of fire, appeared among them, and a tongue rested on each of them. All of them were filled with the Holy Spirit and began to speak in other languages, as the Spirit gave them ability.

- The power comes: By no effort of their own, those present are remade as persons of faith and deep, lasting conviction. The Spirit is surprising, elusive, free.

- The Holy Spirit is a thorn in the side for the Christian, and for the church. How open am I to this Spirit?

Monday 28th May

Mark 10:17–22

As he was setting out on a journey, a man ran up and knelt before him, and asked him, "Good Teacher, what must I do to inherit eternal life?" Jesus said to him, "Why do you call me good? No one is good but God alone. You know the commandments: 'You shall not murder; You shall not commit adultery; You shall not steal; You shall not bear false witness; You shall not defraud; Honor your father and mother.'" He said to him, "Teacher, I have kept all these since my youth." Jesus, looking at him, loved him and said, "You lack one thing; go, sell what you own, and give the money to the poor, and you will have treasure in heaven; then come, follow me." When he heard this, he was shocked and went away grieving, for he had many possessions.

- Am I like that rich man? I am led beyond talk of possessions to poverty of spirit: to stand before the Lord empty, impoverished, with nothing of which I can boast.

- Jesus looked on that man, loved him, and invited him. When he held back from that invitation, Jesus was sad but did not pursue him. He was left with his freedom, as I am with mine.

Tuesday 29th May   **Ecclesiasticus 35:10–12**

Honor the Lord with generosity, do not stint the first fruits you bring. Add a smiling face to all your gifts, and be cheerful as you dedicate your tithes. Give to the Most High as he has given to you, generously as you as your means can afford; for the Lord is a good rewarder, he will reward you seven times over. Offer him no bribe, he will not accept it, do not put your faith in an unvirtuous sacrifice; since the Lord is a judge who is no respecter of personages.

- All through the day I am in a position to give—with my attention, talk, energy. My gifts can be reluctant, cranky; or they can be warmed by a cheerful face, so that they are a blessing to another.

- How do I answer the phone, greet an acquaintance, make a sale or purchase, or receive care in my helplessness? I can choose to be a blessing or grump. Does my smile make a difference?

Wednesday 30th May   **Mark 10:32, 35–40**

They were on the road, going up to Jerusalem, and Jesus was walking ahead of them; James and John, the sons of Zebedee, came forward to Jesus and said to him, "Teacher, we want you to do for us whatever we ask of you." And he said to them, "What is it you want me to do for you?" And they said to him, "Grant us to sit, one at your right hand and one at your left, in your glory." But Jesus said to them, "You do not know what you are asking. Are you able to drink the cup that I drink, or be baptized with the baptism that I am baptized with?" They replied, "We are able." Then Jesus said to them, "The cup that I drink you will drink; and with the baptism with which I am baptized, you will be baptized; but to sit at my right hand or at my left is not mine to grant, but it is for those for whom it has been prepared."

- Jesus tried to prepare his friends for the passion and death he fore-saw. But could they hear him? James and John stayed with their own fantasies of the kingdom, sitting on thrones in glory.

- My own fantasies sometimes go the same way: towards short-term satisfaction in my life, forgetting your call, Lord. Only you know if I can drink the cup that you drink. When you offer it to me, help me to recognize where it comes from.

Thursday 31st May, Visitation of the Virgin Mary to Elizabeth
Luke 1:39–47

In those days Mary set out and went with haste to a Judean town in the hill country, where she entered the house of Zechariah and greeted Elizabeth. When Elizabeth heard Mary's greeting, the child leaped in her womb. And Elizabeth was filled with the Holy Spirit and exclaimed with a loud cry, "Blessed are you among women, and blessed is the fruit of your womb. And why has this happened to me, that the mother of my Lord comes to me? For as soon as I heard the sound of your greeting, the child in my womb leaped for joy. And blessed is she who believed that there would be a fulfillment of what was spoken to her by the Lord." And Mary said, "My soul magnifies the Lord, and my spirit rejoices in God my Savior."

- Stay with the scene. Both of the women are aware that something awesome is at work in them.

- In their meeting there is the ordinariness of friends meeting, and also a profound sense of destiny.

- Can I explore how they are responding?

Friday 1st June   Mark 11:15–19

Then they came to Jerusalem. And he entered the temple and began to drive out those who were selling and those who were buying in the temple, and he overturned the tables of the money changers and the seats of those who sold doves; and he would not allow anyone to carry anything through the temple. He was teaching and saying, "Is it not written, 'My house shall be called a house of prayer for all the nations'? But you have made it a den of robbers." And when the chief priests and the scribes heard it, they kept looking for a way to kill him; for they were afraid of him, because the whole crowd was spellbound by his teaching. And when evening came, Jesus and his disciples went out of the city.

- Shocking behavior in a holy place: tables overturned, money rolling across the Temple floor, the chief priests and the scribes fearful and angry. Jesus hit on the destructive link between religion and money, and targeted it with passion and power.

- How do I guard against this trap, Lord? Is the party afterwards more important to me than the sacrament—the wedding, the baptism or even the funeral? This gospel hits where it hurts.

Saturday 2nd June   **Ecclesiasticus 51:12–13, 19–20**
I will thank you and praise you, and bless the name of the Lord. When I was still a youth, before I went travelling, in my prayers I asked outright for wisdom. My soul has fought to possess her, I have been scrupulous in keeping the law; I have stretched out my hands to heaven and bewailed my ignorance of her; I have directed my soul towards her, and in purity have found her.

- Purity of heart prepares me to seek wisdom. It is no accident that in every culture, east and west, wise people work hard to win the freedom of their bodies, and the control of their appetites.

- How do I purify myself, to come to this wisdom; how do I remove the blinkers imposed by prejudice or lust?

june 3–9

Something to think and pray about each day this week:

Still in the Spirit

We are caught up into the Blessed Trinity in the same way as our brother Jesus. The Holy Spirit was the bond of communion and love between Jesus and his father. That same spirit, dwelling in me, also joins me to the Father. St. Paul (Romans 8:26) explains: "When we cannot choose words in order to pray properly, the Spirit himself expresses our plea in a way that could never be put into words."

My best prayer is when I tune into this non-stop, wordless communion between the Holy Spirit speaking for me and my father in heaven. For that I must be still.

The Presence of God
I pause for a moment, aware that God is here.
I think of how everything around me,
the air I breathe, my whole body,
is tingling with the presence of God.

Freedom
I ask for the grace
to let go of my own concerns
and be open to what God is asking of me,
to let myself be guided and formed by my loving Creator.

Consciousness
Knowing that God loves me unconditionally,
I can afford to be honest about how I am.
How has the last day been, and how do I feel now?
I share my feelings openly with the Lord.

The Word
I read the Word of God slowly, a few times over, and I listen to what God is saying to me. (Please turn to your scripture on the following pages. Inspiration points are there should you need them. When you are ready, return here to continue.)

Conversation
Remembering that I am still in God's presence,
I imagine Jesus himself standing or sitting beside me,
and say whatever is on my mind, whatever is in my heart,
speaking as one friend to another.

Conclusion
Glory be to the Father, and to the Son, and to the Holy Spirit,
As it was in the beginning, is now and ever shall be,
World without end. Amen

Sunday 3rd June, Trinity Sunday — Romans 5:1–5

Therefore, since we are justified by faith, we have peace with God through our Lord Jesus Christ, through whom we have obtained access to this grace in which we stand; and we boast in our hope of sharing the glory of God. And not only that, but we also boast in our sufferings, knowing that suffering produces endurance, and endurance produces character, and character produces hope, and hope does not disappoint us, because God's love has been poured into our hearts through the Holy Spirit that has been given to us.

- Today can I sit humbly before this mystery of the Trinity, as taught by St. Paul?

- I can be at peace with God through our Lord Jesus Christ.

- I am offered a hope that will not let me down because "the love of God has been poured into (my) heart by the Holy Spirit."

- How am I moved as I ponder this?

Monday 4th June — Tobit 1:3, 2:1–7

I, Tobit, have walked in paths of truth and in good works all the days of my life. At our feast of Pentecost (the feast of Weeks) there was a good dinner. I took my place for the meal; the table was brought to me and various dishes were brought. Then I said to my son Tobias, "Go, my child, and seek out some poor, loyal-hearted man among our brothers exiled in Nineveh, and bring him to share my meal. I will wait until you come back, my child." So Tobias went out to again and said, "Father!" I answered, "What is it, my child?" He went on, "Father, one of our nation has just been murdered; he has been strangled and then thrown down in the market place; he is there still." I sprang up at once, left my meal untouched, took the man from the market place and laid him in one of my rooms, waiting until sunset to bury him. I came in again and washed myself and ate my bread in sorrow, remembering the words of the prophet Amos concerning Bethel: "Your feasts will be turned to mourning, and all your songs to lamentation." And I wept. When the sun was down, I went and dug a grave and buried him.

- The book of Tobit tells the story of a just man, who, before he can sit down comfortably to a good dinner, feels he must share it with those who have less; a man who buries the dead at personal risk to himself. Not a theologian, but a man of God.

- What can I learn about this, about the links between faith, love and justice?

Tuesday 5th June   Tobit 2:11–14

My wife Anna then undertook woman's work; she would spin wool and take cloth to weave; she used to deliver whatever had been ordered from her and then receive payment. Now on March the seventh she finished a piece of work and delivered it to her customers. They paid her all that was due, and into the bargain presented her with a kid for a meal. When the kid came into my house, it began to bleat. I called to my wife and said, "Where does this creature come from? Suppose it has been stolen! Quick, let the owners have it back; we have no right to eat stolen goods." She said, "No, it was a present given me over and above my wages." I did not believe her, and told her to give it back to the owners (I felt deeply ashamed of her.)

- This curious story reveals the flip side of Tobit's righteousness: He jumps to a rash judgment on his wife, accuses her wrongly, and even blushes for her.

- How easily I can go beyond the evidence to judge others, and how slow I am to recognize that others are probably better than me. Through my quiet prayer, can I try to see my neighbors as God sees them, with an eye of love, always making allowances.

Wednesday 6th June — Mark 12:18–27

Some Sadducees, who say there is no resurrection, came to Jesus and asked him a question, saying, "Teacher, Moses wrote for us that 'if a man's brother dies, leaving a wife but no child, the man shall marry the widow and raise up children for his brother.' There were seven brothers; the first married and, when he died, left no children; and the second married her and died, leaving no children; and the third likewise; none of the seven left children. Last of all the woman herself died. In the resurrection whose wife will she be? For the seven had married her." Jesus said to them, "Is not this the reason you are wrong, that you know neither the scriptures nor the power of God? For when they rise from the dead, they neither marry nor are given in marriage, but are like angels in heaven. And as for the dead being raised, have you not read in the book of Moses, in the story about the bush, how God said to him, 'I am the God of Abraham, the God of Isaac, and the God of Jacob'? He is God not of the dead, but of the living; you are quite wrong."

- Belief in resurrection challenges us all. Jesus does not step away from it either.

- How do I think about resurrection; like a scientist, a theologian, or like one who believes in the power and presence of God?

Thursday 7th June — Mark 12:28–34

One of the scribes came near and heard them disputing with one another, and seeing that he answered them well, he asked Jesus, "Which commandment is the first of all?" Jesus answered, "The first is, 'Hear, O Israel: the Lord our God, the Lord is one; you shall love the Lord your God with all your heart, and with all your soul, and with all your mind, and with all your strength.' The second is this, 'You shall love your neighbor as yourself.' There is no other commandment greater than these." Then the scribe said to him, "You are right, Teacher; you have truly said that 'he is one, and besides him there is no other'; and 'to love him with all the heart, and with all the understanding, and with all the strength,' and 'to love one's neighbor as oneself,'—this is much more important than all whole burnt offerings and sacrifices." When Jesus saw that he answered wisely, he said to him, "You are not far from the kingdom of God." After that no one dared to ask him any question.

- It is an honest question we should all ask: Which commandment is the first?

- The answer is love, but love that is deeply personal and complete—heart, mind, strength; everything we have got.

- How do I limit my love?

Friday 8th June   Mark 12:35–37

While Jesus was teaching in the temple, he said, "How can the scribes say that the Messiah is the son of David? David himself, by the Holy Spirit, declared: 'The Lord said to my Lord, "Sit at my right hand, until I put your enemies under your feet."' David himself calls him Lord; so how can he be his son?" And the large crowd was listening to him with delight.

- Jesus challenges the scribes, as he challenges us, to understand who he is, to understand the true nature of his presence with us.

- Do I take up the challenge to go beyond my present knowledge and understanding?

- Am I delighted to be in Jesus' presence?

Saturday 9th June   Tobit 12:1, 5–15, 20

When the wedding celebration came to an end, Tobit called his son Tobiah and said to him, "Son, see to it that you give what is due to the man who made the journey with you; give him a bonus too." So Tobiah called Raphael and said, "Take as your wages half of all that you have brought back, and go in peace." Raphael called the two men aside privately and said to them: "Thank God! Give him the praise and the glory. Before all the living, acknowledge the many good things he has done for you, by blessing and extolling his name in song. Before all men, honor and proclaim God's deeds, and do not be slack in praising him. A king's secret it is prudent to keep, but the works of God are to be declared and made known. Praise them with due honor. Do good, and evil will not find its way to you. Prayer and fasting are good, but better than either is almsgiving accompanied by righteousness. A little with righteousness is better than abundance with wickedness. It is better to give alms than to store up gold; for almsgiving saves one from death and expiates every sin. Those who regularly give alms shall enjoy a full life; but those habitually guilty of sin are their own worst enemies. "I will now tell you the whole truth; I will conceal nothing at all from you. I have already said to you, 'A king's secret it is prudent to keep, but the works of God are to be made known with due honor.' I can now tell you that when you, Tobit, and Sarah prayed, it was I who presented and read the record of your prayer before the Glory of the Lord; and I did the same thing when you used to bury the dead. When you did not hesitate to get up and leave your dinner in order to go and bury the dead, I was sent to put you to the test. At the same time, however, God commissioned me to heal you and your daughter-in-law Sarah. I am Raphael, one of the seven angels who enter and serve before the Glory of the Lord." So now get up from the ground and praise God. Behold, I am about to ascend to him who sent me; write down all these things that have happened to you."

- The angel Raphael is a healing presence in the lives of Tobit and his wife Sarah. For a lovely evocation of Raphael, read *Miss Garnet's Angel* by Salley Vickers.

- When Tobias tries to offer a gift to his loved and trusted companion, the angel Raphael reveals himself as a messenger of God. That is how we think of our guardian angel: When we are immersed in the routine of survival, wrestling with the day's complications, trying to get through without too much damage to ourselves or others, our angel is reading our deepest desires and turning them into prayer.

- Is an angel a figure of fear for me, or the presence of God's healing power?

june 10–16

Something to think and pray about each day this week:

Living together

This week we recall the extraordinary gift of the Eucharist, with its rich symbolism. Bread fills our hunger; it is a symbol of our life and work. Wine gives vigor and vitality, fuses us together, quenches our thirst. God enters into the material world through the consecration of bread and wine, a memorial of Jesus' passion, and nourishment for each of us.

Not just an individual food; the symbolic transcends the nutritional. Cicero contrasted the Greek for a meal: *sundeipnon (syndeipnon)* and *sumposion (synposion)*, meaning eating together or drinking together, with the Latin convivium, which means living together. It is at meals that our lives are most closely joined. The Eucharist is a celebration of our kinship in the Lord, sisters and brothers of Jesus.

Meals punctuate the Gospels: at Cana, with Martha and Mary, with Simon the Pharisee, and with Matthew. So it is no surprise that Jesus said his goodbyes at this meal, this *sacrum convivium*. We do the same in memory of him: slake our hunger and thirst on this holy food, and through this come closest to meeting our deepest desire, for union with God.

The Presence of God

For a few moments, I think of God's veiled presence in things:
in the elements, giving them existence;
in plants, giving them life; in animals, giving them sensation;
and finally, in me, giving me all this and more,
making me a temple, a dwelling-place of the Spirit.

Freedom

I ask for the grace to believe
in what I could be and do
if I only allowed God, my loving Creator,
to continue to create me, guide me and shape me.

Consciousness

In the presence of my loving Creator,
I look honestly at my feelings over the last day,
the highs, the lows and the level ground.
Can I see where the Lord has been present?

The Word

I take my time to read the Word of God, slowly, a few times, allowing myself to dwell on anything that strikes me. (Please turn to your scripture on the following pages. Inspiration points are there should you need them. When you are ready, return here to continue.)

Conversation

How has God's Word moved me? Has it left me cold?
Has it consoled me or moved me to act in a new way?
I imagine Jesus standing or sitting beside me,
I turn and share my feelings with him.

Conclusion

Glory be to the Father, and to the Son, and to the Holy Spirit,
As it was in the beginning, is now and ever shall be,
World without end. Amen

Sunday 10th June, The Body and Blood of Christ
Luke 9:11–17

The day was drawing to a close, and the twelve came to him and said, "Send the crowd away, so that they may go into the surrounding villages and countryside, to lodge and get provisions; for we are here in a deserted place." But he said to them, "You give them something to eat." They said, "We have no more than five loaves and two fish—unless we are to go and buy food for all these people." For there were about five thousand men. And he said to his disciples, "Make them sit down in groups of about fifty each." They did so and made them all sit down. And taking the five loaves and the two fish, he looked up to heaven, and blessed and broke them, and gave them to the disciples to set before the crowd. And all ate and were filled. What was left over was gathered up, twelve baskets of broken pieces.

- Can I imagine myself in this scene? Am I one of the disciples? Am I one of the crowd, watching to see what will happen next?

- What do I see and hear?

- How do I feel about it?

- If I see God's great bounty in this scene, what about my own life?

Monday 11th June
Matthew 5:1–12

When Jesus saw the crowds, he went up the mountain; and after he sat down, his disciples came to him. Then he began to speak, and taught them, saying: "Blessed are the poor in spirit, for theirs is the kingdom of heaven. Blessed are those who mourn, for they will be comforted. Blessed are the meek, for they will inherit the earth. Blessed are those who hunger and thirst for righteousness, for they will be filled. Blessed are the merciful, for they will receive mercy. Blessed are the pure in heart, for they will see God. Blessed are the peacemakers, for they will be called children of God. Blessed are those who are persecuted for righteousness' sake, for theirs is the kingdom of heaven. Blessed are you when people revile you and persecute you and utter all kinds of evil against you falsely on my account. Rejoice and be glad, for your reward is great in heaven, for in the same way they persecuted the prophets who were before you."

- We see here the interior landscape of Jesus: poor in spirit, gentle, merciful, hungry for justice, pure in heart, a peacemaker, yet prepared to grieve and suffer persecution in the cause of right.

- Think about the qualities that are not included—ambitious, greedy, obedient, organized, controlled; not that these are necessarily undesirable, but they are not part of Christian beatitude.

- Am I shaping my heart with Jesus' values?

Tuesday 12th June   Matthew 5:13–16

Jesus said to the disciples, "You are the salt of the earth; but if salt has lost its taste, how can its saltiness be restored? It is no longer good for anything, but is thrown out and trampled under foot. You are the light of the world. A city built on a hill cannot be hid. No one after lighting a lamp puts it under the bushel basket, but on the lampstand, and it gives light to all in the house. In the same way, let your light shine before others, so that they may see your good works and give glory to your Father in heaven."

- Light and salt—these are contrasting metaphors for Christian life which apply at different times in life of each person, and in the church's life.

- We may be in the spotlight, and have our fifteen minutes of fame: briefly we are the light of the world, and we can pray that when we are in such focus, we may be worthy of our Christian vocation.

- But most of the time we are more like salt, or leaven, working for good even when unseen. Salt is a less attractive image than light.

- What is asked of me: to be light or salt, to shine in public, or to work invisibly? Am I growing in the role assigned me?

Wednesday 13th June, St. Anthony of Padua
Isaiah 61:1–3a

The spirit of the Lord God is upon me, because the Lord has anointed me; he has sent me to bring good news to the oppressed, to bind up the brokenhearted, to proclaim liberty to the captives, and release to the prisoners; to proclaim the year of the Lord's favor, and the day of vengeance of our God; to comfort all who mourn; to provide for those who mourn in Zion—to give them a garland instead of ashes, the oil of gladness instead of mourning, the mantle of praise instead of a faint spirit.

- We need saints, the heroes and heroines who express the ideals we aspire to.

- The saints are just like us; they are forgiven sinners. They rejoiced in forgiveness and refused to be overwhelmed by their sin. That gives me hope.

Thursday 14th June　　　2 Corinthians 3:15–4:1, 3–6

Indeed, to this very day whenever Moses is read, a veil lies over their minds; but when one turns to the Lord, the veil is removed. Now the Lord is the Spirit, and where the Spirit of the Lord is, there is freedom. And all of us, with unveiled faces, seeing the glory of the Lord as though reflected in a mirror, are being transformed into the same image from one degree of glory to another; for this comes from the Lord, the Spirit. Therefore, since it is by God's mercy that we are engaged in this ministry, we do not lose heart. And even if our gospel is veiled, it is veiled to those who are perishing. In their case the god of this world has blinded the minds of the unbelievers, to keep them from seeing the light of the gospel of the glory of Christ, who is the image of God. For we do not proclaim ourselves; we proclaim Jesus Christ as Lord and ourselves as your slaves for Jesus' sake. For it is the God who said, "Let light shine out of darkness," who has shone in our hearts to give the light of the knowledge of the glory of God in the face of Jesus Christ.

- "It is not ourselves that we are preaching, but Christ Jesus." There is something to learn here for me.

- In my search for Jesus, my ego remains a distraction. I want to be admired, to make an impression. And as the saying goes, if you try to make an impression, that's the impression you make.

- Can I keep my ego under wraps, to let the love of Jesus shine through? Is that how I can bring real life to others?

Friday 15th June, Feast of the Sacred Heart   Luke 15:3–7

Jesus told them this parable: "Which one of you, having a hundred sheep and losing one of them, does not leave the ninety-nine in the wilderness and go after the one that is lost until he finds it? When he has found it, he lays it on his shoulders and rejoices. And when he comes home, he calls together his friends and neighbors, saying to them, 'Rejoice with me, for I have found my sheep that was lost.' Just so, I tell you, there will be more joy in heaven over one sinner who repents than over ninety-nine righteous persons who need no repentance."

- "Heart" is a primal concept in the Bible and great literature, an archetype. This in not the bodily organ but the origin and kernel of everything else in the human person.

- As Jesus reveals himself through the Gospels, we discover that the basic attitude of his heart is one of unconditional love, not hatred or ambivalence.

- The first and last message of the Gospel is that God loves this world and every person in it. He sent his son Jesus as a shepherd, with a large and compassionate heart for each and every person, especially those who are lost.

- What does this mean for me?

Saturday 16th June   Matthew 5:33–37

J esus said to the crowds, "Again, you have heard that it was said to those of ancient times, 'You shall not swear falsely, but carry out the vows you have made to the Lord.' But I say to you, Do not swear at all, either by heaven, for it is the throne of God, or by the earth, for it is his footstool, or by Jerusalem, for it is the city of the great King. And do not swear by your head, for you cannot make one hair white or black. Let your word be 'Yes, Yes' or 'No, No'; anything more than this comes from the evil one."

- For most of us, our style of language becomes habitual. Do I take time to review the way I speak? Perhaps I swear habitually, or for 'effect'?

- Swearing does not add to what I say; it just inflates it with the illusion of eloquence. Think of the friends whose Yes is Yes, and No is No. I respect them, though they may be few in number.

- If I learn to look into the eyes of Jesus and think and say to him only what I know to be true, then I might do the same with other people, and with myself.

june 17–23

Something to think and pray about each day this week:

Seeking the voice

When Elijah listened for the voice of the Lord (I Kings 19:9), he heard it not in an earthquake, a mighty wind or a fire, but in a still, small voice. Jesus too, walking on the water, reduced the raging sea to calm. To be in touch with him, we quiet our bodies, our racing minds, our turbulent hearts. We use the advice of old teachers, Christians and others, to achieve that silence in which we reach out towards God. Our bodily posture, our breathing, our strategy with distractions, all contribute to prayer. Sacred Space offers daily help on this work of preparation.

The Presence of God
I remind myself that, as I sit here now,
God is gazing on me with love and holding me in being.
I pause for a moment and think of this.

Freedom
I need to close out the noise, to rise above the noise;
The noise that interrupts, that separates,
The noise that isolates.
I need to listen to God again.

Consciousness
In God's loving presence I unwind the past day,
starting from now and looking back, moment by moment.
I gather in all the goodness and light, in gratitude.
I attend to the shadows and what they say to me,
seeking healing, courage, forgiveness.

The Word
I take my time to read the Word of God, slowly, a few times,
allowing myself to dwell on anything that strikes me. (Please
turn to your scripture on the following pages. Inspiration points
are there should you need them. When you are ready, return
here to continue.)

Conversation
Do I notice myself reacting as I pray with the Word of God?
Do I feel challenged, comforted, angry?
Imagining Jesus sitting or standing by me,
I speak out my feelings, as one trusted friend to another.

Conclusion
Glory be to the Father, and to the Son, and to the Holy Spirit,
As it was in the beginning, is now and ever shall be,
World without end. Amen

Sunday 17th June, Eleventh Sunday in Ordinary Time
Galatians 2:16, 19–21

We know that a person is justified not by the works of the law but through faith in Jesus Christ. And we have come to believe in Christ Jesus, so that we might be justified by faith in Christ, and not by doing the works of the law, because no one will be justified by the works of the law. For through the law I died to the law, so that I might live to God. I have been crucified with Christ; and it is no longer I who live, but it is Christ who lives in me. And the life I now live in the flesh I live by faith in the Son of God, who loved me and gave himself for me. I do not nullify the grace of God; for if justification comes through the law, then Christ died for nothing.

- To live in faith is to risk looking and feeling like nothing—nothing that can be possessed, sold, measured, merited, or even accurately communicated.

- The consumer, functional, and materialistic age finds this faith almost impossible.

- Do I want religion, but resist faith?

Monday 18th June   Matthew 5:38–42

Jesus said to the crowds, "You have heard that it was said, 'An eye for an eye and a tooth for a tooth.' But I say to you, Do not resist an evildoer. But if anyone strikes you on the right cheek, turn the other also; and if anyone wants to sue you and take your coat, give your cloak as well; and if anyone forces you to go one mile, go also the second mile. Give to everyone who begs from you, and do not refuse anyone who wants to borrow from you."

- This is a hard one: to offer the wicked no resistance, but turn the other cheek. Where will that approach leave us?

- What do you mean by it, Lord? I watched when your face was slapped before the high priest Caiaphas. You answered calmly: "If I have spoken rightly, why do you strike me?" Your resistance was moral, not physical or violent. That calls for greater courage and strength than taking up arms: Gandhi, not those who make war.

Tuesday 19th June   Matthew 5:43–48

Jesus said to the crowds, "You have heard that it was said, 'You shall love your neighbor and hate your enemy.' But I say to you, Love your enemies and pray for those who persecute you, so that you may be children of your Father in heaven; for he makes his sun rise on the evil and on the good, and sends rain on the righteous and on the unrighteous. For if you love those who love you, what reward do you have? Do not even the tax collectors do the same? And if you greet only your brothers and sisters, what more are you doing than others? Do not even the Gentiles do the same? Be perfect, therefore, as your heavenly Father is perfect."

- I'm asked to be perfect: In my heart I should bless even those who hate me and wrong me. The love of God can be poured out in our hearts through the Holy Spirit who is given to us.

- How do I respond to this? When I may feel far from blessed myself, even when old age makes me feel there is little I can do for others, I can still give my approval and blessing to those I meet; that will lift them. Jesus lifts us beyond what we thought possible.

Wednesday 20th June   Matthew 6:1–6, 16–18

Jesus said to the disciples, "Beware of practicing your piety before others in order to be seen by them; for then you have no reward from your Father in heaven. So whenever you give alms, do not sound a trumpet before you, as the hypocrites do in the synagogues and in the streets, so that they may be praised by others. Truly I tell you, they have received their reward. But when you give alms, do not let your left hand know what your right hand is doing, so that your alms may be done in secret; and your Father who sees in secret will reward you. And whenever you pray, do not be like the hypocrites; for they love to stand and pray in the synagogues and at the street corners, so that they may be seen by others. Truly I tell you, they have received their reward. But whenever you pray, go into your room and shut the door and pray to your Father who is in secret; and your Father who sees in secret will reward you. And whenever you fast, do not look dismal, like the hypocrites, for they disfigure their faces so as to show others that they are fasting. Truly I tell you, they have received their reward. But when you fast, put oil on your head and wash your face, so that your fasting may be seen not by others but by your Father who is in secret; and your Father who sees in secret will reward you."

- My left hand is not just curious about what my right is doing; part of me wants to go public, with my own good news. If I am doing something creditable, I am too anxious to broadcast it.

- Jesus teaches me to ignore my image, and to aim at doing what is right. The best work in the world never hits the headlines.

Thursday 21st June, St. Aloysius Gonzaga   Mark 10:23–27

Then Jesus looked around and said to his disciples, "How hard it will be for those who have wealth to enter the kingdom of God!" And the disciples were perplexed at these words. But Jesus said to them again, "Children, how hard it is to enter the kingdom of God! It is easier for a camel to go through the eye of a needle than for someone who is rich to enter the kingdom of God." They were greatly astounded and said to one another, "Then who can be saved?" Jesus looked at them and said, "For mortals it is impossible, but not for God; for God all things are possible."

- Do these words seem extreme?

- If you tend to accept that those who enjoy material prosperity are favored by God, then Jesus' words are especially shocking.

- Salvation originates through God's gracious offer and not from my own efforts. Can I just sit back? How am I cooperating each day in my own salvation?

Friday 22nd June — Matthew 6:19–23

Jesus said to his disciples, "Do not store up for yourselves treasures on earth, where moth and rust consume and where thieves break in and steal; but store up for yourselves treasures in heaven, where neither moth nor rust consumes and where thieves do not break in and steal. For where your treasure is, there your heart will be also. The eye is the lamp of the body. So, if your eye is healthy, your whole body will be full of light; but if your eye is unhealthy, your whole body will be full of darkness. If then the light in you is darkness, how great is the darkness!"

- Where do my thoughts and behavior gravitate when there is no job to be done, no routine to guide me? Some people go to sleep, some make love, some read, watch TV, go fishing, talk to friends. What is my magnetic North when there is no pressure on me?

- Do my thoughts move towards my family or friends? My hobbies, my work? Or towards money?

- Where does Jesus rank in my normal daily routine?

Saturday 23rd June — Matthew 6:24–34

Jesus said to his disciples, "No one can serve two masters; for a slave will either hate the one and love the other, or be devoted to the one and despise the other. You cannot serve God and wealth. Therefore I tell you, do not worry about your life, what you will eat or what you will drink, or about your body, what you will wear. Is not life more than food, and the body more than clothing? Look at the birds of the air; they neither sow nor reap nor gather into barns, and yet your heavenly Father feeds them. Are you not of more value than they? And can any of you by worrying add a single hour to your span of life? And why do you worry about clothing? Consider the lilies of the field, how they grow; they neither toil nor spin, yet I tell you, even Solomon in all his glory was not clothed like one of these. But if God so clothes the grass of the field, which is alive today and tomorrow is thrown into the oven, will he not much more clothe you—you of little faith? Therefore do not worry, saying, 'What will we eat?' or 'What will we drink?' or 'What will we wear?' For it is the Gentiles who strive for all these things; and indeed your heavenly Father knows that you need all these things. But strive first for the kingdom of God and his right-eousness, and all these things will be given to you as well. So do not worry about tomorrow, for tomorrow will bring worries of its own. Today's trouble is enough for today."

- The young Jesus, living in the flowering countryside and relative prosperity of Galilee, tests the real necessities and true values of life. He enjoys the beauty around him, but sees people so concerned with Mammon (a Semitic word for money or wealth), and worry about tomorrow, that they cannot be in tune with the God who reaches us only in the Now.

- How do I live in the present moment? What are my priorities and my worries? Do I seek Jesus, here and now?

Something to think and pray about each day this week:

Knocked off balance

When Caravaggio painted the *Call of St. Matthew*, he placed himself in the centre of the picture, a handsome, richly robed man sitting with friends at his money table, with an attractive boy leaning intimately against his shoulder. Over in the shadows is the silhouette of Jesus. Matthew looks up startled and incredulous as he notices the beckoning finger of Jesus. St. Peter protests with upraised hands, aghast at Jesus' action: "You cannot mean that guy, Lord!" Jesus destabilizes everyone in the picture, Matthew, his friends, his young lover, his tax business, and Peter. These moments when we are knocked off our balance, out of our routine, are potentially entry points for grace.

Lord, you have done the same to me on occasion, thrown me out of kilter in a way that I found uncomfortable, embarrassing or infuriating: with an accident, an accusation, a change of job, a failure, being bad-mouthed, losing a friend. They are not moments I like to dwell on; but when I do think of them, I can see you there, calling me closer to you.

The Presence of God
In the silence of my innermost being,
in the fragments of my yearned-for wholeness,
can I hear the whispers of God's presence?
Can I remember when I felt God's nearness?
When we walked together and I let myself be embraced by God's love.

Freedom
I will ask God's help,
to be free from my own preoccupations,
to be open to God in this time of prayer,
to come to love and serve him more.

Consciousness
I exist in a web of relationships—links to nature, people, God.
I trace out these links, giving thanks for the life that flows through them.
Some links are twisted or broken: I may feel regret, anger, disappointment.
I pray for the gift of acceptance and forgiveness.

The Word
God speaks to each one of us individually. I need to listen to what he is saying to me. (Please turn to your scripture on the following pages. Inspiration points are there should you need them. When you are ready, return here to continue.)

Conversation
Remembering that I am still in God's presence,
I imagine Jesus himself standing or sitting beside me,
and say whatever is on my mind, whatever is in my heart,
speaking as one friend to another.

Conclusion
Glory be to the Father, and to the Son, and to the Holy Spirit,
As it was in the beginning, is now and ever shall be,
World without end. Amen

Sunday 24th June, Birth of St. John the Baptist
Luke 1:57–66

Now the time came for Elizabeth to give birth, and she bore a son. Her neighbors and relatives heard that the Lord had shown his great mercy to her, and they rejoiced with her. On the eighth day they came to circumcise the child, and they were going to name him Zechariah after his father. But his mother said, "No; he is to be called John." They said to her, "None of your relatives has this name." Then they began motioning to his father to find out what name he wanted to give him. He asked for a writing tablet and wrote, "His name is John." And all of them were amazed. Immediately his mouth was opened and his tongue freed, and he began to speak, praising God.

- Can I imagine I am one of the relatives who comes to Elizabeth's house to celebrate their new baby?

- There is controversy about the name.

- What happens? How has this couple been changed by what has happened in their lives?

- How am I moved by all of this?

Monday 25th June   Matthew 7:1–5

Jesus said to the crowds, "Do not judge, so that you may not be judged. For with the judgment you make you will be judged, and the measure you give will be the measure you get. Why do you see the speck in your neighbor's eye, but do not notice the log in your own eye? Or how can you say to your neighbor, 'Let me take the speck out of your eye,' while the log is in your own eye? You hypocrite, first take the log out of your own eye, and then you will see clearly to take the speck out of your neighbor's eye."

- What do you mean Lord, when you tell me not to judge? I cannot make everyday decisions without forming judgments. The sort of judgment that you tell me to avoid is when I forget how tentative and inadequate my knowledge of other people is.

- How often do I try to impute motives and usurp the definitive judgment of God, who alone reads the heart. Do I take the role of lawyer and judge, rather than accept the call to give witness?

Tuesday 26th June   Matthew 7:6, 12–14

Jesus said to the crowds, "Do not give what is holy to dogs; and do not throw your pearls before swine, or they will trample them under foot and turn and maul you. In everything do to others as you would have them do to you; for this is the law and the prophets. Enter through the narrow gate; for the gate is wide and the road is easy that leads to destruction, and there are many who take it. For the gate is narrow and the road is hard that leads to life, and there are few who find it."

- What does Jesus mean by casting "pearls before swine"? The Word of God should not be thrown around indiscriminately. Not everyone is ready. The soil needs to be ready for the seed.

- We remember Bishop Helder Camara's words to his catechists: "Watch how you live. Your lives may be the only Gospel your hearers will ever read."

Wednesday 27th June   Matthew 7:15–20

Jesus told the crowds, "Beware of false prophets, who come to you in sheep's clothing but inwardly are ravenous wolves. You will know them by their fruits. Are grapes gathered from thorns, or figs from thistles? In the same way, every good tree bears good fruit, but the bad tree bears bad fruit. A good tree cannot bear bad fruit, nor can a bad tree bear good fruit. Every tree that does not bear good fruit is cut down and thrown into the fire. Thus you will know them by their fruits."

- Jesus asks that our lives reflect our words; or even replace them. Saint Francis of Assisi told his followers: "Go and spread the good news. Sometimes you may use words."

- At a time when there are more prophets and gurus than ever claiming our attention, it is wise to look hard at their lives. Sometimes their behavior shouts so loud that we cannot hear what they are saying. What is my life saying to those who watch?

Thursday 28th June   Matthew 7:21–29

Jesus said to his disciples, "Not everyone who says to me, 'Lord, Lord,' will enter the kingdom of heaven, but only the one who does the will of my Father in heaven. On that day many will say to me, 'Lord, Lord, did we not prophesy in your name, and cast out demons in your name, and do many deeds of power in your name?' Then I will declare to them, 'I never knew you; go away from me, you evildoers.' Everyone then who hears these words of mine and acts on them will be like a wise man who built his house on rock. The rain fell, the floods came, and the winds blew and beat on that house, but it did not fall, because it had been founded on rock. And everyone who hears these words of mine and does not act on them will be like a foolish man who built his house on sand. The rain fell, and the floods came, and the winds blew and beat against that house, and it fell—and great was its fall!" Now when Jesus had finished saying these things, the crowds were astounded at his teaching, for he taught them as one having authority, and not as their scribes.

- You see charismatic preachers who can rouse a congregation to wave their arms, pray with tongues and chant in ecstasy. That is a blessing, a gift of God that lifts us out of ourselves. But if our lives do not reflect the Gospel, if we do not hear Jesus' words and act on them, it is empty and false.

Friday 29th June, Sts. Peter and Paul   Matthew 16:13–19

Now when Jesus came into the district of Caesarea Philippi, he asked his disciples, "Who do people say that the Son of Man is?" And they said, "Some say John the Baptist, but others Elijah, and still others Jeremiah or one of the prophets." He said to them, "But who do you say that I am?" Simon Peter answered, "You are the Messiah, the Son of the living God." And Jesus answered him, "Blessed are you, Simon son of Jonah! For flesh and blood has not revealed this to you, but my Father in heaven. And I tell you, you are Peter, and on this rock I will build my church, and the gates of Hades will not prevail against it. I will give you the keys of the kingdom of heaven, and whatever you bind on earth will be bound in heaven, and whatever you loose on earth will be loosed in heaven."

- The traditional setting for this memorable encounter in Caesarea Philippi is a lovely riverbank under a huge rocky cliff. It is here that the impetuous Peter, always ready to speak out and take risks, confesses Jesus as the Messiah. It is an inspired confession.

- This uneducated fisherman, who was to prove so shaky when Jesus was arrested, is rewarded with a new name, suggested by the great solid rock above them; and with a new role, leading the people of God.

- His strength is not in his warm, impetuous nature, but in the power of God. Is the Lord my strength?

Saturday 30th June   Matthew 8:5–13

When he entered Capernaum, a centurion came to him, appealing to him and saying, "Lord, my servant is lying at home paralyzed, in terrible distress." And he said to him, "I will come and cure him." The centurion answered, "Lord, I am not worthy to have you come under my roof; but only speak the word, and my servant will be healed. For I also am a man under authority, with soldiers under me; and I say to one, 'Go,' and he goes, and to another, 'Come,' and he comes, and to my slave, 'Do this,' and the slave does it." When Jesus heard him, he was amazed and said to those who followed him, "Truly I tell you, in no one in Israel have I found such faith. I tell you, many will come from east and west and will eat with Abraham and Isaac and Jacob in the kingdom of heaven, while the heirs of the kingdom will be thrown into the outer darkness, where there will be weeping and gnashing of teeth." And to the centurion Jesus said, "Go; let it be done for you according to your faith." And the servant was healed in that hour.

- Can we capture the style of the centurion, a Roman officer, commander in an occupying force, who with the utmost politeness asks this Jewish teacher for help?

- His humility and sensitivity—he felt an observant Jew might be reluctant to enter the house of a Gentile—so astonished early Christians that they incorporated his words into the liturgy of the Eucharist: "Lord I am not worthy to receive you under my roof."

july 1–7

Something to think and pray about each day this week:

Finding our rhythm

After our holidays are over or when our children return to school after a long break, we have to settle into a fresh rhythm of work, of family routine. In the Gospel readings from St. Luke there is a feeling of newness, and finding rhythm: Peter leaving his nets to follow Jesus, walking with him through the wheat fields and casually plucking the grain, and Jesus' own words about new wine and new wineskins.

Do I have it in me to be a new wineskin, open to the incessant movement and ideas of those younger than me? Or am I incurably an old skin? We need help in this. François Mauriac describes a father who finds that his daughter is terrified of him, and he wants to change. "But do you imagine a man is free, at 68 years of age, to lay aside an implacable air? At that age the expression of his traits is not going to change any more. And the soul loses courage when it cannot express itself outwardly. A man cannot, all on his own, preserve confidence in himself. Each of us needs a witness to our powers."

Perhaps there are others around me who want to change, but need me as a witness and support to their good intentions.

The Presence of God
God is with me, but more,
God is within me, giving me existence.
Let me dwell for a moment on God's life-giving presence
in my body, my mind, my heart
and in the whole of my life.

Freedom
God is not foreign to my freedom.
Instead the Spirit breathes life into my most intimate desires,
gently nudging me towards all that is good.
I ask for the grace to let myself be enfolded by the Spirit.

Consciousness
How am I really feeling? Light-hearted? Heavy-hearted?
I may be very much at peace, happy to be here.
Equally, I may be frustrated, worried or angry.
I acknowledge how I really am. It is the real me that the Lord loves.

The Word
I read the Word of God slowly, a few times over, and I listen to what God is saying to me. (Please turn to your scripture on the following pages. Inspiration points are there should you need them. When you are ready, return here to continue.)

Conversation
How has God's Word moved me? Has it left me cold?
Has it consoled me or moved me to act in a new way?
I imagine Jesus standing or sitting beside me,
I turn and share my feelings with him.

Conclusion
Glory be to the Father, and to the Son, and to the Holy Spirit,
As it was in the beginning, is now and ever shall be,
World without end. Amen

Sunday 1st July, Thirteenth Sunday in Ordinary Time
Luke 9:51–62

As they were going along the road, someone said to Jesus, "I will follow you wherever you go." And Jesus said to him, "Foxes have holes, and birds of the air have nests; but the Son of Man has nowhere to lay his head." To another he said, "Follow me." But he said, "Lord, first let me go and bury my father." But Jesus said to him, "Let the dead bury their own dead; but as for you, go and proclaim the kingdom of God." Another said, "I will follow you, Lord; but let me first say farewell to those at my home." Jesus said to him, "No one who puts a hand to the plow and looks back is fit for the kingdom of God."

- When these people approach Jesus really eager to follow him, he certainly doesn't make it easy for them. Why?

- Does he spot resistances in them that they are hardly aware of themselves?

- Does the call of Jesus spark off resistances in me? Is there anything that I'm not prepared to let go?

- Perhaps I can pray for light about this.

Monday 2nd July
Matthew 8:18–22

Now when Jesus saw great crowds around him, he gave orders to go over to the other side. A scribe then approached and said, "Teacher, I will follow you wherever you go." And Jesus said to him, "Foxes have holes, and birds of the air have nests; but the Son of Man has nowhere to lay his head." Another of his disciples said to him, "Lord, first let me go and bury my father." But Jesus said to him, "Follow me, and let the dead bury their own dead."

- This highly educated scribe offers himself as Jesus' disciple. What is it that makes Jesus slow to jump at the offer? Perhaps it was a suspicion that the scribe was exchanging the stability of a scholar for the stability of a disciple, still a student of God's word.

- The great biblical student Karl Barth said: "To understand the scriptures we must stop acting like mere spectators."

- Do I want to hear the voice that challenges me? Do I seek that voice even when it unsettles me?

Tuesday 3rd July, St. Thomas   John 20:24–29

But Thomas (who was called the Twin), one of the twelve, was not with them when Jesus came. So the other disciples told him, "We have seen the Lord." But he said to them, "Unless I see the mark of the nails in his hands, and put my finger in the mark of the nails and my hand in his side, I will not believe." A week later his disciples were again in the house, and Thomas was with them. Although the doors were shut, Jesus came and stood among them and said, "Peace be with you." Then he said to Thomas, "Put your finger here and see my hands. Reach out your hand and put it in my side. Do not doubt but believe." Thomas answered him, "My Lord and my God!" Jesus said to him, "Have you believed because you have seen me? Blessed are those who have not seen and yet have come to believe."

- Can I imagine that I am among those listening to Thomas when he says, "I will not believe"?

- What is my reaction to his skepticism?

- How do I then respond when Thomas says, "My Lord and my God"? Do I doubt Thomas, or join with him?

Wednesday 4th July   Matthew 8:28–34

When Jesus came to the other side, to the country of the Gadarenes, two demoniacs coming out of the tombs met him. They were so fierce that no one could pass that way.

Suddenly they shouted, "What have you to do with us, Son of God? Have you come here to torment us before the time?" Now a large herd of swine was feeding at some distance from them. The demons begged him, "If you cast us out, send us into the herd of swine." And he said to them, "Go!" So they came out and entered the swine; and suddenly, the whole herd rushed down the steep bank into the lake and perished in the water. The swineherds ran off, and on going into the town, they told the whole story about what had happened to the demoniacs. Then the whole town came out to meet Jesus; and when they saw him, they begged him to leave their neighborhood.

- The story shows that Jesus has power over the whole world: even over demons, pagan religion and the Roman world.

- Do I welcome Jesus into my world, into my daily life? Or does the liberating Jesus threaten the world I am used to?

Thursday 5th July   **Matthew 9:1–2**

And after getting into a boat Jesus crossed the sea and came to his own town. And just then some people were carrying a paralyzed man lying on a bed. When Jesus saw their faith, he said to the paralytic, "Take heart, son; your sins are forgiven."

- So much joy is hidden in those words: "Take heart, son; your sins are forgiven."

- Jesus' response was to the faith shown by the paralytic's friends, and the healing started there.

- How do my friends experience my faith? Do I let the Lord touch my life in the same way?

Friday 6th July   **Matthew 9:9–13**

As Jesus was walking along, he saw a man called Matthew sitting at the tax booth; and he said to him, "Follow me." And he got up and followed him. And as he sat at dinner in the house, many tax collectors and sinners came and were sitting with him and his disciples. When the Pharisees saw this, they said to his disciples, "Why does your teacher eat with tax collectors and sinners?" But when he heard this, he said, "Those who are well have no need of a physician, but those who are sick. Go and learn what this means, 'I desire mercy, not sacrifice.' For I have come to call not the righteous but sinners."

- Tax collectors were despised, along with ass-drivers, tanners and bath-attendants. They tended to be social outcasts.

- Jesus saw need and goodness where others saw disreputable villainy. Do I have a private list of social outcasts, people I do not like to be with? Or do I try to chose my friends differently, as Jesus did?

- Do I have to do some serious work on this?

Saturday 7th July   **Matthew 9:14–17**

Then the disciples of John came to him, saying, "Why do we and the Pharisees fast often, but your disciples do not fast?" And Jesus said to them, "The wedding guests cannot mourn as long as the bridegroom is with them, can they? The days will come when the bridegroom is taken away from them, and then they will fast. No one sews a piece of unshrunk cloth on an old cloak, for the patch pulls away from the cloak, and a worse tear is made. Neither is new wine put into old wineskins; otherwise, the skins burst, and the wine is spilled, and the skins are destroyed; but new wine is put into fresh wineskins, and so both are preserved."

- There are rich overtones in the words used here: A "patch" is pleroma (fullness); and a "tear" is schism (schism).

- What is Jesus teaching me? What do the seasons of Advent, Christmas, Lent, and Easter teach me?

- How do I preserve both the old and the new; the need to fast and to celebrate?

july 8–14

Something to think and pray about each day this week:

The work of service

When Jesus chooses the apostles, scripture records it as one of the rare occasions when Jesus seems to be organizing for the future. With great deliberation he chooses twelve apostles who will share his work. What is that work? Not organizing, not pulling people into line; not judging or blaming or coercing into proper behavior, but compassionate service. Jesus' move towards the crowds was because they were harassed and dejected. His mission, and that of the Twelve, was not to organize or dominate people, but to serve them, especially the lost sheep, to lift their dejection and spare them harassment.

Lord, when I look at my life in your service, how much of it is compassionate service? This week let me make others' needs, not my ego, the trigger of my activity.

The Presence of God

To be present is to arrive as one is and open up to the other.
At this instant, as I arrive here, God is present waiting for me.
God always arrives before me, desiring to connect with me
even more than my most intimate friend.
I take a moment and greet my loving God.

Freedom

Everything has the potential to draw forth from me a fuller love
and life.
Yet my desires are often fixed, caught, on illusions of fulfillment.
I ask that God, through my freedom, may orchestrate
my desires in a vibrant loving melody rich in harmony.

Consciousness

Knowing that God loves me unconditionally,
I can afford to be honest about how I am.
How has the last day been, and how do I feel now?
I share my feelings openly with the Lord.

The Word

I take my time to read the Word of God, slowly, a few times,
allowing myself to dwell on anything that strikes me. (Please
turn to your scripture on the following pages. Inspiration points
are there should you need them. When you are ready, return
here to continue.)

Conversation

What feelings are rising in me
as I pray and reflect on God's Word?
I imagine Jesus himself sitting or standing beside me,
and open my heart to him.

Conclusion

Glory be to the Father, and to the Son, and to the Holy Spirit,
As it was in the beginning, is now and ever shall be,
World without end. Amen

Sunday 8th July, Fourteenth Sunday in Ordinary Time
Luke 10:1–9

After this the Lord appointed seventy others and sent them on ahead of him in pairs to every town and place where he himself intended to go. He said to them, "The harvest is plentiful, but the laborers are few; therefore ask the Lord of the harvest to send out laborers into his harvest. Go on your way. See, I am sending you out like lambs into the midst of wolves. Carry no purse, no bag, no sandals; and greet no one on the road. Whatever house you enter, first say, 'Peace to this house!' And if anyone is there who shares in peace, your peace will rest on that person; but if not, it will return to you. Remain in the same house, eating and drinking whatever they provide, for the laborer deserves to be paid. Do not move about from house to house. Whenever you enter a town and its people welcome you, eat what is set before you; cure the sick who are there, and say to them, 'The kingdom of God has come near to you.'"

- Jesus sent his disciples ahead in pairs. Do I see how I am being sent out by Jesus?

- What is the "plentiful harvest" that needs a response from me?

- Do I sometimes feel like a "lamb in the midst of wolves"?

- Can I say with conviction, "The Kingdom of God has come near to you"?

Monday 9th July   Matthew 9:18–19, 23–26

While he was saying these things to them, suddenly a leader of the synagogue came in and knelt before him, saying, "My daughter has just died; but come and lay your hand on her, and she will live." And Jesus got up and followed him, with his disciples. When Jesus came to the leader's house and saw the flute players and the crowd making a commotion, he said, "Go away; for the girl is not dead but sleeping." And they laughed at him. But when the crowd had been put outside, he went in and took her by the hand, and the girl got up. And the report of this spread throughout that district.

- It is the same hunger for sensation and shock that sells the tabloids: The crowd was eager for a tragedy, a death, while Jesus kept hope alive: "The girl is not dead but sleeping."

- Do I seek out the hope within me, that glimmer of vitality that can be fanned into flame? Do I hear those words: "Get up. Live."?

Tuesday 10th July   **Matthew 9:32–35**

After they had gone away, a demoniac who was mute was brought to Jesus. And when the demon had been cast out, the one who had been mute spoke; and the crowds were amazed and said, "Never has anything like this been seen in Israel." But the Pharisees said, "By the ruler of the demons he casts out the demons." Then Jesus went about all the cities and villages, teaching in their synagogues, and proclaiming the good news of the kingdom, and curing every disease and every sickness.

- The rule of God brings liberation of both spirit and body. Jesus' healing is a blow struck against those forces that confine us.

- Do I speak up for God's power in the face of the helplessness and harassment that many suffer, or am I mute? Do I turn to our father and say: "Thank you for giving me a share in this work"?

Wednesday 11th July, St. Benedict   **Matthew 19:27–29**

Then Peter said in reply, "Look, we have left everything and followed you. What then will we have?" Jesus said to them, "Truly I tell you, at the renewal of all things, when the Son of Man is seated on the throne of his glory, you who have followed me will also sit on twelve thrones, judging the twelve tribes of Israel. And everyone who has left houses or brothers or sisters or father or mother or children or fields, for my name's sake, will receive a hundredfold, and will inherit eternal life."

• This was the invitation which Benedict followed. He was named the patron of Europe because the peaceful order of his monasteries helped to reshape it from the chaos of the dark ages, and to create oases of tranquility in which civilization could be reborn.

• For Benedict, monastic life was an opportunity to have leisure for God, vacare Deo. May I find some leisure for God in my life. Let Sacred Space be my monastery.

Thursday 12th July   Matthew 10:7–11

Jesus said to the twelve, "As you go, proclaim the good news, 'The kingdom of heaven has come near.' Cure the sick, raise the dead, cleanse the lepers, cast out demons. You received without payment; give without payment. Take no gold, or silver, or copper in your belts, no bag for your journey, or two tunics, or sandals, or a staff; for laborers deserve their food. Whatever town or village you enter, find out who in it is worthy, and stay there until you leave."

• When we spread the good news, what we say matters less than how we live. Can people look at my life and say: "That life would not make sense if God did not exist?"

Friday 13th July   Genesis 46:1–7, 28–30

When Israel set out on his journey with all that he had and came to Beer-sheba, he offered sacrifices to the God of his father Isaac. God spoke to Israel in visions of the night, and said, "Jacob, Jacob." And he said, "Here I am." Then he said, "I am God, the God of your father; do not be afraid to go down to Egypt, for I will make of you a great nation there. I myself will go down with you to Egypt, and I will also bring you up again; and Joseph's own hand shall close your eyes." Joseph made ready his chariot and went up to meet his father Israel in Goshen. He presented himself to him, fell on his neck, and wept on his neck a good while. Israel said to Joseph, "I can die now, having seen for myself that you are still alive."

- We cannot control death—the way we die, the place, the hour or the company. Blessed are those who die among friends. Blessed are those who die alone.

- May I be "alive" when I come towards death, alert still, and thankful for the Lord's constant hand on me while I lived.

Saturday 14th July   Matthew 10:24–25a

Jesus said to his Twelve, "A disciple is not above the teacher, nor a slave above the master; it is enough for the disciple to be like the teacher, and the slave like the master."

- With other teachers we may reach a point where we have learned all that they have to offer us. We may even go beyond them. Not so with Jesus.

- What sort of pupil do I make—alert? inattentive? diligent? easily distracted?

Something to think and pray about each day this week:

Returning to the Samaritan

We often think of the Good Samaritan as a symbol of the Christ, but perhaps we should try another view—that the real Christ symbol is the person lying by the side of the road.

He is the person who is converting, who shakes us up, who tips our worldview upside down, who confronts us with a new reality. He challenges us. Do we just want to remain the people we are, or the people we are called to be—people of Jesus who are stretched beyond their current boundaries and taken well beyond where they feel at home?

It may seem that we live today with personal or national aggression as a first response to others. To us then, the challenge of the Samaritan is the peace that Jesus announces, and that peace knows no nationality or denomination. It is people left for dead on the side of the road who can teach us that.

The Presence of God

What is present to me is what has a hold on my becoming.
I reflect on the presence of God always there in love,
amidst the many things that have a hold on me.
I pause and pray that I may let God
affect my becoming in this precise moment.

Freedom

There are very few people
who realize what God would make of them
if they abandoned themselves into his hands,
and let themselves be formed by his grace. (St. Ignatius)
I ask for the grace to trust myself totally to God's love.

Consciousness

In the presence of my loving Creator,
I look honestly at my feelings over the last day,
the highs, the lows and the level ground.
Can I see where the Lord has been present?

The Word

God speaks to each one of us individually. I need to listen to
what he is saying to me. (Please turn to your scripture on the following pages. Inspiration points are there should you need
them. When you are ready, return here to continue.)

Conversation

What is stirring in me as I pray?
Am I consoled, troubled, left cold?
I imagine Jesus himself standing or sitting at my side,
and share my feelings with him.

Conclusion

Glory be to the Father, and to the Son, and to the Holy Spirit,
As it was in the beginning, is now and ever shall be,
World without end. Amen

Sunday 15th July, Fifteenth Sunday in Ordinary Time
Luke 10:25–37

Just then a lawyer stood up to test Jesus. "Teacher," he said, "what must I do to inherit eternal life?" He said to him, "What is written in the law? What do you read there?" He answered, "You shall love the Lord your God with all your heart, and with all your soul, and with all your strength, and with all your mind; and your neighbor as yourself." And he said to him, "You have given the right answer; do this, and you will live." But wanting to justify himself, he asked Jesus, "And who is my neighbor?" Jesus replied, "A man was going down from Jerusalem to Jericho, and fell into the hands of robbers, who stripped him, beat him, and went away, leaving him half dead. Now by chance a priest was going down that road; and when he saw him, he passed by on the other side. So likewise a Levite, when he came to the place and saw him, passed by on the other side. But a Samaritan while traveling came near him; and when he saw him, he was moved with pity. He went to him and bandaged his wounds, having poured oil and wine on them. Then he put him on his own animal, brought him to an inn, and took care of him. The next day he took out two denarii, gave them to the innkeeper, and said, 'Take care of him; and when I come back, I will repay you whatever more you spend.' Which of these three, do you think, was a neighbor to the man who fell into the hands of the robbers?" He said, "The one who showed him mercy." Jesus said to him, "Go and do likewise."

- Can I let Jesus tell me this story, and listen to it as if I am hearing it for the first time?

- What resonance does it have with the life I am living right now?

Monday 16th July   Matthew 10:37–39

Jesus said to his disciples, "Whoever loves father or mother more than me is not worthy of me; and whoever loves son or daughter more than me is not worthy of me; and whoever does not take up the cross and follow me is not worthy of me. Those who find their life will lose it, and those who lose their life for my sake will find it."

- Have I ever risked standing out from the crowd, or experienced discomfort or embarrassment for Jesus' sake?

- Is that what the call to "take up the cross" or "lose" my life might mean for me?

Tuesday 17th July — Matthew 11:20–24

Then Jesus began to reproach the cities in which most of his deeds of power had been done, because they did not repent. "Woe to you, Chorazin! Woe to you, Bethsaida! For if the deeds of power done in you had been done in Tyre and Sidon, they would have repented long ago in sackcloth and ashes. But I tell you, on the day of judgment it will be more tolerable for Tyre and Sidon than for you. And you, Capernaum, will you be exalted to heaven? No, you will be brought down to Hades. For if the deeds of power done in you had been done in Sodom, it would have remained until this day. But I tell you that on the day of judgment it will be more tolerable for the land of Sodom than for you."

- It is almost the voice of the Baptist we hear, as Jesus foreshadows the rejection of Israel for the message that the Messiah brings. The pagans of Tyre and Sidon, had they seen these "deeds of power," would have not have remained so unmoved.

- How am I moved by Jesus' reproach? By fear?

- What "deeds of power" is Jesus doing around me? Can I ask for the grace to see them, recognize them, respond to them?

Wednesday 18th July   **Matthew 11:25–27**

At that time Jesus said, "I thank you, Father, Lord of heaven and earth, because you have hidden these things from the wise and the intelligent and have revealed them to infants; yes, Father, for such was your gracious will. All things have been handed over to me by my Father; and no one knows the Son except the Father, and no one knows the Father except the Son and anyone to whom the Son chooses to reveal him."

- In the knowledge of each other that Father and Son share, there is deep intimacy and approval. All the teaching and healing that Jesus does is ultimately the revelation of the Father's desire to save us.

- Do I claim wisdom and intelligence for myself? Wherever I may be in my journey towards knowing the Son, can I be like a child and open my heart?

Thursday 19th July   **Exodus 3:13–20**

Moses said to God, "If I come to the Israelites and say to them, 'The God of your ancestors has sent me to you,' and they ask me, 'What is his name?' what shall I say to them?" God said to Moses, "I AM WHO I AM." He said further, "Thus you shall say to the Israelites, 'I AM has sent me to you.'" God also said to Moses, "Thus you shall say to the Israelites, 'The Lord, the God of your ancestors, the God of Abraham, the God of Isaac, and the God of Jacob, has sent me to you': This is my name forever, and this my title for all generations."

- Here we face the mystery of God. We cannot imagine the One who exists before time or space, the uncreated origin of all that exists. We cannot imagine the answer to the child's question: "Who made God?"

- Thomas Aquinas said: "This is the test of human knowledge of God, that we do not know God."

Friday 20th July   **Matthew 12:1–8**

A t that time Jesus went through the grainfields on the sabbath; his disciples were hungry, and they began to pluck
heads of grain and to eat. When the Pharisees saw it, they said to
him, "Look, your disciples are doing what is not lawful to do on
the sabbath." He said to them, "Have you not read what David
did when he and his companions were hungry? He entered the
house of God and ate the bread of the Presence, which it was not
lawful for him or his companions to eat, but only for the priests.
Or have you not read in the law that on the sabbath the priests
in the temple break the sabbath and yet are guiltless? I tell you,
something greater than the temple is here. But if you had known
what this means, 'I desire mercy and not sacrifice,' you would
not have condemned the guiltless. For the Son of Man is lord of
the sabbath."

- The Bible gave a simple command: Keep the Sabbath holy. The
  rabbis went on to classify 39 sorts of work which were not permit-
  ted on the Sabbath.

- Jesus always draws us back to the simplicity of God's command.
  Am I reluctant to follow?

- How often do I judge others for breaking "the rules"? Can I look
  at their actions through Jesus' eyes?

Saturday 21st July   **Matthew 12:14–21**

B ut the Pharisees went out and conspired against him, how to
destroy him. When Jesus became aware of this, he departed.
Many crowds followed him, and he cured all of them, and he
ordered them not to make him known. This was to fulfill what
had been spoken through the prophet Isaiah: "Here is my servant, whom I have chosen, my beloved, with whom my soul is
well pleased. I will put my Spirit upon him, and he will proclaim
justice to the Gentiles. He will not wrangle or cry aloud, nor will

anyone hear his voice in the streets. He will not break a bruised reed or quench a smoldering wick until he brings justice to victory. And in his name the Gentiles will hope."

- A crucial choice facing the enemies of injustice all over the world: to go the way of violence or non-violence? Che Guevara chose the former, Gandhi the latter. Both paid a heavy price.

- Jesus' way is gentle, not crying aloud or breaking the bruised reed. His way is patient, and will bring justice to victory. Do I struggle with that assurance?

july 22–28

Something to think and pray about each day this week:

Resting our burdens

Matthew's Gospel (11: 28–30) sets the tone for our prayer this week. Jesus opens his arms to comfort those who labor and are burdened. The invitation is almost motherly: He is the giver of rest and consolation. His yoke is easy—the contrast is between the complicated yoke of the Jewish Torah, with hundreds of instructions, and the simple message of Jesus, to love God and our neighbor. "And you will find rest for your souls." St. Augustine reflected his own wayward experience when he wrote: "You have made us for yourself, O Lord, and our hearts are restless till they rest in you."

The Presence of God

God is with me, but more, God is within me.
Let me dwell for a moment on God's life-giving presence
in my body, in my mind, in my heart,
as I sit here, right now.

Freedom

A thick and shapeless tree-trunk would never believe
that it could become a statue, admired as a miracle of sculpture,
and would never submit itself to the chisel of the sculptor,
who sees by her genius what she can make of it. (St. Ignatius)
I ask for the grace to let myself be shaped by my loving Creator.

Consciousness

Knowing that God loves me unconditionally,
I look honestly over the last day, its events and my feelings.
Do I have something to be grateful for? Then I give thanks.
Is there something I am sorry for? Then I ask forgiveness.

The Word

I read the Word of God slowly, a few times over, and I listen to
what God is saying to me. (Please turn to your scripture on the
following pages. Inspiration points are there should you need
them. When you are ready, return here to continue.)

Conversation

Do I notice myself reacting as I pray with the Word of God?
Do I feel challenged, comforted, angry?
Imagining Jesus sitting or standing by me,
I speak out my feelings, as one trusted friend to another.

Conclusion

Glory be to the Father, and to the Son, and to the Holy Spirit,
As it was in the beginning, is now and ever shall be,
World without end. Amen

258

Sunday 22nd July, Sixteenth Sunday in Ordinary Time
Luke 10:38–42

Now as they went on their way, Jesus entered a certain village, where a woman named Martha welcomed him into her home. She had a sister named Mary, who sat at the Lord's feet and listened to what he was saying. But Martha was distracted by her many tasks; so she came to him and asked, "Lord, do you not care that my sister has left me to do all the work by myself? Tell her then to help me." But the Lord answered her, "Martha, Martha, you are worried and distracted by many things; there is need of only one thing. Mary has chosen the better part, which will not be taken away from her."

- Can I imagine myself as either Martha or Mary? Am I naturally like Martha, in charge of things, organizing everything? Or, do I see myself happily sitting at the Lord's feet?

- Jesus gave Martha a gentle challenge.

- What challenge does he have for me?

Monday 23rd July, St. Bridget   Galatians 2:19–20

I have been crucified with Christ; and it is no longer I who live, but it is Christ who lives in me. And the life I now live in the flesh I live by faith in the Son of God, who loved me and gave himself for me.

- What does it mean to "live in you," and for Christ to "live in me"?

- Can I be at ease with Jesus, find my strength in him, and be ready to explain to others what he is in my life?

Tuesday 24th July   Matthew 12:46–50

While Jesus was still speaking to the crowds, his mother and his brothers were standing outside, wanting to speak to him. Someone told him, "Look, your mother and your brothers are standing outside, wanting to speak to you." But to the one who had told him this, Jesus replied, "Who is my mother, and who are my brothers?" And pointing to his disciples, he said, "Here are my mother and my brothers! For whoever does the will of my Father in heaven is my brother and sister and mother."

- Jesus' beloved family comes by as he is preaching. He seizes the chance, not to deny his family ties, but to widen that group.

- When he points to the group of disciples, can I imagine that I am standing among them? How do I respond?

Wednesday 25th July, St. James, Apostle
Matthew 20:20–23

Then the mother of the sons of Zebedee came to him with her sons, and kneeling before him, she asked a favor of him. And he said to her, "What do you want?" She said to him, "Declare that these two sons of mine will sit, one at your right hand and one at your left, in your kingdom." But Jesus answered, "You do not know what you are asking. Are you able to drink the cup that I am about to drink?" They said to him, "We are able." He said to them, "You will indeed drink my cup, but to sit at my right hand and at my left, this is not mine to grant, but it is for those for whom it has been prepared by my Father."

- How easily we ask God for the wrong things. How quickly we apply the world's standards to the church, and see her leaders— Pope, bishops, priests—on the lines of presidents and politicians.

- But Christ-like authority is a form of service, and that those who exercise it must be prepared to suffer.

- Can I see the suffering in my life as a sharing in the cup from which Jesus drank?

Thursday 26th July, Sts. Joachim and Ann

Matthew 13:16–17

Jesus said to the disciples, "But blessed are your eyes, for they see, and your ears, for they hear. Truly I tell you, many prophets and righteous people longed to see what you see, but did not see it, and to hear what you hear, but did not hear it."

- Mary's parents, Joachim and Ann, and the disciples, saw and heard Jesus. They are blessed.

- When Jesus speaks about conversion and healing, do I "see" and "hear"?

Friday 27th July

Exodus 20:1–17

Then God spoke all these words: I am the Lord your God, who brought you out of the land of Egypt, out of the house of slavery; you shall have no other gods before me. You shall not make for yourself an idol, whether in the form of anything that is in heaven above, or that is on the earth beneath, or that is in the water under the earth. You shall not bow down to them or worship them; for I the Lord your God am a jealous God, punishing children for the iniquity of parents, to the third and the fourth generation of those who reject me, but showing steadfast love to the thousandth generation of those who love me and keep my commandments. You shall not make wrongful use of the name of the Lord your God, for the Lord will not acquit anyone who misuses his name. Remember the Sabbath day, and keep it holy. Six days you shall labour and do all your work. But the seventh day is a Sabbath to the Lord your God; you shall not do any work—you, your son or your daughter, your male or female slave, your livestock, or the alien resident in your towns. For in six days the Lord made heaven and earth, the sea, and all that is in them, but rested the seventh day; therefore the Lord blessed the Sabbath day and consecrated it. Honor your father and your mother, so that your days may be long in the land that the Lord your God is giving you. You shall not murder. You shall not commit adultery. You shall not steal. You shall not bear false witness against your neighbor. You shall not covet your neighbor's house; you shall not covet your neighbor's wife, or male or female slave, or ox, or donkey, or anything that belongs to your neighbor.

- What is the impact of the Ten Commandments on me, today? Do I shift uneasily at being ordered around? How do they stand against the personal freedom I cherish?

- Something in my ego squirms at having limits put on my behavior. Can I speak to the Lord about this?

Saturday 28th July   Matthew 13:24–30

Jesus put before them another parable: "The kingdom of heaven may be compared to someone who sowed good seed in his field; but while everybody was asleep, an enemy came and sowed weeds among the wheat, and then went away. So when the plants came up and bore grain, then the weeds appeared as well. And the slaves of the householder came and said to him, 'Master, did you not sow good seed in your field? Where, then, did these weeds come from?' He answered, 'An enemy has done this.' The slaves said to him, 'Then do you want us to go and gather them?' But he replied, 'No; for in gathering the weeds you would uproot the wheat along with them. Let both of them grow together until the harvest; and at harvest time I will tell the reapers, Collect the weeds first and bind them in bundles to be burned, but gather the wheat into my barn.'"

- Do I struggle to understand why God's kingdom does not flourish in this world? Am I downhearted about that?

- God shows the patience of the farmer. Can I be patient? With myself? With others?

Something to think and pray about each day this week:

Awakening God's grace

When I slow down in preparation for prayer, when I quiet my body and allow thoughts to bubble up in me, they are sometimes nasty thoughts. Resentments that are normally dormant seem to come awake in me. In order to regain balance, I need to offer an absolution to the people I resent, and let them go. The absolution will not come if I feel that they alone are guilty and I am blameless. I must see myself as being co-responsible with the offender for each offence that I have been the victim of. Rather than casting stones—I have beams in my own eye, Lord—I dispense amnesties and pardons. So I make the offence a channel of grace for both the offender and for me.

The Presence of God
As I sit here, the beating of my heart,
the ebb and flow of my breathing, the movements of my mind
are all signs of God's ongoing creation of me.
I pause for a moment, and become aware
of this presence of God within me.

Freedom
I ask for the grace
to let go of my own concerns
and be open to what God is asking of me,
to let myself be guided and formed by my loving Creator.

Consciousness
How do I find myself today?
Where am I with God? With others?
Do I have something to be grateful for? Then I give thanks.
Is there something I am sorry for? Then I ask forgiveness.

The Word
I take my time to read the Word of God, slowly, a few times,
allowing myself to dwell on anything that strikes me. (Please
turn to your scripture on the following pages. Inspiration points
are there should you need them. When you are ready, return
here to continue.)

Conversation
Remembering that I am still in God's presence,
I imagine Jesus himself standing or sitting beside me,
and say whatever is on my mind, whatever is in my heart,
speaking as one friend to another.

Conclusion
Glory be to the Father, and to the Son, and to the Holy Spirit,
As it was in the beginning, is now and ever shall be,
World without end. Amen

Sunday 29th July, Seventeenth Sunday in Ordinary Time
Luke 11:1–8

Jesus was praying in a certain place, and after he had finished, one of his disciples said to him, "Lord, teach us to pray, as John taught his disciples." He said to them, "When you pray, say: Father, hallowed be your name. Your kingdom come. Give us each day our daily bread. And forgive us our sins, for we ourselves forgive everyone indebted to us. And do not bring us to the time of trial." And he said to them, "Suppose one of you has a friend, and you go to him at midnight and say to him, 'Friend, lend me three loaves of bread; for a friend of mine has arrived, and I have nothing to set before him.' And he answers from within, 'Do not bother me; the door has already been locked, and my children are with me in bed; I cannot get up and give you anything.' I tell you, even though he will not get up and give him anything because he is his friend, at least because of his persistence he will get up and give him whatever he needs."

- These simple lines sum up the relationship with God that Jesus wanted for each one of us.

- Can I take one of these phrases and let it teach me?

Monday 30th July   **Matthew 13:31–35**

Jesus put before them another parable: "The kingdom of heaven is like a mustard seed that someone took and sowed in his field; it is the smallest of all the seeds, but when it has grown it is the greatest of shrubs and becomes a tree, so that the birds of the air come and make nests in its branches." He told them another parable: "The kingdom of heaven is like yeast that a woman took and mixed in with three measures of flour until all of it was leavened." Jesus told the crowds all these things in parables; without a parable he told them nothing. This was to fulfil what had been spoken through the prophet: "I will open my mouth to speak in parables; I will proclaim what has been hidden from the foundation of the world."

- These two stories are so short, and their subjects—mustard seeds and yeast—so small and insignificant; humble beginnings, yet extraordinary outcomes. Jesus is not a warrior Messiah, but quiet and unobtrusive.

- How do I respond to this?

Tuesday 31st July, St. Ignatius Loyola Luke 9:23–26

Then Jesus said to the disciples, "If any want to become my followers, let them deny themselves and take up their cross daily and follow me. For those who want to save their life will lose it, and those who lose their life for my sake will save it. What does it profit them if they gain the whole world, but lose or forfeit themselves? Those who are ashamed of me and of my words, of them the Son of Man will be ashamed when he comes in his glory and the glory of the Father and of the holy angels."

- Following Jesus involves struggle and some painful choices. Ignatius knew worldly comfort, but following Jesus meant accepting that Jesus wants us to be impressed with things quite at odds with material riches.

- Where is the cross in my life? Can I let Jesus encourage and strengthen me? Can I trust him to accept me and lead me into true life?

Wednesday 1st August Matthew 13:44–46

Jesus said to the disciples, "The kingdom of heaven is like treasure hidden in a field, which someone found and hid; then in his joy he goes and sells all that he has and buys that field. Again, the kingdom of heaven is like a merchant in search of fine pearls; on finding one pearl of great value, he went and sold all that he had and bought it."

- This gospel is uncompromising. There is joy in finding Jesus, but that is only the first step. To become free to possess "the pearl of great price," the asking price is all that I have.

- Can I sustain my effort, each step of the way? Can I make Jesus my priority all through my life, in every decision I take?

Thursday 2nd August   Psalm 83(84)

My heart and my soul ring out their joy to God, the living God. They are happy whose strength is in you. They walk with ever growing strength.

- Is my strength in the Lord? Or is it invested in these mortal limbs, this limited mind of mine?

- Can I trust in the Lord's strength to be fully alive? Can I let the God's love work through me in all my encounters, rather than seek my own path?

Friday 3rd August   Matthew 13:54–58

Jesus came to his home town and began to teach the people in their synagogue, so that they were astounded and said, "Where did this man get this wisdom and these deeds of power? Is not this the carpenter's son? Is not his mother called Mary? And are not his brothers James and Joseph and Simon and Judas? And are not all his sisters with us? Where then did this man get all this?" And they took offense at him. But Jesus said to them, "Prophets are not without honor except in their own country and in their own house." And he did not do many deeds of power there, because of their unbelief.

- Let me imagine myself in this scene, as someone who grew up with Jesus. He was a boy of this town, and is now a man.

- Can I discern anything of the divine in this man, in his preaching and miracles? Does my astonishment overcome me? What prejudice blocks my belief?

Saturday 4th August **Matthew 14:1–12**

At that time Herod the ruler heard reports about Jesus; and he said to his servants, "This is John the Baptist; he has been raised from the dead, and for this reason these powers are at work in him." For Herod had arrested John, bound him, and put him in prison on account of Herodias, his brother Philip's wife, because John had been telling him, "It is not lawful for you to have her." Though Herod wanted to put him to death, he feared the crowd, because they regarded him as a prophet. But when Herod's birthday came, the daughter of Herodias danced before the company, and she pleased Herod so much that he promised on oath to grant her whatever she might ask. Prompted by her mother, she said, "Give me the head of John the Baptist here on a platter." The king was grieved, yet out of regard for his oaths and for the guests, he commanded it to be given; he sent and had John beheaded in the prison. The head was brought on a platter and given to the girl, who brought it to her mother. His disciples came and took the body and buried it; then they went and told Jesus.

- In Herod, "that fox" (Luke 13:32), we see a ruler who abuses his power, treats religion as a spectacle or news item, makes grandiose promises which he regrets, then kills on a whim. We have known such in our day.

- What word would you use for me, Lord? I am not worthy to be in your company, not as straight as I would wish to be. I wish for true integrity, like yours.

Something to think and pray about each day this week:

Being at home

In one of the gospel parables, the rich man is mulling over his treasures, and plans to build even bigger barns to store all his crops. He relishes his security: "My soul, you have plenty of good things laid by for many years to come." Jesus reflects: "A person's life is not made secure by what he owns."

As we grow quiet in prayer, our hearts can be invaded in the same way by false securities. In the measure that my heart is in past treasures, I am fossilized and dead, for life is only in the present. So to each of these past treasures, I say goodbye, explaining that, grateful though I am that it came into my life, it must move out, or my heart will never learn to love the present.

We draw energy from prayer to the extent that it draws us into the here and now. The only place I can meet God is in this body, with this heart and mind, in this room. It is not an exercise of fantasy, or placing myself above the clouds in some imaginary heaven. I find God, or rather God finds me, when I am home to myself.

The Presence of God

I pause for a moment
and reflect on God's life-giving presence
in every part of my body, in everything around me,
in the whole of my life.

Freedom

I ask for the grace to believe
in what I could be and do
if I only allowed God, my loving Creator,
to continue to create me, guide me and shape me.

Consciousness

In God's loving presence I unwind the past day,
starting from now and looking back, moment by moment.
I gather in all the goodness and light, in gratitude.
I attend to the shadows and what they say to me,
seeking healing, courage, forgiveness.

The Word

God speaks to each one of us individually. I need to listen to
what he is saying to me. (Please turn to your scripture on the following pages. Inspiration points are there should you need
them. When you are ready, return here to continue.)

Conversation

How has God's Word moved me? Has it left me cold?
Has it consoled me or moved me to act in a new way?
I imagine Jesus standing or sitting beside me,
I turn and share my feelings with him.

Conclusion

Glory be to the Father, and to the Son, and to the Holy Spirit,
As it was in the beginning, is now and ever shall be,
World without end. Amen

Sunday 5th August, Eighteenth Sunday in Ordinary Time
Luke 12:13–21

Someone in the crowd said to Jesus, "Teacher, tell my brother to divide the family inheritance with me." But he said to him, "Friend, who set me to be a judge or arbitrator over you?" And he said to them, "Take care! Be on your guard against all kinds of greed; for one's life does not consist in the abundance of possessions." Then he told them a parable: "The land of a rich man produced abundantly. And he thought to himself, 'What should I do, for I have no place to store my crops?' Then he said, 'I will do this: I will pull down my barns and build larger ones, and there I will store all my grain and my goods. And I will say to my soul, 'Soul, you have ample goods laid up for many years; relax, eat, drink, be merry.' But God said to him, 'You fool! This very night your life is being demanded of you. And the things you have prepared, whose will they be?' So it is with those who store up treasures for themselves but are not rich toward God."

- Does this seem an outlandish parable? Can I imagine anyone—even me—allowing the beautiful things of life to come between me and God?

- Is there anything that I hoard?

- What does being "rich toward God" mean in my case?

Monday 6th August, Transfiguration of the Lord
Luke 9:28b–36

Jesus took with him Peter and John and James, and went up on the mountain to pray. And while he was praying, the appearance of his face changed, and his clothes became dazzling white. Suddenly they saw two men, Moses and Elijah, talking to him. They appeared in glory and were speaking of his departure, which he was about to accomplish at Jerusalem. Now Peter and his companions were weighed down with sleep; but since they had stayed awake, they saw his glory and the two men who stood with him. Just as they were leaving him, Peter said to Jesus, "Master, it is good for us to be here; let us make three dwellings, one for you, one for Moses, and one for Elijah"—not knowing what he said. While he was saying this, a cloud came and overshadowed them; and they were terrified as they entered the cloud. Then from the cloud came a voice that said, "This is my Son, my Chosen; listen to him!" When the voice had spoken, Jesus was found alone. And they kept silent and in those days told no one any of the things they had seen.

- In our journey towards God we experience high moments, spots when we find ourselves on holy ground, and God shows himself. That was the state of St. Peter as he witnessed the transfiguration of Jesus: Peter wanted the party to go on for ever.

- Jesus brought him down to earth, led him down the mountain, told him to stop talking about the vision and instead be ready for Calvary.

- Our life journey takes us from one little piece of holy ground to the next. Lord, give me the strength to keep going in between.

Tuesday 7th August   **Matthew 14:22–33**

Jesus made the disciples get into the boat and go on ahead to the other side, while he dismissed the crowds. And after he had dismissed the crowds, he went up the mountain by himself to pray. When evening came, he was there alone, but by this time the boat, battered by the waves, was far from the land, for the wind was against them. And early in the morning he came walking toward them on the sea. But when the disciples saw him walking on the sea, they were terrified, saying, "It is a ghost!" And they cried out in fear. But immediately Jesus spoke to them and said, "Take heart, it is I; do not be afraid." Peter answered him, "Lord, if it is you, command me to come to you on the water." He said, "Come." So Peter got out of the boat, started walking on the water, and came toward Jesus. But when he noticed the strong wind, he became frightened, and beginning to sink, he cried out, "Lord, save me!" Jesus immediately reached out his hand and caught him, saying to him, "You of little faith, why did you doubt?" When they got into the boat, the wind ceased. And those in the boat worshiped him, saying, "Truly you are the Son of God."

- Jesus was on the mountain alone. At the end of a busy day he needed space to be alone with God. In human terms, that was where he found his strength.

- What a strength Peter is to us! He is so vulnerable, with his mix of emotional impulse and faith weakened by doubt. He loves Jesus and wants to come to him, but has not reckoned with the continuing violence of the wind and waves.

- What a mixture our faith is: bold and ready to take risks, yet vulnerable.

Wednesday 8th August   Matthew 15:21–28

Jesus left that place and went away to the district of Tyre and Sidon. Just then a Canaanite woman from that region came out and started shouting, "Have mercy on me, Lord, Son of David; my daughter is tormented by a demon." But he did not answer her at all. And his disciples came and urged him, saying, "Send her away, for she keeps shouting after us." He answered, "I was sent only to the lost sheep of the house of Israel." But she came and knelt before him, saying, "Lord, help me." He answered, "It is not fair to take the children's food and throw it to the dogs." She said, "Yes, Lord, yet even the dogs eat the crumbs that fall from their masters' table." Then Jesus answered her, "Woman, great is your faith! Let it be done for you as you wish." And her daughter was healed instantly.

- This woman is different from the scribes who often tried to trap Jesus with arguments. She is begging for her daughter. There is something almost cold about Jesus' first reply to her.

- His first response is what we often experience in prayer: no give. But a mother seeking health for her child is not easily deterred, and Jesus rewards her persistence—we can imagine him smiling as he blesses her.

- Lord I want to remember this. When I want something badly, I will keep after you and if necessary give out to you.

Thursday 9th August   Matthew 16:13–20

Now when Jesus came into the district of Caesarea Philippi, he asked his disciples, "Who do people say that the Son of Man is?" And they said, "Some say John the Baptist, but others Elijah, and still others Jeremiah or one of the prophets." He said to them, "But who do you say that I am?" Simon Peter answered, "You are the Messiah, the Son of the living God." And Jesus answered him, "Blessed are you, Simon son of Jonah! For flesh and blood has not revealed this to you, but my Father in heaven. And I tell you, you are Peter, and on this rock I will build my church, and the gates of Hades will not prevail against it. I will give you the keys of the kingdom of heaven, and whatever you bind on earth will be bound in heaven, and whatever you loose on earth will be loosed in heaven." Then he sternly ordered the disciples not to tell anyone that he was the Messiah.

- Let me imagine myself there, under the cliff-face in Caesarea Philippi, as Jesus asks his momentous question: "Who do you say that I am?" Suddenly the mission expanded. He is handing over to us (the people of God) the task of continuing his mission.

- We are not, as is sometimes phrased, "followers of the church." We are the church, served by bishops and others, but with our own wisdom.

Friday 10th August, St. Lawrence   2 Corinthians 9:6–10

The point is this: The one who sows sparingly will also reap sparingly, and the one who sows bountifully will also reap bountifully. Each of you must give as you have made up your mind, not reluctantly or under compulsion, for God loves a cheerful giver. And God is able to provide you with every blessing in abundance, so that by always having enough of everything, you may share abundantly in every good work. As it is written, "He scatters abroad, he gives to the poor; his righteousness endures forever."

- When St. Paul writes: "God loves a cheerful giver," he is begging for the poor of Jerusalem.

- How do these words speak to me? Am I reluctant to give? Do I offer gifts to make an impression? Take some time to talk to the Lord about this.

Saturday 11th August   Matthew 17:14–20

When they came to the crowd, a man came to Jesus, knelt before him, and said, "Lord, have mercy on my son, for he is an epileptic and he suffers terribly; he often falls into the fire and often into the water. And I brought him to your disciples, but they could not cure him." Jesus answered, "You faithless and perverse generation, how much longer must I be with you? How much longer must I put up with you? Bring him here to me." And Jesus rebuked the demon, and it came out of him, and the boy was cured instantly. Then the disciples came to Jesus privately and said, "Why could we not cast it out?" He said to them, "Because of your little faith. For truly I tell you, if you have faith the size of a mustard seed, you will say to this mountain, 'Move from here to there,' and it will move; and nothing will be impossible for you."

- Here is a short story with many elements: a boy in great distress; his father on his knees at his wit's end; Jesus' disciples, doing the best they can, but coming up short.

- Jesus is frustrated with the disciples' failure to understand and believe. To Jesus the healing has a minor part in this encounter; the real struggle is with their—and our—limited faith.

- How do I fit in to this story? Can I hear the challenge in a way that leads me forward?

august 12–18

Something to think and pray about each day this week:

Painful prayer

"Where your treasure is, there will your heart be also." What are my treasures? What persons, places, occupations, memories, ambitions does my heart gravitate towards when it is free? I take up each of these, picture them, taste their sweetness; and to each I say with tenderness: "You are precious to me, but you are not my life. I have a life to live, and a destiny to meet, that is separate from you."

This may be an agonizing prayer. If we are caught between two loves, it can be torture to choose. Suppose my treasures are things that seem to constitute my very being; can I endure the loss of the people I love most, or my health, my ideals, my good name, even my life? Can I stand before God and say: "You, Lord, are my life. I gave my heart to you." Prayer can be painful.

The Presence of God
The world is charged with the grandeur of God (Gerard Manley Hopkins).
I dwell for a moment on the presence of God
around me, in every part of my body,
and deep within my being.

Freedom
"In these days, God taught me
as a schoolteacher teaches a pupil" (St. Ignatius).
I remind myself that there are things God has to teach me yet,
and ask for the grace to hear them and let them change me.

Consciousness
I exist in a web of relationships—links to nature, people, God.
I trace out these links, giving thanks for the life that flows through them.
Some links are twisted or broken: I may feel regret, anger, disappointment.
I pray for the gift of acceptance and forgiveness.

The Word
I read the Word of God slowly, a few times over, and I listen to what God is saying to me. (Please turn to your scripture on the following pages. Inspirations points are there should you need them. When you are ready, return here to continue.)

Conversation
What feelings are rising in me
as I pray and reflect on God's Word?
I imagine Jesus himself sitting or standing beside me,
and open my heart to him.

Conclusion
Glory be to the Father, and to the Son, and to the Holy Spirit,
As it was in the beginning, is now and ever shall be,
World without end. Amen

Sunday 12th August, Nineteenth Sunday in Ordinary Time
Luke 12:32–34

Jesus said to the disciples, "Do not be afraid, little flock, for it is your Father's good pleasure to give you the kingdom. Sell your possessions, and give alms. Make purses for yourselves that do not wear out, an unfailing treasure in heaven, where no thief comes near and no moth destroys. For where your treasure is, there your heart will be also.

- Can I get my head around this? The Father really wants to give me everything.

- Can I honestly pose the question: "Where is my treasure? What is really important to me?"

- What am I being called to?

Monday 13th August   Deuteronomy 10:14–20

Moses said to the people, "The Lord your God executes justice for the orphan and the widow, and loves the strangers, providing them food and clothing. You shall also love the stranger, for you were strangers in the land of Egypt. You shall fear the Lord your God; him alone you shall worship; to him you shall hold fast, and by his name you shall swear."

- God has chosen the poor and the stranger as my brothers and sisters. What does this mean for me? Strangers include immigrants, gypsies, the homeless, the vagrants, who make us uneasy if we are native, settled and housed.

- Lord, open my heart to what you want of me, to see you in the needy and have energy for them.

Tuesday 14th August, St. Maximilian Kolbe
John 15:16–17

Jesus said to the disciples, "You did not choose me but I chose you. And I appointed you to go and bear fruit, fruit that will last, so that the Father will give you whatever you ask him in my name. I am giving you these commands so that you may love one another."

- How do I respond to the idea that Jesus chooses me—every moment of every day? Can I let that truth sink in?

- Let me take some time to talk with the Lord about how I bear fruit? I might ask him to show me where and how.

Wednesday 15th August, The Assumption
of the Blessed Virgin Mary
Luke 1:39–41a

In those days Mary set out and went with haste to a Judean town in the hill country, where she entered the house of Zechariah and greeted Elizabeth. When Elizabeth heard Mary's greeting, the child leaped in her womb.

- It is difficult to imagine Mary in heaven—after all she lived her life keeping house. Here is an image from a Czech poet, Vladimir Holan:

    Forgive me, God, but I console myself
    that the beginning and resurrection of all us dead
    will simply be announced by the crowing of the cock.
    After that we'll remain lying down a while...
    The first to get up will be Mother... We'll hear her
    quietly laying the fire,
    quietly putting the kettle on the stove
    and cosily taking the teapot out of the cupboard.
    We'll be home once more.

280

Thursday 16th August   **Matthew 18:21–22**

Then Peter came and said to Jesus, "Lord, if another member of the church sins against me, how often should I forgive? As many as seven times?" Jesus said to him, "Not seven times, but, I tell you, seventy-seven times."

• Jesus returns to the need for forgiveness so often because it is so difficult. It is easy to see the need in others; but when I have been deeply and intentionally hurt by somebody close to me, it tears me apart to forgive them. Yet the burden of unforgiven grievance lies heavy on my heart, not on the other's.

• Lord, teach me to recognize my resentments and grievances, and then take the first steps to shed them.

Friday 17th August   **Matthew 19:3–6**

Some Pharisees came to Jesus, and to test him they asked, "Is it lawful for a man to divorce his wife for any cause?" He answered, "Have you not read that the one who made them at the beginning 'made them male and female,' and said, 'For this reason a man shall leave his father and mother and be joined to his wife, and the two shall become one flesh'? So they are no longer two, but one flesh. Therefore what God has joined together, let no one separate."

• "Is it lawful for a man to divorce his wife for any cause?" How many good Christians wish you had never uttered these words, Lord! They put me in mind of friends and acquaintances who feel cut off from the church because they have separated what God joined together.

• When the vocation to full Christian marriage works, and lasts for decades, it is a miracle of grace. Those who fail to make it work can still be sure of your love and compassion.

• I pray for them, as suffering members of Christ's body.

Saturday 18th August   **Matthew 19:13–15**

Then little children were being brought to Jesus in order that he might lay his hands on them and pray. The disciples spoke sternly to those who brought them; but Jesus said, "Let the little children come to me, and do not stop them; for it is to such as these that the kingdom of heaven belongs." And he laid his hands on them and went on his way.

- I can imagine the chatter and laughter of children drowning Jesus' voice as he talked to a crowd of adults on the hillside. I can see the disciples trying to quiet the kids and pushing them away, until you intervene.

- You gave them what all children need: attention and touch, the knowledge that they are loved and blessed.

Something to think and pray about each day this week:

Being acceptable

As Christians we cannot avoid the puzzle of inclusion and exclusion. Jesus, who at first confined his mission to the Jews, later spoke of the gospel for all nations. Does God have time and love for all his creatures? We wonder about the billions of humans who were born before or have lived since Christ, but never heard of him. Many of them tried to be good according to their lights. Many of them followed other pieties. How is it possible for God to have time for each one of the billions who have toiled on this planet since the beginning of time? St. Peter (Acts 10:34) spoke of his growing realization: "I truly understand that God shows no partiality, but in every nation anyone who fears him and does what is right is acceptable to him."

The Presence of God
As I sit here, God is present,
breathing life into me and into everything around me.
For a few moments, I sit silently,
and become aware of God's loving presence.

Freedom
If God were trying to tell me something, would I know?
If God were reassuring me or challenging me, would I notice?
I ask for the grace to be free of my own preoccupations
and open to what God may be saying to me.

Consciousness
How am I really feeling? Light-hearted? Heavy-hearted?
I may be very much at peace, happy to be here.
Equally, I may be frustrated, worried or angry.
I acknowledge how I really am. It is the real me that the Lord loves.

The Word
I take my time to read the Word of God, slowly, a few times, allowing myself to dwell on anything that strikes me. (Please turn to your scripture on the following pages. Inspiration points are there should you need them. When you are ready, return here to continue.)

Conversation
What is stirring in me as I pray?
Am I consoled, troubled, left cold?
I imagine Jesus himself standing or sitting at my side,
and share my feelings with him.

Conclusion
Glory be to the Father, and to the Son, and to the Holy Spirit,
As it was in the beginning, is now and ever shall be,
World without end. Amen

Sunday 19th August, Twentieth Sunday in Ordinary Time
Luke 12:49–53

"I came to bring fire to the earth, and how I wish it were already kindled! I have a baptism with which to be baptized, and what stress I am under until it is completed! Do you think that I have come to bring peace to the earth? No, I tell you, but rather division! From now on five in one household will be divided, three against two and two against three; they will be divided: father against son and son against father, mother against daughter and daughter against mother, mother-in-law against her daughter-in-law and daughter-in-law against mother-in-law."

• Why would someone bringing good news cause such trouble?

• Can I imagine how someone who spoke the truth in love could bring upset to my world?

• Are there ways in which I avoid the truth because of the disturbance it might cause?

• Can I talk to the Lord about these things?

Monday 20th August   Matthew 19:16–22

Then someone came to Jesus and said, "Teacher, what good deed must I do to have eternal life?" And he said to him, "Why do you ask me about what is good? There is only one who is good. If you wish to enter into life, keep the commandments." He said to him, "Which ones?" And Jesus said, "You shall not murder; You shall not commit adultery; You shall not steal; You shall not bear false witness; Honor your father and mother; also, You shall love your neighbor as yourself." The young man said to him, "I have kept all these; what do I still lack?" Jesus said to him, "If you wish to be perfect, go, sell your possessions, and give the money to the poor, and you will have treasure in heaven; then come, follow me." When the young man heard this word, he went away grieving, for he had many possessions.

- The young man was a good person; he very much wanted to be united with God and to gain eternal life. However, he stumbled at the next step. His attachment to possessions was not obvious to him before he met Jesus.

- Are there any attachments in my life that stand between me and God, especially any that are not obvious?

Tuesday 21st August   Psalm 84:9, 11–14

Let me hear what God the Lord will speak, for he will speak peace to his people, to his faithful, to those who turn to him in their hearts. Surely his salvation is at hand for those who fear him, that his glory may dwell in our land. Steadfast love and faithfulness will meet; righteousness and peace will kiss each other. Faithfulness will spring up from the ground, and righteousness will look down from the sky. The Lord will give what is good, and our land will yield its increase. Righteousness will go before him, and will make a path for his steps.

- God wants to shower blessings and give hope to his people, "to those who turn to him in their hearts."

- Is there any one of the words or images here that catches my attention? Can I just sit with that word and let its promise touch me?

Wednesday 22nd August   Matthew 20:1–16

Jesus said to his disciples, "For the kingdom of heaven is like a landowner who went out early in the morning to hire laborers for his vineyard. After agreeing with the laborers for the usual daily wage, he sent them into his vineyard. When he went out about nine o'clock, he saw others standing idle in the marketplace; and he said to them, 'You also go into the vineyard, and I will pay you whatever is right.' So they went. When he went out again about noon and about three o'clock, he did the same. And about five o'clock he went out and found others standing around; and he said to them, 'Why are you standing here idle all day?' They said to him, 'Because no one has hired us.' He said to them, 'You also go into the vineyard.' When evening came, the owner of the vineyard said to his manager, 'Call the laborers and give them their pay, beginning with the last and then going to the first.' When those hired about five o'clock came, each of them received the usual daily wage. Now when the first came, they thought they would receive more; but each of them also received the usual daily wage. And when they received it, they grumbled against the landowner, saying, 'These last worked only one hour, and you have made them equal to us who have borne the burden of the day and the scorching heat.' But he replied to one of them, 'Friend, I am doing you no wrong; did you not agree with me for the usual daily wage? Take what belongs to you and go; I choose to give to this last the same as I give to you. Am I not allowed to do what I choose with what belongs to me? Or are you envious because I am generous?' So the last will be first, and the first will be last."

- Whom do I identify with in this parable? Am I the landowner trying to get a job done, but with a feeling for those I employ? Am I the unemployed waiting disconsolately in the market place? Am I a laborer who feels hard-done-by? How do I feel in my role?

- The parable touches our envy and sibling rivalry, the feeling that others have not had to work as hard or suffer as much as we had.

- Lord, I am not proud of feeling envious or resentful of others. I trust that you do not ask of me more than I can give, and that in all that befalls me, I can see your love.

Thursday 23rd August   **Matthew 22:1–14**

Once more Jesus spoke to them in parables, saying: "The kingdom of heaven may be compared to a king who gave a wedding banquet for his son. Then he said to his slaves, 'The wedding is ready. Go therefore into the main streets, and invite everyone you find to the wedding banquet.' Those slaves went out into the streets and gathered all whom they found, both good and bad; so the wedding hall was filled with guests. But when the king came in to see the guests, he noticed a man there who was not wearing a wedding robe, and he said to him, 'Friend, how did you get in here without a wedding robe?' And he was speechless. Then the king said to the attendants, 'Bind him hand and foot, and throw him into the outer darkness, where there will be weeping and gnashing of teeth.' For many are called, but few are chosen."

- This parable, spoken when Jesus saw that his own people were moving to reject him, seems to be responding to the invitation offered, and about not taking privileges for granted. The kingdom, the "banquet" is the in the future but the invitation is to live in anticipation of that kingdom.

- The invitation is cast wide, and includes saints and sinners. But it is an invitation to work for the kingdom. Can I avoid the trap of taking the community and salvation for granted, without any real change in my life?

Friday 24th August, St. Bartholomew   **John 1:45–51**

Philip found Nathanael and said to him, "We have found him about whom Moses in the law and also the prophets wrote, Jesus son of Joseph from Nazareth." Nathanael said to him, "Can anything good come out of Nazareth?" Philip said to him, "Come and see." When Jesus saw Nathanael coming toward him, he said of him, "Here is truly an Israelite in whom there is no deceit!" Nathanael asked him, "Where did you get to know me?" Jesus answered, "I saw you under the fig tree before Philip called you." Nathanael replied, "Rabbi, you are the Son of God! You are the King of Israel!" Jesus answered, "Do you believe because I told you that I saw you under the fig tree? You will see greater things than these." And he said to him, "Very truly, I tell you, you will see heaven opened and the angels of God ascending and descending upon the Son of Man."

- "Can anything good come out of Nazareth?" How often, Lord, have I tried to pigeon-hole people by looking down at their gender, .origin, race or family. Nathanael could have missed the chance to meet you, but for Philip's gentle invitation: "Come and see."

- Save me, Lord, from the stupidity of those who try to seem smart by despising others. May I heed Philip, and invite others to walk your way.

Saturday 25th August   Matthew 23:8–12

Jesus addressed the people and his disciples, he said, "But you are not to be called rabbi, for you have one teacher, and you are all students. And call no one your father on earth, for you have one Father the one in heaven. Nor are you to be called instructors, for you have one instructor, the Messiah. The greatest among you will be your servant. All who exalt themselves will be humbled, and all who humble themselves will be exalted."

- The modern, competitive world is in love with hierarchies and qualifications, status and standing. What a stark contrast with Jesus' vision of equality and mutual service!

- Am I seduced by titles and deflected from the inner core? I take no comfort in labels. Just keep my inner reality in line with you.

august 26 – september 1

Something to think and pray about each day this week:

Daily treasure

We never tire of the childhood game of having three wishes. The internet is awash with variations on the theme, and every night TV advertisements invite us to imagine what we would do if we won the lottery. Our first choices, our priorities, change as we grow older. When King Solomon was offered the choice by God, he opted for wisdom. Jesus visits the theme in the parables of the treasure hidden in a field, and the pearl of great price. What do I treasure most? What is my precious pearl? We learn much about ourselves if we study our daily choices.

The Presence of God
As I sit here with my book, God is here.
Around me, in my sensations, in my thoughts and deep within me.
I pause for a moment, and become aware
of God's life-giving presence.

Freedom
I need to close out the noise, to rise above the noise;
The noise that interrupts, that separates,
The noise that isolates.
I need to listen to God again.

Consciousness
Knowing that God loves me unconditionally,
I can afford to be honest about how I am.
How has the last day been, and how do I feel now?
I share my feelings openly with the Lord.

The Word
God speaks to each one of us individually. I need to listen to what he is saying to me. (Please turn to your scripture on the following pages. Inspiration points are there should you need them. When you are ready, return here to continue.)

Conversation
Do I notice myself reacting as I pray with the Word of God?
Do I feel challenged, comforted, angry?
Imagining Jesus sitting or standing by me,
I speak out my feelings, as one trusted friend to another.

Conclusion
Glory be to the Father, and to the Son, and to the Holy Spirit,
As it was in the beginning, is now and ever shall be,
World without end. Amen

Sunday 26th August, Twenty-first Sunday in Ordinary Time
Luke 13:22–30

Jesus went through one town and village after another, teaching as he made his way to Jerusalem. Someone asked him, "Lord, will only a few be saved?" He said to them, "Strive to enter through the narrow door; for many, I tell you, will try to enter and will not be able. When once the owner of the house has got up and shut the door, and you begin to stand outside and to knock at the door, saying, 'Lord, open to us,' then in reply he will say to you, 'I do not know where you come from.' Then you will begin to say, 'We ate and drank with you, and you taught in our streets.' But he will say, 'I do not know where you come from; go away from me, all you evildoers!' There will be weeping and gnashing of teeth when you see Abraham and Isaac and Jacob and all the prophets in the kingdom of God, and you yourselves thrown out. Then people will come from east and west, from north and south, and will eat in the kingdom of God. Indeed, some are last who will be first, and some are first who will be last."

- Here Jesus is uncompromising in his challenge about the serious demands of true discipleship.

- What's my reaction to this challenge? Do I need to be pushed a little bit? Do I feel resentful and misunderstood by Jesus?

- Can I speak to Jesus from my heart?

Monday 27th August   Matthew 23:13–15

Jesus said to the crowds and his disciples, "But woe to you, scribes and Pharisees, hypocrites! For you lock people out of the kingdom of heaven. For you do not go in yourselves, and when others are going in, you stop them. Woe to you, scribes and Pharisees, hypocrites! For you cross sea and land to make a single convert, and you make the new convert twice as much a child of hell as yourselves."

- When Jesus saw hypocrisy, his words cut like a knife through butter. They applied not just to the Pharisees, nor just to the rabbinic school which Matthew was attacking. They reach out to warn all who dare to preach to others.

- These words challenge me: Does my life reflect what I profess?

Tuesday 28th August, St. Augustine   Matthew 23:8–12

Jesus said to the crowds and to his disciples, "But you are not to be called rabbi, for you have one teacher, and you are all students. And call no one your father on earth, for you have one Father—the one in heaven. Nor are you to be called instructors, for you have one instructor, the Messiah. The greatest among you will be your servant. All who exalt themselves will be humbled, and all who humble themselves will be exalted."

- Jesus is unmasking the perennial tendency of leaders to lord it over others. Among his followers the authentic leadership would be exercised by servants.

- What does this say to me? Do I need to change my attitude, whether as a leader or as a follower?

Wednesday 29th August   Matthew 23:27–28

Jesus said, "Woe to you, scribes and Pharisees, hypocrites! For you are like whitewashed tombs, which on the outside look beautiful, but inside they are full of the bones of the dead and of all kinds of filth. So you also on the outside look righteous to others, but inside you are full of hypocrisy and lawlessness."

- "What really matters is to look good!" Does this ring a bell with me?

- Can I allow my preoccupation with appearances to be examined? What can I begin to change here?

Thursday 30th August   **Matthew 24:42–44**

Jesus said to the disciples, "Keep awake therefore, for you do not know on what day your Lord is coming. But understand this: if the owner of the house had known in what part of the night the thief was coming, he would have stayed awake and would not have let his house be broken into. Therefore you also must be ready, for the Son of Man is coming at an unexpected hour."

- Unlike the early Christians, I am not expecting the Second Coming of Jesus at any moment. For 2000 years we have heard prophecies that the end is nigh.
- Your message, Lord, was always: "Be ready. Live in such a way that you can meet the Lord with love."

Friday 31st August   **Matthew 25:1–13**

Jesus said to his disciples, "Then the kingdom of heaven will be like this. Ten bridesmaids took their lamps and went to meet the bridegroom. Five of them were foolish, and five were wise. When the foolish took their lamps, they took no oil with them; but the wise took flasks of oil with their lamps. As the bridegroom was delayed, all of them became drowsy and slept. But at midnight there was a shout, 'Look! Here is the bridegroom! Come out to meet him.' Then all those bridesmaids got up and trimmed their lamps. The foolish said to the wise, 'Give us some of your oil, for our lamps are going out.' But the wise replied, 'No! there will not be enough for you and for us; you had better go to the dealers and buy some for yourselves.' And while they went to buy it, the bridegroom came, and those who were ready went with him into the wedding banquet; and the door was shut. Later the other bridesmaids came also, saying, 'Lord, lord, open to us.' But he replied, 'Truly I tell you, I do not know you.' Keep awake therefore, for you know neither the day nor the hour."

- The oil in the lamps is often understood as the good works which each of us may have to show when called to account. The answer of the wise virgins—"Buy some for yourselves"—implies that people cannot work out their salvation by proxy, creeping in on the coat-tails of a holy person. I have to use my own wisdom and show my own record.

- Can I pray that I work to be prepared for the Lord's coming?

Saturday 1st September   Matthew 25:14–30

Jesus told his disciples this parable, "For it is as if a man, going on a journey, summoned his slaves and entrusted his property to them; to one he gave five talents, to another two, to another one, to each according to his ability. Then he went away. The one who had received the five talents went off at once and traded with them, and made five more talents. In the same way, the one who had the two talents made two more talents. But the one who had received the one talent went off and dug a hole in the ground and hid his master's money. After a long time the master of those slaves came and settled accounts with them. Then the one who had received the five talents came forward, bringing five more talents, saying, 'Master, you handed over to me five talents; see, I have made five more talents.' His master said to him, 'Well done, good and trustworthy slave; you have been trustworthy in a few things, I will put you in charge of many things; enter into the joy of your master.' And the one with the two talents also came forward, saying, 'Master, you handed over to me two talents; see, I have made two more talents.' His master said to him, 'Well done, good and trustworthy slave; you have been trustworthy in a few things, I will put you in charge of many things; enter into the joy of your master.' Then the one who had received the one talent also came forward, saying, 'Master, I knew that you were a harsh man, reaping where you did not sow, and gathering where you did not scatter seed; so I was afraid, and I went and hid your talent in the ground. Here you have what is yours.' But his master replied, 'You wicked and lazy slave! You knew, did you, that I reap where I did not sow, and gather where I did not scatter? Then you ought to have invested my money with the bankers, and on my return I would have received what was my own with interest. So take the talent from him, and give it to the one with the ten talents.'"

- What can I take from your story, Lord? The cards you dealt me, the talents with which I grew up, are different from other people's.

- Am I to take risks with them? Try out different paths, with the danger of failing? And then learn from my failures?

- You are telling me not to bury my gifts, not to curl up in safe inertia, but to take risks and use them to the full.

september 2–8

Something to think and pray about each day this week:

Breaking open the Word

This week the daily Gospels are taken from St. Luke, starting with the fourth chapter. Luke is a thoughtful, gifted writer, worth reading and re-reading. His early chapters focus on continuity with the Old Testament, while his last chapter links up with the story of the early Christian community in the Acts of the Apostles. He shows how God through Jesus Christ is faithful to promises made to Israel, but extends his goodness. The gospel throws unexpected light on Jesus' relations with women, Gentiles, the unclean, the poor, Samaritans, rich tax collectors and assorted others who had a marginal place in Israel. Luke was writing in pluralistic Syrian Antioch, for a primarily Gentile audience; his words and style resonate well with us over the centuries.

The Presence of God
I pause for a moment, aware that God is here.
I think of how everything around me,
the air I breathe, my whole body,
is tingling with the presence of God.

Freedom
I will ask God's help,
to be free from my own preoccupations,
to be open to God in this time of prayer,
to come to love and serve him more.

Consciousness
In the presence of my loving Creator,
I look honestly at my feelings over the last day,
the highs, the lows and the level ground.
Can I see where the Lord has been present?

The Word
I read the Word of God slowly, a few times over, and I listen to what God is saying to me. (Please turn to your scripture on the following pages. Inspiration points are there should you need them. When you are ready, return here to continue.)

Conversation
Remembering that I am still in God's presence,
I imagine Jesus himself standing or sitting beside me,
and say whatever is on my mind, whatever is in my heart,
speaking as one friend to another.

Conclusion
Glory be to the Father, and to the Son, and to the Holy Spirit,
As it was in the beginning, is now and ever shall be,
World without end. Amen

Sunday 2nd September, Twenty-second Sunday in Ordinary Time
Luke 14:1, 7–14

On one occasion when Jesus was going to the house of a leader of the Pharisees to eat a meal on the sabbath, they were watching him closely. When he noticed how the guests chose the places of honor, he told them a parable. "When you are invited by someone to a wedding banquet, do not sit down at the place of honor, in case someone more distinguished than you has been invited by your host; and the host who invited both of you may come and say to you, 'Give this person your place,' and then in disgrace you would start to take the lowest place. But when you are invited, go and sit down at the lowest place, so that when your host comes, he may say to you, 'Friend, move up higher'; then you will be honored in the presence of all who sit at the table with you. For all who exalt themselves will be humbled, and those who humble themselves will be exalted."

- Has this ever happened to me? Where do I rank myself in relation to others?

- Do I always look for the place of honor, or on the other hand do I let people walk all over me?

- I imagine myself at the table with Jesus after everyone else has left, and talk to him about this.

Monday 3rd September
Luke 4:16–21

When he came to Nazareth, where he had been brought up, he went to the synagogue on the sabbath day, as was his custom. He stood up to read, and the scroll of the prophet Isaiah was given to him. He unrolled the scroll and found the place where it was written: "The Spirit of the Lord is upon me, because he has anointed me to bring good news to the poor. He has sent me to proclaim release to the captives and recovery of sight to the blind, to let the oppressed go free, to proclaim the year of the Lord's favor." And he rolled up the scroll, gave it back to the attendant, and sat down. The eyes of all in the synagogue were fixed on him. Then he began to say to them, "Today this scripture has been fulfilled in your hearing."

• This Sabbath is a moment of light and grace. In imagination I join the synagogue congregation, and hear this charismatic young man speaking the prophecy of Isaiah as his own mission statement. As I listen, I sense with excitement that he is reaching out to me to join him.

• Lord, let me be part of that unending mission, to bring good news, vision and freedom to those who need them.

Tuesday 4th September   1 Corinthians 2:10–12

These things God has revealed to us through the Spirit; for the Spirit searches everything, even the depths of God. For what human being knows what is truly human except the human spirit that is within? So also no one comprehends what is truly God's except the Spirit of God. Now we have received not the spirit of the world, but the Spirit that is from God, so that we may understand the gifts bestowed on us by God.

• These opaque words of St. Paul lead us beyond human experience and language. Let me allow the inner truth of these sentences to germinate and grow.

• I will sow it where the soil is rich, sow it in my heart, and give it time. As St. Augustine wrote: God has ears that listen to what our heart is saying.

Wednesday 5th September   Luke 4:38–39

After leaving the synagogue Jesus entered Simon's house. Now Simon's mother-in-law was suffering from a high fever, and they asked him about her. Then he stood over her and rebuked the fever, and it left her. Immediately she got up and began to serve them.

- "He stood over her and rebuked the fever, and it left her." There is authority in Jesus' action, even at the start of his ministry.

- Healing meant not just the absence of pathology, but wholeness, energy, and the readiness to serve. Lord, lay your hand on the fevers in my heart, and fit me to work for you.

Thursday 6th September   Luke 5:4–11

When Jesus had finished speaking, he said to Simon, "Put out into the deep water and let down your nets for a catch." Simon answered, "Master, we have worked all night long but have caught nothing. Yet if you say so, I will let down the nets." When they had done this, they caught so many fish that their nets were beginning to break. So they signaled their partners in the other boat to come and help them. And they came and filled both boats, so that they began to sink. But when Simon Peter saw it, he fell down at Jesus' knees, saying, "Go away from me, Lord, for I am a sinful man!" For he and all who were with him were amazed at the catch of fish that they had taken; and so also were James and John, sons of Zebedee, who were partners with Simon. Then Jesus said to Simon, "Do not be afraid; from now on you will be catching people." When they had brought their boats to shore, they left everything and followed him.

- Jesus has already been rebuffed by his own townspeople in Nazareth. Here for the first time, in Simon and Andrew, he meets an astonishing response, a huge act of faith: "They left everything and followed him." Simon, weary from a night's futile fishing, is still ready to push out again from the shore.

- Lord, it is only when I take risks and push myself for you that I realize it is not me giving to you, but you enriching me.

Friday 7th September   Luke 5:33–39

Then the Pharisees and the scribes said to Jesus, "John's disciples, like the disciples of the Pharisees, frequently fast and
pray, but your disciples eat and drink. Jesus said to them, "You
cannot make wedding guests fast while the bridegroom is with
them, can you? The days will come when the bridegroom will be
taken away from them, and then they will fast in those days."
He also told them a parable: "No one tears a piece from a new
garment and sews it on an old garment; otherwise the new will
be torn, and the piece from the new will not match the old. And
no one puts new wine into old wineskins; otherwise the new
wine will burst the skins and will be spilled, and the skins will be
destroyed. But new wine must be put into fresh wineskins. And
no one after drinking old wine desires new wine, but says, 'The
old is good.'"

• Jesus did not want to cut his disciples off from the world. He did
not want them to dissociate themselves from the people and form
closed communities. He sent his disciples out into the world.
Peter and the other apostles took their wives with them when they
went to preach the Gospel.

• How does this apply in my life? Have I used my circumstances to
put limits on my discipleship?

Saturday 8th September,
Birthday of the Blessed Virgin Mary   Matthew 1:18–23

Now the birth of Jesus the Messiah took place in this way.
When his mother Mary had been engaged to Joseph, but
before they lived together, she was found to be with child from
the Holy Spirit. Her husband Joseph, being a righteous man and
unwilling to expose her to public disgrace, planned to dismiss
her quietly. But just when he had resolved to do this, an angel of
the Lord appeared to him in a dream and said, "Joseph, son of
David, do not be afraid to take Mary as your wife, for the child

conceived in her is from the Holy Spirit. She will bear a son, and you are to name him Jesus, for he will save his people from their sins." All this took place to fulfill what had been spoken by the Lord through the prophet: "Look, the virgin shall conceive and bear a son, and they shall name him Emmanuel," which means, "God is with us."

- Mary symbolizes the people of God—humanity in need of God. Let me take some time to think about the mystery of Mary's motherhood.

- Her life is tipped upside down, then Joseph's, then . . .

september 9–15

Something to think and pray about each day this week:

Making a statement

The early chapters of Luke's Gospel contain what would now be called Jesus' mission statement: He chooses the Twelve, then starts to open his vision to them, in the beatitudes and the parables of the Kingdom. These chapters give us a glimpse of the inner life of Jesus.

All sorts of organizations publish mission statements nowadays: high-sounding words about the service that they hope to offer, and how they will work. Even banks and businesses try out mission statements. Have I one for myself? Nobody, neither employer nor priest, can write my mission statement for me. I may subscribe in theory to Jesus' words, but that only becomes real when people can read them in my life. This week I am going to work on what I would like to do with my life, my totally personal mission statement, not for publication, but for my and God's eyes only.

The Presence of God

For a few moments, I think of God's veiled presence in things:
in the elements, giving them existence;
in plants, giving them life; in animals, giving them sensation;
and finally, in me, giving me all this and more,
making me a temple, a dwelling-place of the Spirit.

Freedom

God is not foreign to my freedom.
Instead the Spirit breathes life into my most intimate desires,
gently nudging me towards all that is good.
I ask for the grace to let myself be enfolded by the Spirit.

Consciousness

Knowing that God loves me unconditionally,
I look honestly over the last day, its events and my feelings.
Do I have something to be grateful for? Then I give thanks.
Is there something I am sorry for? Then I ask forgiveness.

The Word

I take my time to read the Word of God, slowly, a few times,
allowing myself to dwell on anything that strikes me. (Please
turn to your scripture on the following pages. Inspiration points
are there should you need them. When you are ready, return
here to continue.)

Conversation

How has God's Word moved me? Has it left me cold?
Has it consoled me or moved me to act in a new way?
I imagine Jesus standing or sitting beside me,
I turn and share my feelings with him.

Conclusion

Glory be to the Father, and to the Son, and to the Holy Spirit,
As it was in the beginning, is now and ever shall be,
World without end. Amen

308

Sunday 9th September, Twenty-third Sunday in Ordinary Time   Luke 14:25–33

Now large crowds were traveling with Jesus; and he turned and said to them, "Whoever comes to me and does not hate father and mother, wife and children, brothers and sisters, yes, and even life itself, cannot be my disciple. Whoever does not carry the cross and follow me cannot be my disciple. For which of you, intending to build a tower, does not first sit down and estimate the cost, to see whether he has enough to complete it? Otherwise, when he has laid a foundation and is not able to finish, all who see it will begin to ridicule him, saying, 'This fellow began to build and was not able to finish.' Or what king, going out to wage war against another king, will not sit down first and consider whether he is able with ten thousand to oppose the one who comes against him with twenty thousand? If he cannot, then, while the other is still far away, he sends a delegation and asks for the terms of peace. So therefore, none of you can become my disciple if you do not give up all your possessions."

- Jesus is saying to me: "If you want to be a follower of mine you will have to be prepared for the cross."

- Do I find these words arresting or have they lost their power to shock because of familiarity?

- Am I open to the cross? Do I dread it?

- What do I want to say to Jesus about this?

Monday 10th September   Luke 6:6–11

On another sabbath Jesus entered the synagogue and taught, and there was a man there whose right hand was withered. The scribes and the Pharisees watched him to see whether he would cure on the sabbath, so that they might find an accusation against him. Even though he knew what they were thinking, he said to the man who had the withered hand, "Come and stand here." He got up and stood there. Then Jesus said to them, "I ask you, is it lawful to do good or to do harm on the sabbath, to save life or to destroy it?" After looking around at all of them, he said to him, "Stretch out your hand." He did so, and his hand was restored. But they were filled with fury and discussed with one another what they might do to Jesus.

- There are two strong emotions stirred in this drama: The Pharisees show anger; Jesus feel compassion. We can marvel at the courage and freedom with which Jesus again confronts his critics.

- Am I on the side of health and compassion?

Tuesday 11th September   Luke 6:12–16

Now during those days he went out to the mountain to pray; and he spent the night in prayer to God. And when day came, he called his disciples and chose twelve of them, whom he also named apostles: Simon, whom he named Peter, and his brother Andrew, and James, and John, and Philip, and Bartholomew, and Matthew, and Thomas, and James son of Alphaeus, and Simon, who was called the Zealot, and Judas son of James, and Judas Iscariot, who became a traitor.

- Jesus, you prayed all night to prepare for this momentous decision, choosing the Twelve apostles. What came out of it? These Jewish workers, without any special qualifications except the knowledge and love of you, and with no power or money to back them, went out to carry your good news to the world.

- Sacred Space continues that work. I share that work too.

Wednesday 12th September   Luke 6:20–23a

Then Jesus looked up at his disciples and said: "Blessed are you who are poor, for yours is the kingdom of God. Blessed are you who are hungry now, for you will be filled. Blessed are you who weep now, for you will laugh. Blessed are you when people hate you, and when they exclude you, revile you, and defame you on account of the Son of Man. Rejoice in that day and leap for joy, for surely your reward is great in heaven."

- Let me think about people I know who are poor in spirit, who live a simple life, would not take long to pack up and move house, have no superfluities or huge attachments to complicate their life. They travel light, and therefore can travel far and fast. I think of Francis of Assisi shedding his clothes with a cry: "Now I can truly call God my father."

- Jesus is speaking to those who know rejection and sorrow. His words seem to turn our understanding of "the good life" on its head.

Thursday 13th September — Colossians 3:12–17

As God's chosen ones, holy and beloved, clothe yourselves with compassion, kindness, humility, meekness, and patience. Bear with one another and, if anyone has a complaint against another, forgive each other; just as the Lord has forgiven you, so you also must forgive. Above all, clothe yourselves with love, which binds everything together in perfect harmony. And let the peace of Christ rule in your hearts, to which indeed you were called in the one body. And be thankful. Let the word of Christ dwell in you richly; teach and admonish one another in all wisdom; and with gratitude in your hearts sing psalms, hymns, and spiritual songs to God. And whatever you do, in word or deed, do everything in the name of the Lord Jesus, giving thanks to God the Father through him.

- "Just as the Lord has forgiven you, so you also must forgive." Forgiveness is the beginning, middle, and end of gospel life.

- The experience of being forgiven renews us when we feel broken; it is as important to offer forgiveness as it is to receive it.

- Can I talk to the Lord about this? Is there some action I need to take right now?

Friday 14th September, Exaltation of the Holy Cross
Philippians 2:6–8

Jesus, though he was in the form of God, did not regard equality with God as something to be exploited, but emptied himself, taking the form of a slave, being born in human likeness. And being found in human form, he humbled himself and became obedient to the point of death—even death on a cross.

- In these words of St. Paul is the most unforgettable and baffling statement of Jesus' Incarnation: that he not merely took on human flesh, but knew the taste of salt in the bottom of the mouth, the taste of abandonment.

- Lord, you emptied yourself completely. You let yourself be powerless, ineffective, at the mercy of others.

Saturday 15th September, Our Lady of Sorrows
Luke 2:33–35

And the child's father and mother were amazed at what was being said about him. Then Simeon blessed them and said to his mother Mary, "This child is destined for the falling and the rising of many in Israel, and to be a sign that will be opposed so that the inner thoughts of many will be revealed—and a sword will pierce your own soul too."

- We name this encounter among the joyful mysteries of the Rosary. I wonder if Mary in her old age would have felt it a joyful memory. "A sword will pierce your own soul too." Hidden in Simeon's stage whisper is the shadow of the rejection and crucifixion of her son.

- You could have said it to me, Lord. I have known sorrowful mysteries, but did not always see your hand in them.

september 16–22

Something to think and pray about each day this week:

Using the moment
This week brings us to the Equinox: Night is as long as day. Where am I in my life? Past the equinox?

But at my back I always hear

Time's winged chariot hurrying near.

Lord, I cannot find you in time past or time future; only in this present moment. Teach me to use it to the full. That use may be writing or sleeping or making love or talking or playing or working—or praying. It is no use looking before and after, and pining for what is not. The now is all that I have. It is a sacrament, a sign of inward grace. A friend who came close to death said that as she felt God's love sweep irresistibly over her, all the past, its sins and its achievements, became irrelevant. It is only in this moment that I can come close to God.

The Presence of God
I pause for a moment
and think of the love and the grace that God showers on me,
creating me in his image and likeness, making me his temple.

Freedom
Everything has the potential to draw forth from me a fuller love
and life.
Yet my desires are often fixed, caught, on illusions of fulfillment.
I ask that God, through my freedom, may orchestrate
my desires in a vibrant loving melody rich in harmony.

Consciousness
How do I find myself today?
Where am I with God? With others?
Do I have something to be grateful for? Then I give thanks.
Is there something I am sorry for? Then I ask forgiveness.

The Word
God speaks to each one of us individually. I need to listen to
what he is saying to me. (Please turn to your scripture on the following pages. Inspiration points are there should you need
them. When you are ready, return here to continue.)

Conversation
What feelings are rising in me
as I pray and reflect on God's Word?
I imagine Jesus himself sitting or standing beside me,
and open my heart to him.

Conclusion
Glory be to the Father, and to the Son, and to the Holy Spirit,
As it was in the beginning, is now and ever shall be,
World without end. Amen

Sunday 16th September, Twenty-fourth Sunday
in Ordinary Time   Luke 15:1–7

Now all the tax collectors and sinners were coming near to listen to him. And the Pharisees and the scribes were grumbling and saying, "This fellow welcomes sinners and eats with them." So he told them this parable: "Which one of you, having a hundred sheep and losing one of them, does not leave the ninety-nine in the wilderness and go after the one that is lost until he finds it? When he has found it, he lays it on his shoulders and rejoices. And when he comes home, he calls together his friends and neighbors, saying to them, 'Rejoice with me, for I have found my sheep that was lost.' Just so, I tell you, there will be more joy in heaven over one sinner who repents than over ninety-nine righteous persons who need no repentance."

- Can I imagine the flock of 99 in the wilderness and the shepherd heading off in search of the lost one? Then there's the image of him coming back with the stray across his shoulders.

- Jesus is putting these pictures before my mind in order to touch my heart.

- Can I let myself be moved by the compassion and mercy of God?

Monday 17th September   Luke 7:1–10

After Jesus had finished all his sayings in the hearing of the people, he entered Capernaum. A centurion there had a slave whom he valued highly, and who was ill and close to death. When he heard about Jesus, he sent some Jewish elders to him, asking him to come and heal his slave. When they came to Jesus, they appealed to him earnestly, saying, "He is worthy of having you do this for him, for he loves our people, and it is he who built our synagogue for us." And Jesus went with them, but when he was not far from the house, the centurion sent friends to say to him, "Lord, do not trouble yourself, for I am not worthy to have you come under my roof; therefore I did not presume to come to you. But only speak the word, and let my servant be healed. For I also am a man set under authority, with soldiers under me; and I say to one, 'Go,' and he goes, and to another, 'Come,' and he comes, and to my slave, 'Do this,' and the slave does it." When Jesus heard this he was amazed at him, and turning to the crowd that followed him, he said, "I tell you, not even in Israel have I found such faith." When those who had been sent returned to the house, they found the slave in good health.

- The centurion was powerful, at the core of the powerful Roman army. Their law instructed them to see slaves as living tools, without rights, people to be used and then thrown out when they were old or broken.

- You saw something different and remarkable in this man: not merely power; not merely compassion and justice; but faith. Your followers preserved his precious words and insight.

- Let me take time to sit with these thoughts of our authority, your healing power, and your intimate presence with me.

Tuesday 18th September   Luke 7:11–17

Soon afterwards he went to a town called Nain, and his disciples and a large crowd went with him. As he approached the gate of the town, a man who had died was being carried out. He was his mother's only son, and she was a widow; and with her was a large crowd from the town. When the Lord saw her, he had compassion for her and said to her, "Do not weep." Then he came forward and touched the bier, and the bearers stood still. And he said, "Young man, I say to you, rise!" The dead man sat up and began to speak, and Jesus gave him to his mother. Fear seized all of them; and they glorified God, saying, "A great prophet has risen among us!" and "God has looked favorably on his people!" This word about him spread throughout Judea and all the surrounding country.

- On the bier was the only son of a widow. In a man's world, this woman was left undefended.

- Lord, you saw that this was more than just a funeral; you broke through the barriers of ritual purity, you laid your hand on the bier, and gave the man back to his mother.

- Teach me, Lord, to respond to human misery with your touch.

Wednesday 19th September   1 Timothy 3:14–16

I hope to come to you soon, but I am writing these instructions to you so that, if I am delayed, you may know how one ought to behave in the household of God, which is the church of the living God, the pillar and bulwark of the truth. Without any doubt, the mystery of our religion is great: He was revealed in flesh, vindicated in spirit, seen by angels, proclaimed among Gentiles, believed in throughout the world, taken up in glory.

- "Without any doubt, the mystery of our religion is great." What inspired words Paul leaves us.

- Can I hold this summary in my heart?

Thursday 20th September   1 Timothy 4:12–16

Let no one despise your youth, but set the believers an example in speech and conduct, in love, in faith, in purity. Until I arrive, give attention to the public reading of scripture, to exhorting, to teaching. Do not neglect the gift that is in you, which was given to you through prophecy with the laying on of hands by the council of elders. Put these things into practice, devote yourself to them, so that all may see your progress. Pay close attention to yourself and to your teaching; continue in these things, for in doing this you will save both yourself and your hearers.

- "Do not neglect the gift that is in you." The gifts we have are many, but we all have the gift of prayer within us. The Spirit is the gift of prayer within us.

- Do I concern myself with where I am in my prayer, what stage I have reached? Isn't it more important that I have the desire to pray?

Friday 21st September, St. Matthew   Matthew 9:9–13

As Jesus was walking along, he saw a man called Matthew sitting at the tax booth; and he said to him, "Follow me." And he got up and followed him. And as he sat at dinner in the house, many tax collectors and sinners came and were sitting with him and his disciples. When the Pharisees saw this, they said to his disciples, "Why does your teacher eat with tax collectors and sinners?" But when he heard this, he said, "Those who are well have no need of a physician, but those who are sick. Go and learn what this means, 'I desire mercy, not sacrifice.' For I have come to call not the righteous but sinners."

- Jesus came along, Matthew was at his place of work: a normal, everyday setting for God's grace to find an opening. Sitting at your computer is another such setting. The Lord can speak there.

- Many tax collectors and sinners came to sit and eat with Jesus. It is characteristic of holy people that others feel easy in their company. Jesus accepted people as they were, where they were.

- Am I as easy and accepting?

Saturday 22nd September   Luke 8:4–8

When a great crowd gathered and people from town after town came to him, Jesus said in a parable: "A sower went out to sow his seed; and as he sowed, some fell on the path and was trampled on, and the birds of the air ate it up. Some fell on the rock; and as it grew up, it withered for lack of moisture. Some fell among thorns, and the thorns grew with it and choked it. Some fell into good soil, and when it grew, it produced a hundredfold." As he said this, he called out, "Let anyone with ears to hear listen!"

- "Let anyone with ears to hear listen!" Becoming "good soil" means listening humbly, and being willing to begin, and then begin again.

- How patient am I with those who do not seem to listen? How patient am I with myself? How patient is the Lord?

Something to think and pray about each day this week:

A channel of grace

When I slow down in preparation for prayer, when I quiet my body and allow thoughts to bubble up in me, they are sometimes nasty thoughts. Resentments that are normally dormant seem to come awake in me. In order to regain balance, I need to offer an absolution to the people I resent, and let them go. The absolution will not come if I feel that they alone are guilty and I am blameless. I must see myself as being co-responsible with the offender for each offence that I have been the victim of. Rather than casting stones—I have beams in my own eye, Lord—I dispense amnesties and pardons. So I make the offence a channel of grace for both the offender and for me.

The Presence of God

I reflect for a moment on God's presence around me and in me.
Creator of the universe, the sun and the moon, the earth,
every molecule, every atom, everything that is:
God is in every beat of my heart. God is with me, now.

Freedom

There are very few people
who realize what God would make of them
if they abandoned themselves into his hands,
and let themselves be formed by his grace. (St. Ignatius)
I ask for the grace to trust myself totally to God's love.

Consciousness

In God's loving presence I unwind the past day,
starting from now and looking back, moment by moment.
I gather in all the goodness and light, in gratitude.
I attend to the shadows and what they say to me,
seeking healing, courage, forgiveness.

The Word

I read the Word of God slowly, a few times over, and I listen to
what God is saying to me. (Please turn to your scripture on the
following pages. Inspiration points are there should you need
them. When you are ready, return here to continue.)

Conversation

What is stirring in me as I pray?
Am I consoled, troubled, left cold?
I imagine Jesus himself standing or sitting at my side,
and share my feelings with him.

Conclusion

Glory be to the Father, and to the Son, and to the Holy Spirit,
As it was in the beginning, is now and ever shall be,
World without end. Amen

Sunday 23rd September, Twenty-fifth Sunday in Ordinary Time
Amos 8:4–7

Hear this, you that trample on the needy, and bring to ruin the poor of the land, saying, "When will the new moon be over so that we may sell grain; and the sabbath, so that we may offer wheat for sale? We will make the ephah small and the shekel great, and practice deceit with false balances, buying the poor for silver and the needy for a pair of sandals, and selling the sweepings of the wheat." The Lord has sworn by the pride of Jacob: Surely I will never forget any of their deeds.

- Can I allow myself to hear the rugged voice of the prophet Amos with its fiery passion and righteous anger?

- He speaks for the Lord when he says that cheating the poor and the weak is truly a shameful sin.

- Can I allow myself to be moved by the passion of Amos, the passion of God, for justice and for the poor?

Monday 24th September
Luke 8:16–18

Jesus said to his disciples, "No one after lighting a lamp hides it under a jar, or puts it under a bed, but puts it on a lampstand, so that those who enter may see the light. For nothing is hidden that will not be disclosed, nor is anything secret that will not become known and come to light. Then pay attention to how you listen; for to those who have, more will be given; and from those who do not have, even what they seem to have will be taken away."

- Jesus spoke plainly, hiding nothing, letting the truth appear. Following him is not entering a secret cult, nor relying on hidden prayers, formulas, or mysterious and ancient codes.

- Can I try with an open and honest heart to listen to the truth and learn from experience?

- Can I pay careful attention to how I listen?

Tuesday 25th September   Luke 8:19–21

Then his mother and his brothers came to him, but they could not reach him because of the crowd. And he was told, "Your mother and your brothers are standing outside, wanting to see you." But he said to them, "My mother and my brothers are those who hear the word of God and do it."

- There is Jesus' family: Mary, and the others of the household.

- Then Jesus widens it. We become part of that family not by birth, nor by rituals, but by hearing and acting on God's word.

- Just think for a few moments: Jesus welcomes me into the same intimate relationship he has with Mary his mother.

Wednesday 26th September   Luke 9:1–6

Jesus called the twelve together and gave them power and authority over all demons and to cure diseases, and he sent them out to proclaim the kingdom of God and to heal. He said to them, "Take nothing for your journey, no staff, nor bag, nor bread, nor money—not even an extra tunic. Whatever house you enter, stay there, and leave from there. Wherever they do not welcome you, as you are leaving that town shake the dust off your feet as a testimony against them." They departed and went through the villages, bringing the good news and curing diseases everywhere.

- Jesus did not tell the Twelve what to say; instead, his instruction was to take nothing and receive hospitality as it is offered to you. There is no mention of sermon notes.

- This passage was an inspiration to Francis of Assisi: He did not want his friars to preach salvation so much as "be" salvation.

Thursday 27th September   Luke 9:7–9

Now Herod the ruler heard about all that had taken place, and he was perplexed, because it was said by some that John had been raised from the dead, by some that Elijah had appeared, and by others that one of the ancient prophets had arisen. Herod said, "John I beheaded; but who is this about whom I hear such things?" And he tried to see him.

- Herod appears as a politician: He has an eye to self-publicity, on contact with somebody who is making news. Jesus was talked about, so Herod had to see him, but not involve himself.

- God's word demands that we engage our lives with him. Remember Karl Barth: "To understand the scriptures we must stop acting like mere spectators."

Friday 28th September   Luke 9:18–22

Once when Jesus was praying alone, with only the disciples near him, he asked them, "Who do the crowds say that I am?" They answered, "John the Baptist; but others, Elijah; and still others, that one of the ancient prophets has arisen." He said to them, "But who do you say that I am?" Peter answered, "The Messiah of God." He sternly ordered and commanded them not to tell anyone, saying, "The Son of Man must undergo great suffering, and be rejected by the elders, chief priests, and scribes, and be killed, and on the third day be raised."

- Can I hear Jesus' question to me too: "Who do you say that I am?" Jesus' life and words are not just for chatting about. Can I let them change my life?

Saturday 29th September, Sts. Michael, Gabriel and Raphael   John 1:47–51

When Jesus saw Nathanael coming toward him, he said of him, "Here is truly an Israelite in whom there is no deceit!" Nathanael asked him, "Where did you get to know me?" Jesus answered, "I saw you under the fig tree before Philip called you." Nathanael replied, "Rabbi, you are the Son of God! You are the King of Israel!" Jesus answered, "Do you believe because I told you that I saw you under the fig tree? You will see greater things than these." And he said to him, "Very truly, I tell you, you will see heaven opened and the angels of God ascending and descending upon the Son of Man."

- If I came towards you, Lord, what would you say of me? I tremble at the thought.

- I would wish to show a heart without deceit, and remember the words of Rumi, the Sufi poet: "In the presence of His Glory, closely watch your heart, so your thoughts won't shame you, for He sees guilt, opinion, and desire as plainly as a hair in pure milk."

Something to think and pray about each day this week:

Sharing the table
You could eat your way through the Gospels, especially Luke, so frequent are the stories about meals and parties. Apart from the intimacy of lovers, there are few human actions that bind people to one another more closely than what the Romans called a convivium, their word for a banquet that literally means "living together." We drop our defenses, feel grateful to the hands that have prepared the meal, we argue and discuss and quarrel and tease and laugh. But we stay at the table. It is there that children watch their parents and learn about living. From the marriage feast of Cana, to the Last Supper, to his post-resurrection breakfast on the shore of the lake, Jesus loved to eat and drink with his friends. And he used the imagery of the banquet for the Eucharist in which he leaves us his abiding presence.

The Presence of God
I remind myself that, as I sit here now,
God is gazing on me with love and holding me in being.
I pause for a moment and think of this.

Freedom
A thick and shapeless tree-trunk would never believe
that it could become a statue, admired as a miracle of sculpture,
and would never submit itself to the chisel of the sculptor,
who sees by her genius what she can make of it. (St. Ignatius)
I ask for the grace to let myself be shaped by my loving Creator.

Consciousness
How am I really feeling? Light-hearted? Heavy-hearted?
I may be very much at peace, happy to be here.
Equally, I may be frustrated, worried or angry.
I acknowledge how I really am. It is the real me that the Lord loves.

The Word
I take my time to read the Word of God, slowly, a few times, allowing myself to dwell on anything that strikes me. (Please turn to your scripture on the following pages. Inspiration points are there should you need them. When you are ready, return here to continue.)

Conversation
Do I notice myself reacting as I pray with the Word of God?
Do I feel challenged, comforted, angry?
Imagining Jesus sitting or standing by me,
I speak out my feelings, as one trusted friend to another.

Conclusion
Glory be to the Father, and to the Son, and to the Holy Spirit,
As it was in the beginning, is now and ever shall be,
World without end. Amen

Sunday 30th September, Twenty-sixth Sunday in Ordinary Time — Luke 16:19–31

Jesus said to the Pharisees, "There was a rich man who was dressed in purple and fine linen and who feasted sumptuously every day. And at his gate lay a poor man named Lazarus, covered with sores, who longed to satisfy his hunger with what fell from the rich man's table; even the dogs would come and lick his sores. The poor man died and was carried away by the angels to be with Abraham. The rich man also died and was buried. In Hades, where he was being tormented, he looked up and saw Abraham far away with Lazarus by his side. He called out, 'Father Abraham, have mercy on me, and send Lazarus to dip the tip of his finger in water and cool my tongue; for I am in agony in these flames.' But Abraham said, 'Child, remember that during your lifetime you received your good things, and Lazarus in like manner evil things; but now he is comforted here, and you are in agony. Besides all this, between you and us a great chasm has been fixed, so that those who might want to pass from here to you cannot do so, and no one can cross from there to us.' He said, 'Then, father, I beg you to send him to my father's house—for I have five brothers—that he may warn them, so that they will not also come into this place of torment.' Abraham replied, 'They have Moses and the prophets; they should listen to them.' He said, 'No, father Abraham; but if someone goes to them from the dead, they will repent.' He said to him, 'If they do not listen to Moses and the prophets, neither will they be convinced even if someone rises from the dead.'"

- If I was an intelligent and fairly well off Pharisee, how would I feel about Jesus' very pointed story? What's he getting at? What did the rich man do wrong?

- What is the crucial insight which people will not understand even if someone should come back from the dead to tell them?

- What is the Lord trying to tell me here?

Monday 1st October   Luke 9:46–48

An argument arose among the disciples as to which one of them was the greatest. But Jesus, aware of their inner thoughts, took a little child and put it by his side, and said to them, "Whoever welcomes this child in my name welcomes me, and whoever welcomes me welcomes the one who sent me; for the least among all of you is the greatest."

- Lord, it seems that when I begin to feel secure, powerful, and on top of things, you unsettle me. You ask me to emulate the powerlessness of children, who cannot plan for themselves. You welcome me as a follower, but warn me that I am not your only follower. There are lots of tracks, lots of ways to you.

- I come with all my baggage, my skepticism, competitiveness, self-regard. Can I put this aside and be like the little child?

Tuesday 2nd October   Luke 9:51–56

When the days drew near for him to be taken up, Jesus set his face to go to Jerusalem. And he sent messengers ahead of him. On their way they entered a village of the Samaritans to make ready for him; but they did not receive him, because his face was set toward Jerusalem. When his disciples James and John saw it, they said, "Lord, do you want us to command fire to come down from heaven and consume them?" But he turned and rebuked them. Then they went on to another village.

- James and John are restless, and feel "what is the use of having power if you do not use it on those who reject you?" They put words on the angry, vengeful feelings that often stir in us when confronted with wickedness: "Lock them up. Hang them. Bomb them."

- Yet that is not your spirit, Lord. You knew the wickedness that awaited you in Jerusalem, but you set your face to meet it.

Wednesday 3rd October   Luke 9:57–62

As they were going along the road, someone said to him, "I will follow you wherever you go." And Jesus said to him, "Foxes have holes, and birds of the air have nests; but the Son of Man has nowhere to lay his head." To another he said, "Follow me." But he said, "Lord, first let me go and bury my father." But Jesus said to him, "Let the dead bury their own dead; but as for you, go and proclaim the kingdom of God." Another said, "I will follow you, Lord; but let me first say farewell to those at my home." Jesus said to him, "No one who puts a hand to the plow and looks back is fit for the kingdom of God."

- Here we see three apparently generous individuals who are ready to become followers. Jesus, in each case, seems to make things more difficult for them. What is my reaction to this? What is Jesus up to? Does he sense a false note in their offer?

- If Jesus is calling his followers to give without the slightest reservation or hesitation, is he perhaps telling us something about himself? A disciple can only learn to love God unconditionally when they have first experienced that kind of love from God.

- Do I find myself hesitating or holding back in my following? How does this sit with the guarantee of God's unconditional love for me?

Thursday 4th October, St. Francis of Assisi
Matthew 11:28–30

Jesus said, "Come to me, all you that are weary and are carrying heavy burdens, and I will give you rest. Take my yoke upon you, and learn from me; for I am gentle and humble in heart, and you will find rest for your souls. For my yoke is easy, and my burden is light."

- Jesus is saying these words to me, now; offering to relieve my weariness.

- Can I share the burdens I carry with Jesus?

- Do I trust him when he says "my burden is light"?

Friday 5th October   Luke 10:13–16

Jesus said to his disciples, "Woe to you, Chorazin! Woe to you, Bethsaida! For if the deeds of power done in you had been done in Tyre and Sidon, they would have repented long ago, sitting in sackcloth and ashes. But at the judgment it will be more tolerable for Tyre and Sidon than for you. And you, Capernaum, will you be exalted to heaven? No, you will be brought down to Hades. Whoever listens to you listens to me, and whoever rejects you rejects me, and whoever rejects me rejects the one who sent me."

- The Lord has done deeds of power in my life. I did not always recognize them, or use the opportunities.

- Can I take confidence in the thought of Jesus looking for the lost sheep, forgiving again and again, loving me as I am in my weakness?

Saturday 6th October   Luke 10:23–24

Then turning to the disciples, Jesus said to them privately, "Blessed are the eyes that see what you see! For I tell you that many prophets and kings desired to see what you see, but did not see it, and to hear what you hear, but did not hear it."

- The disciples of Jesus have a privileged experience; they spent years in Jesus' company.

- I am privileged too. Many people long to have a real, living relationship with God. Jesus is offering it to me freely, now.

october 7–13

Something to think and pray about each day this week:

Living in darkness

Our faith is a mixture of light and darkness. We look to the holy people of history to give us some light on the quest for God. Saint John of the Cross, who reformed the Carmelites and was imprisoned for his pains, "distrusted whatever removed the soul from the obscure faith where the understanding must be left behind in order to go to God by love." One of his greatest Carmelite followers, Thérèse of Lisieux, lived her religious life in darkness. Her biographer described her state in these words: "The whole area of religion seemed remote and unreal to her, not arousing the least response, either friendly or antagonistic, in her mind and heart. It was as though religion had become simply something remembered, grey, cold and unimportant."

St. Paul wrote about our inability to pray (Romans 8:26): "The Spirit helps us in our weakness; when we do not know how to pray as we ought, that very Spirit intercedes with sighs too deep for words. And God, who searches the heart, knows what is the mind of the Spirit, because the Spirit intercedes for the saints according to the will of God." The dialogue with God continues even when our mind and heart are weary.

The Presence of God
In the silence of my innermost being,
in the fragments of my yearned-for wholeness,
can I hear the whispers of God's presence?
Can I remember when I felt God's nearness?
When we walked together and I let myself be embraced by God's love.

Freedom
I ask for the grace
to let go of my own concerns
and be open to what God is asking of me,
to let myself be guided and formed by my loving Creator.

Consciousness
I exist in a web of relationships—links to nature, people, God.
I trace out these links, giving thanks for the life that flows through them.
Some links are twisted or broken: I may feel regret, anger, disappointment.
I pray for the gift of acceptance and forgiveness.

The Word
God speaks to each one of us individually. I need to listen to what he is saying to me. (Please turn to your scripture on the following pages. Inspiration points are there should you need them. When you are ready, return here to continue.)

Conversation
Remembering that I am still in God's presence,
I imagine Jesus himself standing or sitting beside me,
and say whatever is on my mind, whatever is in my heart,
speaking as one friend to another.

Conclusion
Glory be to the Father, and to the Son, and to the Holy Spirit,
As it was in the beginning, is now and ever shall be,
World without end. Amen

Sunday 7th October, Twenty-seventh Sunday in Ordinary Time

2 Timothy 1:6–8

For this reason I remind you to rekindle the gift of God that is within you through the laying on of my hands; for God did not give us a spirit of cowardice, but rather a spirit of power and of love and of self-discipline. Do not be ashamed, then, of the testimony about our Lord or of me his prisoner, but join with me in suffering for the gospel, relying on the power of God.

- If I compare myself with Timothy, what is God's gift in me?

- Can I see it as a little flicker that I can help fan into a flame?

- How is God calling me to let this life in me grow stronger?

Monday 8th October

Luke 10:30–37

Jesus replied, "A man was going down from Jerusalem to Jericho, and fell into the hands of robbers, who stripped him, beat him, and went away, leaving him half dead. Now by chance a priest was going down that road; and when he saw him, he passed by on the other side. So likewise a Levite, when he came to the place and saw him, passed by on the other side. But a Samaritan while traveling came near him; and when he saw him, he was moved with pity. He went to him and bandaged his wounds, having poured oil and wine on them. Then he put him on his own animal, brought him to an inn, and took care of him. The next day he took out two denarii, gave them to the innkeeper, and said, 'Take care of him; and when I come back, I will repay you whatever more you spend.' Which of these three, do you think, was a neighbor to the man who fell into the hands of the robbers?" He said, "The one who showed him mercy." Jesus said to him, "Go and do likewise."

- Jesus' story was in response to a man asking, "Who is my neighbor?" The man received more than he expected.

- What is Jesus trying to say to me? Who is my neighbor—today, here and now? Is it the person whom I view with suspicion and don't like, or who views me with suspicion and doesn't like me?

- Do I have any neighbors in this challenging sense of the word?

Tuesday 9th October   Luke 10:38–42

Now as they went on their way, Jesus entered a certain vil-lage, where a woman named Martha welcomed him into her home. She had a sister named Mary, who sat at the Lord's feet and listened to what he was saying. But Martha was dis-tracted by her many tasks; so she came to him and asked, "Lord, do you not care that my sister has left me to do all the work by myself? Tell her then to help me." But the Lord answered her, "Martha, Martha, you are worried and distracted by many things; there is need of only one thing. Mary has chosen the bet-ter part, which will not be taken away from her."

- Jesus was on his way to Jerusalem, facing the struggle with his own people—would they accept or reject him? He calls on his friends, who are excited to welcome him. Martha rushes about preparing a meal; Mary sits and listens to Jesus.

- Lord teach me to read situations as Mary did, and to listen with love, giving more space to the feelings of others than to my own plans, however generous these may be.

Wednesday 10th October   Luke 11:1–4

Jesus was praying in a certain place, and after he had finished, one of his disciples said to him, "Lord, teach us to pray, as John taught his disciples." He said to them, "When you pray, say: Father, hallowed be your name. Your kingdom come. Give us each day our daily bread. And forgive us our sins, for we our-selves forgive everyone indebted to us. And do not bring us to the time of trial."

- It was the habit of many Jewish rabbis to teach their disciples a simple prayer. This prayer of Jesus has depths we never totally fathom. We can linger on every phrase.
- If we call God "Father," we say that he knows our needs, and wants to give what will help us most. Lord, for tomorrow and its needs I do not pray. Give me your love and grace just for today.

Thursday 11th October **Luke 11:5–10**

And Jesus said to them, "Suppose one of you has a friend, and you go to him at midnight and say to him, 'Friend, lend me three loaves of bread; for a friend of mine has arrived, and I have nothing to set before him.' And he answers from within, 'Do not bother me; the door has already been locked, and my children are with me in bed; I cannot get up and give you anything.' I tell you, even though he will not get up and give him anything because he is his friend, at least because of his persistence he will get up and give him whatever he needs. So I say to you, Ask, and it will be given you; search, and you will find; knock, and the door will be opened for you. For everyone who asks receives, and everyone who searches finds, and for everyone who knocks, the door will be opened."

- Am I thinking, "This isn't my experience. I don't get what I ask for?" God wants what is truly best for us all.
- Can I remember experiences when I got what I asked for, and when I didn't? What was it that I was asking for?

Friday 12th October **Joel 1:19–20**

To you, O Lord, I cry. For fire has devoured the pastures of the wilderness, and flames have burned all the trees of the field. Even the wild animals cry to you because the watercourses are dried up, and fire has devoured the pastures of the wilderness.

- This seems to be a cry of utter desolation. Do I feel that way now, or can I remember a time when I did? The speaker—and even the animals—are turning to God in their time of need. Where do I look for help when I am in trouble?

Saturday 13th October   **Luke 11:27–28**

While Jesus was speaking, a woman in the crowd raised her voice and said to him, "Blessed is the womb that bore you and the breasts that nursed you!" But he said, "Blessed rather are those who hear the word of God and obey it!"

- This woman is like an interjector from the public gallery. She can't contain herself; she has to call out her message.

- We know only her passion, but perhaps her own child had died, or was handicapped. Whatever her circumstances, she is filled with love and admiration for the person of Jesus.

- Jesus returns the compliment, and refers in a subtle way back to his mother. Mary is blessed above all because she believed God's word and made herself his handmaid.

- Can I sit for a while and think about this beautiful scene?

october 14–20

Something to think and pray about each day this week:

Silent night

Night is an ambivalent time. It's the time of death and conflict, a time associated with crime and punishment. It is often a time of distortion of the day that has preceded it. However, it can also be a time of profound, silent prayer.

Such was often the case for Jesus. A favorite theme of St. Luke's gospel is prayer, and he often presents Jesus praying, especially before major events. For example, he chose the Twelve after a night on a mountain in prayer. It is in prayer that we learn the mystery of Christ and the wisdom of the Cross. In prayer we perceive, in all their dimensions, the real needs of our brothers and sisters throughout the world; in prayer we find the strength to face whatever lies ahead; in prayer we get the strength for the mission Christ shares with us. Above all, in prayer we should acknowledge the fullness of our dependence on God.

The Presence of God
God is with me, but more,
God is within me, giving me existence.
Let me dwell for a moment on God's life-giving presence
in my body, my mind, my heart
and in the whole of my life.

Freedom
I ask for the grace to believe
in what I could be and do
if I only allowed God, my loving Creator,
to continue to create me, guide me and shape me.

Consciousness
Knowing that God loves me unconditionally,
I can afford to be honest about how I am.
How has the last day been, and how do I feel now?
I share my feelings openly with the Lord.

The Word
I read the Word of God slowly, a few times over, and I listen to
what God is saying to me. (Please turn to your scripture on the
following pages. Inspiration points are there should you need
them. When you are ready, return here to continue.)

Conversation
How has God's Word moved me? Has it left me cold?
Has it consoled me or moved me to act in a new way?
I imagine Jesus standing or sitting beside me,
I turn and share my feelings with him.

Conclusion
Glory be to the Father, and to the Son, and to the Holy Spirit,
As it was in the beginning, is now and ever shall be,
World without end. Amen

Sunday 14th October, Twenty-eighth Sunday
in Ordinary Time   Luke 17:11–19

On the way to Jerusalem Jesus was going through the region between Samaria and Galilee. As he entered a village, ten lepers approached him. Keeping their distance, they called out, saying, "Jesus, Master, have mercy on us!" When he saw them, he said to them, "Go and show yourselves to the priests." And as they went, they were made clean. Then one of them, when he saw that he was healed, turned back, praising God with a loud voice. He prostrated himself at Jesus' feet and thanked him. And he was a Samaritan. Then Jesus asked, "Were not ten made clean? But the other nine, where are they? Was none of them found to return and give praise to God except this foreigner?" Then he said to him, "Get up and go on your way; your faith has made you well."

- Can I imagine this scene? Ten miserable individuals have to call on Jesus from a distance for fear of contaminating him.

- What is going on in them?

- What happens?

- What does it say to me?

Monday 15th October   Luke 11:29–30

When the crowds were increasing, Jesus began to say, "This generation is an evil generation; it asks for a sign, but no sign will be given to it except the sign of Jonah. For just as Jonah became a sign to the people of Nineveh, so the Son of Man will be to this generation."

- What signs do I seek from God? What demands do I attempt to make on God?

- Lord, open my eyes to your saving presence in my sisters and brothers, especially those who are social outsiders.

Tuesday 16th October Luke 11:37–41

While Jesus was speaking, a Pharisee invited him to dine with him; so he went in and took his place at the table. The Pharisee was amazed to see that he did not first wash before dinner. Then the Lord said to him, "Now you Pharisees clean the outside of the cup and of the dish, but inside you are full of greed and wickedness. You fools! Did not the one who made the outside make the inside also? So give for alms those things that are within; and see, everything will be clean for you."

- The law laid down how much water you should use for washing before meals, the sort of vessel to contain it, the order in which you washed your hands, from the finger-tip to the wrist. The Pharisees considered it sinful to omit the smallest detail. Jesus tells them to give the same attention to cleansing their hearts.

- Lord, I easily lose myself in details of religious behavior, and fail to notice the spots of malice, greed and resentment in my heart. Open my inward eye.

Wednesday 17th October Luke 11:42–44

Jesus said, "Woe to you Pharisees! For you tithe mint and rue and herbs of all kinds, and neglect justice and the love of God; it is these you ought to have practiced, without neglecting the others. Woe to you Pharisees! For you love to have the seat of honour in the synagogues and to be greeted with respect in the marketplaces. Woe to you! For you are like unmarked graves, and people walk over them without realizing it."

- I must heed your words, Lord. I so easily give priority to collecting debts and paying bills, and have little energy left for justice and love.

Thursday 18th October, St. Luke   Luke 10:1–7a

After this the Lord appointed seventy others and sent them on ahead of him in pairs to every town and place where he himself intended to go. He said to them, "The harvest is plentiful, but the labourers are few; therefore ask the Lord of the harvest to send out labourers into his harvest. Go on your way. See, I am sending you out like lambs into the midst of wolves. Carry no purse, no bag, no sandals; and greet no one on the road. Whatever house you enter, first say, 'Peace to this house!' And if anyone is there who shares in peace, your peace will rest on that person; but if not, it will return to you. Remain in the same house, eating and drinking whatever they provide, for the labourer deserves to be paid."

- Jesus' advice to travel light applies to all of us. How simple is life for the person whose goods fit into one bag! That is Jesus' way.

- How many purchases do I make of things that I don't really need, or even use? How much energy do I use in my house or car that I could save?

- Lord, make me content with you as my baggage.

Friday 19th October   Luke 12:1–7

Meanwhile, when the crowd gathered by the thousands, so that they trampled on one another, Jesus began to speak first to his disciples, "Beware of the yeast of the Pharisees, that is, their hypocrisy. Nothing is covered up that will not be uncovered, and nothing secret that will not become known. Therefore whatever you have said in the dark will be heard in the light, and what you have whispered behind closed doors will be proclaimed from the housetops. I tell you, my friends, do not fear those who kill the body, and after that can do nothing more. But I will warn you whom to fear: fear him who, after he has killed, has authority to cast into hell. Yes, I tell you, fear him! Are not five sparrows sold for two pennies? Yet not one of them is forgotten in God's sight. But even the hairs of your head are all counted. Do not be afraid; you are of more value than many sparrows."

- God has an eye for the details, for the monsters as well as the molecules. We mortals are born and die in our millions, many of us quickly forgotten. Yet the Lord cherishes each of us personally.

- "But even the hairs of your head are all counted." Would I despair without that faith? What do I still fear?

Saturday 20th October   Luke 12:8–12

Jesus said to the disciples, "And I tell you, everyone who acknowledges me before others, the Son of Man also will acknowledge before the angels of God; but whoever denies me before others will be denied before the angels of God. And everyone who speaks a word against the Son of Man will be forgiven; but whoever blasphemes against the Holy Spirit will not be forgiven. When they bring you before the synagogues, the rulers, and the authorities, do not worry about how you are to defend yourselves or what you are to say; for the Holy Spirit will teach you at that very hour what you ought to say."

- There are two types of fear that Jesus talks about here. There is a false fear of physical persecution, false because "the Son of Man will acknowledge (you) before the angels of God" and "the Holy Spirit will teach you ... what you ought to say." The second is fear of God, who can threaten our grasp on eternal life—"whoever blasphemes against the Holy Spirit will not be forgiven."

- What is my spontaneous response? Am I encouraged and challenged, or am I frightened and unnerved? Why do I react in this way?

- What words of comfort are here for me?

october 21–27

Something to think and pray about each day this week:

Simply praying

The catechism definition of prayer is useful: the raising of the heart and mind to God. Not that we need a definition. Prayer is something we do in our own way. We breathe, smile and metabolize food, without defining the operations; so too with prayer. But we can consciously put ourselves in the way of prayer.

To start, we quiet the body. One traditional method is to sit with the backbone straight, from your bottom to the top of your head, the eyes half-closed, the breathing slow and easy, the hands on your lap with the palms facing upwards in openness to God's gifts. Then we aim to become present to God as he is always present to us. He has ears to listen to what our heart is saying.

The Presence of God
To be present is to arrive as one is and open up to the other.
At this instant, as I arrive here, God is present waiting for me.
God always arrives before me, desiring to connect with me
even more than my most intimate friend.
I take a moment and greet my loving God.

Freedom
"In these days, God taught me
as a schoolteacher teaches a pupil" (St. Ignatius).
I remind myself that there are things God has to teach me yet,
and ask for the grace to hear them and let them change me.

Consciousness
In the presence of my loving Creator,
I look honestly at my feelings over the last day,
the highs, the lows and the level ground.
Can I see where the Lord has been present?

The Word
I take my time to read the Word of God, slowly, a few times,
allowing myself to dwell on anything that strikes me. (Please
turn to your scripture on the following pages. Inspiration points
are there should you need them. When you are ready, return
here to continue.)

Conversation
What feelings are rising in me
as I pray and reflect on God's Word?
I imagine Jesus himself sitting or standing beside me,
and open my heart to him.

Conclusion
Glory be to the Father, and to the Son, and to the Holy Spirit,
As it was in the beginning, is now and ever shall be,
World without end. Amen

Sunday 21st October, Twenty-ninth Sunday
in Ordinary Time   Luke 18:2–7

Jesus said to his disciples, "In a certain city there was a judge who neither feared God nor had respect for people. In that city there was a widow who kept coming to him and saying, 'Grant me justice against my opponent.' For a while he refused; but later he said to himself, 'Though I have no fear of God and no respect for anyone, yet because this widow keeps bothering me, I will grant her justice, so that she may not wear me out by continually coming.'" And the Lord said, "Listen to what the unjust judge says. And will not God grant justice to his chosen ones who cry to him day and night? Will he delay long in helping them?"

- This woman was socially vulnerable – at the mercy of family and friends. This judge is a person of power and influence.

- God grants justice to those who persist, and grants it speedily. Do I persist in my faith, in my prayer; or do I falter regularly?

- Can I ask the Lord about this?

Monday 22nd October   Luke 12:13–21

Someone in the crowd said to Jesus, "Teacher, tell my brother to divide the family inheritance with me." But he said to him, "Friend, who set me to be a judge or arbitrator over you?" And he said to them, "Take care! Be on your guard against all kinds of greed; for one's life does not consist in the abundance of possessions." Then he told them a parable: "The land of a rich man produced abundantly. And he thought to himself, 'What should I do, for I have no place to store my crops?' Then he said, 'I will do this: I will pull down my barns and build larger ones, and there I will store all my grain and my goods.' And I will say to my soul, 'Soul, you have ample goods laid up for many years; relax, eat, drink, be merry.' But God said to him, 'You fool! This very night your life is being demanded of you. And the things you have prepared, whose will they be?' So it is with those who store up treasures for themselves but are not rich toward God."

- That rich man was talking to himself, not to friends; and his talk was all "I" and "my." His horizon was bounded by his plans and pleasures. He was a Scrooge chasing a phantom of happiness.

- Lord, you are warning me not just about greed but about egotism and the unacknowledged misery that it brings. There is more happiness in giving than in receiving.

Tuesday 23rd October   Luke 12:35–38

Jesus said to his disciples, "Be dressed for action and have your lamps lit; be like those who are waiting for their master to return from the wedding banquet, so that they may open the door for him as soon as he comes and knocks. Blessed are those slaves whom the master finds alert when he comes; truly I tell you, he will fasten his belt and have them sit down to eat, and he will come and serve them. If he comes during the middle of the night, or near dawn, and finds them so, blessed are those slaves."

- "Be dressed for action and have your lamp lit." What exactly is Jesus referring to? Am I to be ready when my end-time comes, or must I be ready now?

- Cardinal Newman said: "Fear not that your life will come to an end; fear rather that it will never come to a beginning."

- Is the Lord calling me to be honest and real about myself in some new way?

Wednesday 24th October   Luke 12:39–42

Jesus said, "But know this: if the owner of the house had known at what hour the thief was coming, he would not have let his house be broken into. You also must be ready, for the Son of Man is coming at an unexpected hour." Peter said, "Lord, are you telling this parable for us or for everyone?" And the Lord said, "Who then is the faithful and prudent manager whom his master will put in charge of his slaves, to give them their allowance of food at the proper time?"

- "The Son of Man is coming at an unexpected hour." Jesus, you tell me to be ready for the hour when you unexpectedly come into my life.

- When that hour comes, may I be at peace with myself, loving myself as you love me. And may I be able to answer with St. Vincent de Paul, who was asked on his death-bed if he forgave his enemies: "I have no enemies."

Thursday 25th October   Luke 12:49–53

Jesus said to his disciples, "I came to bring fire to the earth, and how I wish it were already kindled! I have a baptism with which to be baptized, and what stress I am under until it is completed! Do you think that I have come to bring peace to the earth? No, I tell you, but rather division! From now on five in one household will be divided, three against two and two against three; they will be divided: father against son and son against father, mother against daughter and daughter against mother, mother-in-law against her daughter-in-law and daughter-in-law against mother-in-law."

- We see Jesus now under great stress, almost at the limits of his endurance. He means to purify, and cause us to clean out the dross in our lives. It disturbs me.

- Jesus sensed already what a price he would pay for his teaching, and how bitter would be his baptism, inevitably leading him to his Passion.

- Can I talk with the Lord about this, and what it means for me today?

Friday 26th October   Romans 7:21–24

I do not understand my own actions. I find it to be a law that when I want to do what is good, evil lies close at hand. I delight in the law of God in my inmost self, but I see in my members another law at war with the law of my mind, making me captive to the law of sin that dwells in my members. Wretched man that I am! Who will rescue me from this body of death?

- Paul is very frank, veering almost towards depression. He feels weighed down, enslaved by sin which is deep within him. Though he did not face a world of advertisers and media stirring up his human desires, he was still upset by the tug of the flesh.

- Lord, I know that feeling of conflict, but please do not rescue me just yet from this body of death. It is what I am; it keeps me humble.

Saturday 27th October   Luke 13:6–9

Then Jesus told this parable: "A man had a fig tree planted in his vineyard; and he came looking for fruit on it and found none. So he said to the gardener, 'See here! For three years I have come looking for fruit on this fig tree, and still I find none. Cut it down! Why should it be wasting the soil?' He replied, 'Sir, let it alone for one more year, until I dig around it and put manure on it. If it bears fruit next year, well and good; but if not, you can cut it down.'"

- Jesus saw a useless tree, drawing from the soil but giving no fruit: a parable for those who take out more than they put in. Not like Abraham Lincoln: "Die when I may, I want it said of me that I plucked a weed and planted a flower wherever I thought a flower would grow."

- Lord, give me another chance. I have sometimes been a parasite; dig and manure me around with suffering if you must, but let me bear some fruit.

Something to think and pray about each day this week:

Seeking oneness with God

This is the month when we relish what is called the communion of saints, the oneness of all who have lived and died. We remember them on Cemetery Sundays as we pray at familiar graves. They are not the saints with haloes and floating bodies, but rather those who suffered and survived, who tried and sometimes failed, as Paddy Kavanagh wrote:

> To be a poet and not know the trade,
> To be a lover and repel all women;
> Twin ironies by which great saints are made,
> The agonising pincer-jaws of Heaven.

Presence of God
What is present to me is what has a hold on my becoming.
I reflect on the presence of God always there in love,
amidst the many things that have a hold on me.
I pause and pray that I may let God
affect my becoming in this precise moment.

Freedom
If God were trying to tell me something, would I know?
If God were reassuring me or challenging me, would I notice?
I ask for the grace to be free of my own preoccupations
and open to what God may be saying to me.

Consciousness
Knowing that God loves me unconditionally,
I look honestly over the last day, its events and my feelings.
Do I have something to be grateful for? Then I give thanks.
Is there something I am sorry for? Then I ask forgiveness.

The Word
God speaks to each one of us individually. I need to listen to
what he is saying to me. (Please turn to your scripture on the following pages. Inspiration points are there should you need
them. When you are ready, return here to continue.)

Conversation
What is stirring in me as I pray?
Am I consoled, troubled, left cold?
I imagine Jesus himself standing or sitting at my side,
and share my feelings with him.

Conclusion
Glory be to the Father, and to the Son, and to the Holy Spirit,
As it was in the beginning, is now and ever shall be,
World without end. Amen

Sunday 28th October, Thirtieth Sunday in Ordinary Time   Luke 18:9–14

Jesus also told this parable to some who trusted in themselves that they were righteous and regarded others with contempt: "Two men went up to the temple to pray, one a Pharisee and the other a tax collector. The Pharisee, standing by himself, was praying thus, 'God, I thank you that I am not like other people: thieves, rogues, adulterers, or even like this tax collector. I fast twice a week; I give a tenth of all my income.' But the tax collector, standing far off, would not even look up to heaven, but was beating his breast and saying, 'God, be merciful to me, a sinner!' I tell you, this man went down to his home justified rather than the other; for all who exalt themselves will be humbled, but all who humble themselves will be exalted."

- This parable, addressed to some proud and arrogant people, was meant to sting.

- Can I get in touch with the power of Jesus' rebuke?

- Do I hear the call to a different way of living?

- What does it say to me?

Monday 29th October   Luke 13:10–13

Now Jesus was teaching in one of the synagogues on the sabbath. And just then there appeared a woman with a spirit that had crippled her for eighteen years. She was bent over and was quite unable to stand up straight. When Jesus saw her, he called her over and said, "Woman, you are set free from your ailment." When he laid his hands on her, immediately she stood up straight and began praising God.

- How often, Lord, you faced the tension between human needs and the law's demands. And how consistently you moved to lift the misery of the individual person. Save me from ever loving systems more than humans.

Tuesday 30th October   Luke 13:18–21

Jesus said to the crowds, "What is the kingdom of God like? And to what should I compare it? It is like a mustard seed that someone took and sowed in the garden; it grew and became a tree, and the birds of the air made nests in its branches." And again he said, "To what should I compare the kingdom of God? It is like yeast that a woman took and mixed in with three measures of flour until all of it was leavened."

- These two images of growth are incremental and organic. The kingdom of God grows slowly, but it grows: 1.8 billion Christians today, which includes believers of diverse cultures and experiences, like the myriad birds of heaven nesting in its branches.

- And it often grows unseen, like yeast, giving a hidden dynamism to other movements.

Wednesday 31st October   Romans 8:26–27

The Spirit helps us in our weakness; for we do not know how to pray as we ought, but that very Spirit intercedes with sighs too deep for words. And God, who searches the heart, knows what is the mind of the Spirit, because the Spirit intercedes for the saints according to the will of God.

- "The Spirit helps us in our weakness." For Paul, the fact that we don't know how to pray as we ought is of no concern, provided we let the Spirit come to help.

- Lord, you search me and you know me. When I am sick, distracted, or in other ways unable to pray, the Holy Spirit links me with you, and prays for me with sighs too deep for words. Thank you.

- Teach me to know my weakness, and to welcome the Spirit.

Thursday 1st November, Feast of All Saints   Matthew 5:1–6

When Jesus saw the crowds, he went up the mountain; and after he sat down, his disciples came to him. Then he began to speak, and taught them, saying: "Blessed are the poor in spirit, for theirs is the kingdom of heaven. Blessed are those who mourn, for they will be comforted. Blessed are the meek, for they will inherit the earth. Blessed are those who hunger and thirst for righteousness, for they will be filled."

- Today's feast includes all the saints who were never canonized: mothers and fathers who stayed faithful to one another and their families; single women and men who did good unseen; those who found God through the pain they endured; all those who would never have thought of themselves as holy but whose goodness was clear to those close to them.

- Do I belong there?

Friday 2nd November, Feast of All Souls   Matthew 5:7–12

Jesus said to the crowds, "Blessed are the merciful, for they will receive mercy. Blessed are the pure in heart, for they will see God. Blessed are the peacemakers, for they will be called children of God. Blessed are those who are persecuted for righteousness' sake, for theirs is the kingdom of heaven. Blessed are you when people revile you and persecute you and utter all kinds of evil against you falsely on my account. Rejoice and be glad, for your reward is great in heaven, for in the same way they persecuted the prophets who were before you."

- Our reward is great in heaven, says Jesus. Today we are in communion with the millions who have gone to the Lord. Eye has not seen nor ear heard, nor has it entered into the human heart to conceive what God has prepared for those who love him.

Saturday 3rd November   Luke 14:7–11

When Jesus noticed how the guests chose the places of honor, he told them a parable. "When you are invited by someone to a wedding banquet, do not sit down at the place of honor, in case someone more distinguished than you has been invited by your host; and the host who invited both of you may come and say to you, 'Give this person your place,' and then in disgrace you would start to take the lowest place. But when you are invited, go and sit down at the lowest place, so that when your host comes, he may say to you, 'Friend, move up higher'; then you will be honored in the presence of all who sit at the table with you. For all who exalt themselves will be humbled, and those who humble themselves will be exalted."

- Today humility is neglected and seems quaint; it certainly does not suit the modern media age where pride and self-promotion are essential "virtues."

- Being humble is exhausting; it takes effort because it is difficult to live as a person who always needs God. It also has to be separated from timidity, and letting people walk all over us.

- Can I imagine myself at the table with Jesus after everyone else has left, and talk to him about this.

november 4–10

Something to think and pray about each day this week:

Mary, model for prayer

Of all the books in the New Testament, Luke gives the fullest account of Mary both as mother of Jesus and symbol of humanity. The Jewish girl becomes a mother, and a woman of extraordinary faith.

Mary responds to God in an attitude of listening to what is genuinely real. She attunes herself to the word that is coming to her and she trusts that it is speaking the truth to her. She fully participates in that dialogue, and thus allows the truth which is spoken to become real. She does not hide from the truth; she embraces it so that it unfolds in and through her life.

Mary is therefore a model for prayer for all Christians. Prayer is getting in touch with reality, letting it speak to us, and bringing alive the word which comes to us. We let it happen; we don't make it happen.

The Presence of God
God is with me, but more, God is within me.
Let me dwell for a moment on God's life-giving presence
in my body, in my mind, in my heart,
as I sit here, right now.

Freedom
I need to close out the noise, to rise above the noise;
The noise that interrupts, that separates,
The noise that isolates.
I need to listen to God again.

Consciousness
How do I find myself today?
Where am I with God? With others?
Do I have something to be grateful for? Then I give thanks.
Is there something I am sorry for? Then I ask forgiveness.

The Word
I read the Word of God slowly, a few times over, and I listen to
what God is saying to me. (Please turn to your scripture on the
following pages. Inspiration points are there should you need
them. When you are ready, return here to continue.)

Conversation
Do I notice myself reacting as I pray with the Word of God?
Do I feel challenged, comforted, angry?
Imagining Jesus sitting or standing by me,
I speak out my feelings, as one trusted friend to another.

Conclusion
Glory be to the Father, and to the Son, and to the Holy Spirit,
As it was in the beginning, is now and ever shall be,
World without end. Amen

Sunday 4th November, Thirty-first Sunday
in Ordinary Time   Luke 19:1–10

Jesus entered Jericho and was passing through it. A man was there named Zacchaeus; he was a chief tax collector and was rich. He was trying to see who Jesus was, but on account of the crowd he could not, because he was short in stature. So he ran ahead and climbed a sycamore tree to see him, because he was going to pass that way. When Jesus came to the place, he looked up and said to him, "Zacchaeus, hurry and come down; for I must stay at your house today." So he hurried down and was happy to welcome him. All who saw it began to grumble and said, "He has gone to be the guest of one who is a sinner." Zacchaeus stood there and said to the Lord, "Look, half of my possessions, Lord, I will give to the poor; and if I have defrauded anyone of anything, I will pay back four times as much." Then Jesus said to him, "Today salvation has come to this house, because he too is a son of Abraham. For the Son of Man came to seek out and to save the lost."

- Jesus made Zacchaeus' day, and everybody else began to grumble.
- What is going on here?
- What does it say to me?

Monday 5th November   Luke 14:12–14

Jesus said also to the one who had invited him, "When you give a luncheon or a dinner, do not invite your friends or your brothers or your relatives or rich neighbors, in case they may invite you in return, and you would be repaid. But when you give a banquet, invite the poor, the crippled, the lame, and the blind. And you will be blessed, because they cannot repay you, for you will be repaid at the resurrection of the righteous."

- How often is my giving affected by self-interest and the hope of favors in return? Jesus gives to me without hope of return.

- I can do God no favors, but Jesus' teaching is that love means giving without expectations. Is that how I give?

Tuesday 6th November   Romans 12:5–8

We, who are many, are one body in Christ, and individually we are members one of another. We have gifts that differ according to the grace given to us: prophecy, in proportion to faith; ministry, in ministering; the teacher, in teaching; the exhorter, in exhortation; the giver, in generosity; the leader, in diligence; the compassionate, in cheerfulness. Let love be genuine; hate what is evil, hold fast to what is good; love one another with mutual affection; outdo one another in showing honor. Do not lag in zeal, be ardent in spirit, serve the Lord. Rejoice in hope, be patient in suffering, persevere in prayer. Contribute to the needs of the saints; extend hospitality to strangers. Bless those who persecute you; bless and do not curse them. Rejoice with those who rejoice, weep with those who weep. Live in harmony with one another; do not be haughty, but associate with the lowly; do not claim to be wiser than you are.

- Notice how the focus of these gifts is towards others. We all have individual gifts from the Spirit, and they are directed towards the benefit of the community.

- We need to share these hopes and gifts because we are one body in Christ.

- Do I always share my gifts willingly? Do I hide them away?

Wednesday 7th November   Luke 14:28–33

Jesus said to the crowds, "For which of you, intending to build a tower, does not first sit down and estimate the cost, to see whether he has enough to complete it? Otherwise, when he has laid a foundation and is not able to finish, all who see it will begin to ridicule him, saying, 'This fellow began to build and was not able to finish.' Or what king, going out to wage war against another king, will not sit down first and consider whether he is able with ten thousand to oppose the one who comes against him with twenty thousand? If he cannot, then, while the other is still far away, he sends a delegation and asks for the terms of peace. So therefore, none of you can become my disciple if you do not give up all your possessions."

- Jesus tells two stories—one related to personal life, and one to public or political life—to ask his followers a simple question: Are you serious about following me, or not?

- How do people organize themselves for the things about which they are serious? How do I organize myself for the things about which I am serious?

- What do I want to say to the Lord? Am I committed?

Thursday 8th November   Luke 15:1–7

Now all the tax collectors and sinners were coming near to listen to him. And the Pharisees and the scribes were grumbling and saying, "This fellow welcomes sinners and eats with them." So he told them this parable: "Which one of you, having a hundred sheep and losing one of them, does not leave the ninety-nine in the wilderness and go after the one that is lost until he finds it? When he has found it, he lays it on his shoulders and rejoices. And when he comes home, he calls together his friends and neighbors, saying to them, 'Rejoice with me, for I have found my sheep that was lost.' Just so, I tell you, there will be more joy in heaven over one sinner who repents than over ninety-nine righteous persons who need no repentance."

- The Pharisees were scandalized that Jesus would spend time with sinners whom they did not trust or eat with.

- In reply Jesus challenges their picture of an intolerant, exclusive God, and substitutes the image of the constant, persistent, loving shepherd. This is the Lord I know, who never gives up on me.

Friday 9th November, Dedication
of the Lateran Basilica   John 2:13–16

The Passover of the Jews was near, and Jesus went up to Jerusalem. In the temple he found people selling cattle, sheep, and doves, and the money changers seated at their tables. Making a whip of cords, he drove all of them out of the temple, both the sheep and the cattle. He also poured out the coins of the money changers and overturned their tables. He told those who were selling the doves, "Take these things out of here! Stop making my Father's house a marketplace!"

- In my imagination I am standing there in the courtyard, with its sounds and smells, the rattle of coins on the tables, the reek and cries of the animals. I watch Jesus, see the blood rush to his face. He has come to reverence the temple and to pray.

- Suddenly I sense a whirlwind of anger as he whips the hucksters and scatters their money. This is a new side of Jesus and it shakes me. I stay with it.

Saturday 10th November   Luke 16:10–15

Jesus said to the disciples, "Whoever is faithful in a very little is faithful also in much; and whoever is dishonest in a very little is dishonest also in much. If then you have not been faithful with the dishonest wealth, who will entrust to you the true riches? And if you have not been faithful with what belongs to another, who will give you what is your own? No slave can serve two masters; for a slave will either hate the one and love the other, or be devoted to the one and despise the other. You cannot serve God and wealth." The Pharisees, who were lovers of money, heard all this, and they ridiculed him. So he said to them, "You are those who justify yourselves in the sight of others; but God knows your hearts; for what is prized by human beings is an abomination in the sight of God."

• To be faithful in small things is an expression of our love. When I prepare a gift for the one I love, every detail counts, and I do it with joy. A gentleman excused his lack of religious practice to St. Catherine of Siena, saying he was busy with temporal affairs. She answered: "It is you who make them temporal."

• Lord, let this be my way to you, to do the small things well out of love for you, to show you my love is exclusive.

november 11–17

Something to think and pray about each day this week:

Moving closer

We are never stationary on the path to God. Our prayer changes. Many, many good people move from using well-rehearsed vocal prayers and pious reflections, to a more silent, wordless sort of presence: "Be still and know that I am God. I will not have thy thoughts instead of thee." The old peasant, whom the Curè of Ars found spending hours in the church, explained it: "I look at the good God and the good God looks at me." With our oldest friends we do not need to talk.

The Presence of God
As I sit here, the beating of my heart,
the ebb and flow of my breathing, the movements of my mind
are all signs of God's ongoing creation of me.
I pause for a moment, and become aware
of this presence of God within me.

Freedom
I will ask God's help,
to be free from my own preoccupations,
to be open to God in this time of prayer,
to come to love and serve him more.

Consciousness
In God's loving presence I unwind the past day,
starting from now and looking back, moment by moment.
I gather in all the goodness and light, in gratitude.
I attend to the shadows and what they say to me,
seeking healing, courage, forgiveness.

The Word
I take my time to read the Word of God, slowly, a few times, allowing myself to dwell on anything that strikes me. (Please turn to your scripture on the following pages. Inspiration points are there should you need them. When you are ready, return here to continue.)

Conversation
Remembering that I am still in God's presence,
I imagine Jesus himself standing or sitting beside me,
and say whatever is on my mind, whatever is in my heart,
speaking as one friend to another.

Conclusion
Glory be to the Father, and to the Son, and to the Holy Spirit,
As it was in the beginning, is now and ever shall be,
World without end. Amen

Sunday 11th November, Thirty-second Sunday in Ordinary Time
Luke 20:27–38

Some Sadducees, those who say there is no resurrection, came to Jesus and asked him a question, "Teacher, Moses wrote for us that if a man's brother dies, leaving a wife but no children, the man shall marry the widow and raise up children for his brother. Now there were seven brothers; the first married, and died childless; then the second and the third married her, and so in the same way all seven died childless. Finally the woman also died. In the resurrection, therefore, whose wife will the woman be? For the seven had married her." Jesus said to them, "Those who belong to this age marry and are given in marriage; but those who are considered worthy of a place in that age and in the resurrection from the dead neither marry nor are given in marriage. Indeed they cannot die anymore, because they are like angels and are children of God, being children of the resurrection. And the fact that the dead are raised Moses himself showed, in the story about the bush, where he speaks of the Lord as the God of Abraham, the God of Isaac, and the God of Jacob. Now he is God not of the dead, but of the living; for to him all of them are alive."

• Jesus was being hassled by a trick question from someone who denies the resurrection of the dead.

• How would I deal with this situation?

• Do I hear Jesus' strong affirmation of eternal life? How am I moved by it?

Monday 12th November
Luke 17:1–4

Jesus said to his disciples, "Occasions for stumbling are bound to come, but woe to anyone by whom they come! It would be better for you if a millstone were hung around your neck and you were thrown into the sea than for you to cause one of these little ones to stumble. Be on your guard! If another disciple sins, you must rebuke the offender, and if there is repentance, you must forgive. And if the same person sins against you seven times a day, and turns back to you seven times and says, 'I repent,' you must forgive."

- These are strong words from Jesus. Causing others to stumble, introducing another human to sin: that is something I would not want to live with or die with. I am heir to much sinfulness, and can sometimes fail to shed that inheritance.

- Lord, you will forgive me if I am sorry, even if it happens again and again.

Tuesday 13th November   Wisdom 3:2–5a

But the souls of the righteous are in the hand of God, and no torment will ever touch them. In the eyes of the foolish they seemed to have died, and their departure was thought to be a disaster, and their going from us to be their destruction; but they are at peace. For though in the sight of others they were punished, their hope is full of immortality. Having been disciplined a little, they will receive great good.

- This is a funeral text, often read at requiem Masses; so it touches us all—we will all one day be the body before the altar. Is my hope full of immortality? It is, but my imagination cannot grasp it. Enough for me to be in your hands, Lord.

Wednesday 14th November   Luke 17:11–19

On the way to Jerusalem Jesus was going through the region between Samaria and Galilee. As he entered a village, ten lepers approached him. Keeping their distance, they called out, saying, "Jesus, Master, have mercy on us!" When he saw them, he said to them, "Go and show yourselves to the priests." And as they went, they were made clean. Then one of them, when he saw that he was healed, turned back, praising God with a loud voice. He prostrated himself at Jesus' feet and thanked him. And he was a

Samaritan. Then Jesus asked, "Were not ten made clean? But the other nine, where are they? Was none of them found to return and give praise to God except this foreigner?" Then he said to him, "Get up and go on your way; your faith has made you well."

- Simple social graces make a great difference to daily life, but more than that, they take us closer to God. Is it not easier to pray after an act of friendship or understanding, than after an angry exchange?

- The Samaritan, the outsider, returned and gave thanks to Jesus; the other nine did not.

- Do I forget to thank people when I should? What other social graces do I lack?

Thursday 15th November   **Luke 17:20–21**
Once Jesus was asked by the Pharisees when the kingdom of God was coming, and he answered, "The kingdom of God is not coming with things that can be observed; nor will they say, 'Look, here it is!' or 'There it is!' For, in fact, the kingdom of God is among you."

- We do not need to look for miracles or signs outside us to find the kingdom of God. It is within our personal power to reach, through justice, love and faith. To ask "When" and "Where" is to delay the coming of the kingdom among us.

Friday 16th November   **Wisdom 13:1–5**
Men did not recognize the craftsman while paying heed to his works; but they supposed that either fire or wind or swift air, or the circle of the stars or turbulent water, or the luminaries of heaven were the gods that rule the world. If through delight in the beauty of these things men assumed them to be gods, let them know how much better than these is their Lord, for the author of beauty created them. And if men were amazed at their power and

working, let them perceive from them how much more powerful is the one who formed them. For from the greatness and beauty of created things come a corresponding perception of their Creator.

- Lord, I am happy in the beauty you show me, whether on a large or a small scale. Let my prayer be like Gerard Manly Hopkins:
  Glory be to God for dappled things
  For skies of couple-colour as a brinded cow;
  For rose-moles in all stipple upon trout that swim;
  Fresh-firecoal chestnut-falls; finches' wings;
  Landscape plotted and pieced—fold, fallow, and plough; . . .
  He fathers-forth whose beauty is past change;
  Praise him.

Saturday 17th November, St. Elizabeth of Hungary
Luke 6:31–35

Jesus said to the disciples, "Do to others as you would have them do to you. If you love those who love you, what credit is that to you? For even sinners love those who love them. If you do good to those who do good to you, what credit is that to you? For even sinners do the same. If you lend to those from whom you hope to receive, what credit is that to you? Even sinners lend to sinners, to receive as much again. But love your enemies, do good, and lend, expecting nothing in return. Your reward will be great, and you will be children of the Most High; for he is kind to the ungrateful and the wicked."

- "Do to others as you would have them do to you." Jesus' does not ask us to respond to kindnesses extended to us, but to take the first step. This is a distinguishing mark of the Christian response.

- Are there people in my life from whom I don't expect kindness? Can I ask God for the grace to take the first step, especially if it makes me look foolish?

Something to think and pray about each day this week:

The whole person

We need our minds for prayer, but prayer is not an activity of the mind. God will not have your thoughts instead of you your-self. He does not surrender himself to cerebration. The poet R. S. Thomas described it in *Via negativa*:

> Why no! I never thought other than
> That God is that great absence
> In our lives, the empty silence
> Within, the place where we go
> Seeking, not in hope to
> Arrive or find. He keeps the interstices
> In our knowledge, the darkness
> Between stars. His are the echoes
> We follow, the footprints he has just
> Left.

The Presence of God
As I sit here, the beating of my heart,
the ebb and flow of my breathing, the movements of my mind
are all signs of God's ongoing creation of me.
I pause for a moment, and become aware
of this presence of God within me.

Freedom
I will ask God's help,
to be free from my own preoccupations,
to be open to God in this time of prayer,
to come to love and serve him more.

Consciousness
In God's loving presence I unwind the past day,
starting from now and looking back, moment by moment.
I gather in all the goodness and light, in gratitude.
I attend to the shadows and what they say to me,
seeking healing, courage, forgiveness.

The Word
I take my time to read the Word of God, slowly, a few times,
allowing myself to dwell on anything that strikes me. (Please
turn to your scripture on the following pages. Inspiration points
are there should you need them. When you are ready, return
here to continue.)

Conversation
Remembering that I am still in God's presence,
I imagine Jesus himself standing or sitting beside me,
and say whatever is on my mind, whatever is in my heart,
speaking as one friend to another.

Conclusion
Glory be to the Father, and to the Son, and to the Holy Spirit,
As it was in the beginning, is now and ever shall be,
World without end. Amen

Sunday 18th November, Thirty-third Sunday
in Ordinary Time   Luke 21:12–19

Jesus said, "But before all this occurs, they will arrest you and persecute you; they will hand you over to synagogues and prisons, and you will be brought before kings and governors because of my name. This will give you an opportunity to testify. So make up your minds not to prepare your defense in advance; for I will give you words and a wisdom that none of your opponents will be able to withstand or contradict. You will be betrayed even by parents and brothers, by relatives and friends; and they will put some of you to death. You will be hated by all because of my name. But not a hair of your head will perish. By your endurance you will gain your souls."

• When I hear Jesus speak in this ominous way, how do I react? Does it stir my blood or leave me cold? Does it seem somehow relevant or utterly distant from me?

• What is my experience of conflict and betrayal?

• How does Jesus' promise to be with me all the way move me?

Monday 19th November   Luke 18:35–43

As he approached Jericho, a blind man was sitting by the roadside begging. When he heard a crowd going by, he asked what was happening. They told him, "Jesus of Nazareth is passing by." Then he shouted, "Jesus, Son of David, have mercy on me!" Those who were in front sternly ordered him to be quiet; but he shouted even more loudly, "Son of David, have mercy on me!" Jesus stood still and ordered the man to be brought to him; and when he came near, he asked him, "What do you want me to do for you?" He said, "Lord, let me see again." Jesus said to him, "Receive your sight; your faith has saved you." Immediately he regained his sight and followed him, glorifying God; and all the people, when they saw it, praised God.

- If the Lord asked me: "What do you want me to do for you?" what would I answer? The blind, the starving, the troubled, know what they need and want. Do I live without desires, not too keen to change myself, complacent?

- Lord, you interrupted what you were saying to meet the blind man's cry. For you, acting mattered more than talking. Can I follow your example?

Tuesday 20th November   Luke 19:1–6

Jesus was passing through Jericho, and a man was there named Zacchaeus; he was a chief tax collector and was rich. He was trying to see who Jesus was, but on account of the crowd he could not, because he was short in stature. So he ran ahead and climbed a sycamore tree to see him, because he was going to pass that way. When Jesus came to the place, he looked up and said to him, "Zacchaeus, hurry and come down; for I must stay at your house today." So he hurried down and was happy to welcome him.

- Jesus, as I read this book, you look at me as you looked at Zacchaeus. You call me by name, and invite me to join you.

- You do not make demands—you even invite yourself to eat with sinners—but in your company I want to change something in myself, and to offer it to you.

Wednesday 21st November   Psalm 16(17):1, 6, 8, 15

I call upon you, for you will answer me, O God; incline your ear to me, hear my words. Guard me as the apple of your eye; hide me in the shadow of your wings, As for me, I shall behold your face in righteousness; when I awake I shall be satisfied, beholding your likeness.

- "Guard me as the apple of your eye." Lord, I need to feel I am in the shadow of your wings as I cope with what each day brings.

- More than that, I look forward to that for which I was born. When I awake I shall be satisfied with the sight of your glory.

Thursday 22nd November   Luke 19:41–43

As he came near and saw the city, he wept over it, saying, "If you, even you, had only recognized on this day the things that make for peace! But now they are hidden from your eyes. Indeed, the days will come upon you, when your enemies will set up ramparts around you and surround you, and hem you in on every side.

- Jesus wept over his city. Those who live there—some Arab, some Jewish—still weep over it. We who live far away cannot forget Jesus' city. "If I forget you, O Jerusalem, let my right hand wither! Let my tongue cling to the roof of my mouth, if I do not remember you, if I do not set Jerusalem above my highest joy."

- Lord God of Jews, Moslems and Christians, look with pity on Jerusalem, so that she may cease to be a sign of contradiction, and become a mother to all the children of Abraham.

Friday 23rd November   Luke 19:45–48

Then Jesus entered the temple and began to drive out those who were selling things there; and he said, "It is written, 'My house shall be a house of prayer'; but you have made it a den of robbers." Every day he was teaching in the temple. The chief priests, the scribes, and the leaders of the people kept looking for a way to kill him; but they did not find anything they could do, for all the people were spellbound by what they heard.

- Lord, your anger seldom flared spontaneously; but when you saw money-making invading the temple, you were furious. Money and religion are a dangerous mix. This is a sacred space.

- I try to imagine the scene: Faced with Jesus' indignation, some people were spellbound and others wanted to kill him. What is it about him that gives rise to these reactions? I will encounter those same reactions, if Jesus is real in my life.

Saturday 24th November   Luke 20:37–38

Jesus said to the Sadducees, "The fact that the dead are raised Moses himself showed, in the story about the bush, where he speaks of the Lord as the God of Abraham, the God of Isaac, and the God of Jacob. Now he is God not of the dead, but of the living; for to him all of them are alive."

- You are the God of the living, not the dead; the source of all life, the power of creation, more vital than the blood coursing in my veins, more jubilant than the Alleluia chorus, more intimate to me than my own thoughts or desires, pulsating in an eternal Now.

- I cannot grasp you, Lord, but these words lift my heart.

Something to think and pray about each day this week:

An uncommon king

When we call Christ the King, we have to un-think the trappings of royalty, and picture him as Pilate saw him when he asked: "Are you a king?" He was rejected, in pain, deserted by his followers. He had known fear; he had sweated blood and called on God three times, using the self-same words: "Let this chalice pass from me." Yet Pilate was in awe. Jesus was unafraid now, ready to drain the bitter chalice, but himself untouched by bitterness. Here was a man who could command the loyalty not so much of the successful and popular, as of the great mass of humankind who also pray daily that God spare them the bitter chalice. If he is a king, it is not as the overclothed icon of Byzantine art, but as the naked, crucified one.

The Presence of God
I pause for a moment
and reflect on God's life-giving presence
in every part of my body, in everything around me,
in the whole of my life.

Freedom
God is not foreign to my freedom.
Instead the Spirit breathes life into my most intimate desires,
gently nudging me towards all that is good.
I ask for the grace to let myself be enfolded by the Spirit.

Consciousness
I exist in a web of relationships—links to nature, people, God.
I trace out these links, giving thanks for the life that flows
through them.
Some links are twisted or broken: I may feel regret, anger,
disappointment.
I pray for the gift of acceptance and forgiveness.

The Word
God speaks to each one of us individually. I need to listen to
what he is saying to me. (Please turn to your scripture on the following pages. Inspiration points are there should you need
them. When you are ready, return here to continue.)

Conversation
How has God's Word moved me? Has it left me cold?
Has it consoled me or moved me to act in a new way?
I imagine Jesus standing or sitting beside me,
I turn and share my feelings with him.

Conclusion
Glory be to the Father, and to the Son, and to the Holy Spirit,
As it was in the beginning, is now and ever shall be,
World without end. Amen

Sunday 25th November, Feast of Christ the King
Luke 23:35–43

And the people stood by, watching; but the leaders scoffed at Jesus, saying, "He saved others; let him save himself if he is the Messiah of God, his chosen one!" The soldiers also mocked him, coming up and offering him sour wine, and saying, "If you are the King of the Jews, save yourself!" There was also an inscription over him, "This is the King of the Jews." One of the criminals who were hanged there kept deriding him and saying, "Are you not the Messiah? Save yourself and us!" But the other rebuked him, saying, "Do you not fear God, since you are under the same sentence of condemnation? And we indeed have been condemned justly, for we are getting what we deserve for our deeds, but this man has done nothing wrong." Then he said, "Jesus, remember me when you come into your kingdom." He replied, "Truly I tell you, today you will be with me in Paradise."

- This is a remarkable scene. The King of the Jews crucified between two criminals.

- What happens?

- How do I respond to it?

Monday 26th November
Luke 21:1–4

Jesus looked up and saw rich people putting their gifts into the treasury; he also saw a poor widow put in two small copper coins. He said, "Truly I tell you, this poor widow has put in more than all of them; for all of them have contributed out of their abundance, but she out of her poverty has put in all she had to live on."

- Lord it does not matter what others see of my actions or neglect. You see into my heart and know my generosity or selfishness. Save me, Lord, from sacrifices that cost me nothing. True generosity is not so much giving what I can easily spare as giving what I can't easily do without.

Tuesday 27th November   Luke 21:5–11

When some were speaking about the temple, how it was adorned with beautiful stones and gifts dedicated to God, Jesus said, "As for these things that you see, the days will come when not one stone will be left upon another; all will be thrown down." They asked him, "Teacher, when will this be, and what will be the sign that this is about to take place?" And he said, "Beware that you are not led astray; for many will come in my name and say, 'I am he!' and, 'The time is near!' Do not go after them. When you hear of wars and insurrections, do not be terrified; for these things must take place first, but the end will not follow immediately." Then he said to them, "Nation will rise against nation, and kingdom against kingdom; there will be great earthquakes, and in various places famines and plagues; and there will be dreadful portents and great signs from heaven."

- The temple was not just the centre of the Jews' civilization: It was the place where God lived among them. Yet Jesus told them that it was all going to fall apart!

- Is there any way in which my "secure centre"—either personal or national—threatens to collapse? Terrorism? War? Earthquakes? The key words from Jesus in all of this are: "Do not be terrified." Can I allow Jesus, the Consoler, to speak to me, wherever I am?

Wednesday 28th November   Luke 21:12–19

Jesus said to his disciples, "But before all this occurs, they will arrest you and persecute you; they will hand you over to synagogues and prisons, and you will be brought before kings and governors because of my name. This will give you an opportunity to testify. So make up your minds not to prepare your defense in advance; for I will give you words and a wisdom that none of your opponents will be able to withstand or contradict. You will be betrayed even by parents and brothers, by relatives and friends; and they will put some of you to death. You will be hated by all because of my name. But not a hair of your head will perish. By your endurance you will gain your souls."

- "You will be hated by all because of my name." How do I respond to Jesus' talk of persecution? Do I want to flee? Am I excited by the struggle with these opponents?

- "But not a hair on your head will perish." Can I trust my defense to Jesus?

Thursday 29th November   Luke 21:25–28

Jesus said to the disciples, "There will be signs in the sun, the moon, and the stars, and on the earth distress among nations confused by the roaring of the sea and the waves. People will faint from fear and foreboding of what is coming upon the world, for the powers of the heavens will be shaken. Then they will see 'the Son of Man coming in a cloud' with power and great glory. Now when these things begin to take place, stand up and raise your heads, because your redemption is drawing near."

- In all my years I have seen no signs in the sun and the stars. We seem to be still a long way off from the apocalypse Jesus describes. Lord, it looks like I will see you in person before these things take place.

- Teach me to stand prepared but unworried.

Friday 30th November, St. Andrew   Matthew 4:18–20

As he walked by the Sea of Galilee, he saw two brothers, Simon, who is called Peter, and Andrew his brother, casting a net into the sea—for they were fishermen. And he said to them, "Follow me, and I will make you fish for people." Immediately they left their nets and followed him.

- Dear Andrew, patron saint of young brothers, the one who is always introduced as "the brother of Simon Peter." Though he became the patron saint of Scotland, Russia and Greece, and is remembered for the X-shaped cross on which he died, yet in the Gospels he is always overshadowed by big brother.

- Let me know the grace of living in someone else's shadow, wearing hand-me-downs. Teach me, Andrew, to love where I am in the family.

Saturday 1st December   Luke 21:34–36

Jesus said to his disciples, "Be on guard so that your hearts are not weighed down with dissipation and drunkenness and the worries of this life, and that day catch you unexpectedly, like a trap. For it will come upon all who live on the face of the whole earth. Be alert at all times, praying that you may have the strength to escape all these things that will take place, and to stand before the Son of Man."

- It is a curious phrase, but apt: "weighed down with dissipation and drunkenness." Drink is a narcotic that dulls the heart and blunts the appetites. As for dissipation, while it may be sold as fun, on the morning after most would agree with Nietzsche that "the mother of dissipation is not joy but joylessness."

- Joy and moderation go hand in hand. When our hearts are happy, our own skins are a good place to be; we do not need alcohol or other drugs.

Other Titles of Interest

The Art of Discernment

Making Good Decisions in Your World of Choices
Stefan Kiechle, S.J.
The Art of Discernment is an explanation of the discernment process first developed by St. Ignatius of Loyola: outlining the pros and the cons, considering the decision, listening to our hearts, and doing what is best. It is the second title in the Ignatian Impulse series.
ISBN: 1-59471-035-X / 128 pages / $9.95 / Ave Maria Press

Riding the Dragon

10 Lessons for Inner Strength in Challenging Times
Robert J. Wicks
In this warm, compassionate, and highly personal guidebook, Robert J. Wicks offers encouragement and dragon-riding lessons to help people engage their problems and grow through them.
PAPERBACK / ISBN: 1-893732-94-0 / 160 pages / $12.95 / Sorin Books
HARDCOVER / ISBN: 1-893732-65-7 / 160 pages / $17.95 / Sorin Books

Plain Living

A Quaker Path to Simplicity
Catherine Whitmire
For centuries Quakers have been living out of a spiritual center in a way of life they call "plain living." Their experiences and wisdom have much to offer anyone seeking greater simplicity today.
ISBN: 1-893732-28-2 / 192 pages / $14.95 / Sorin Books

Sacred Refuge

Why and How to Make a Retreat
Thomas M. Santa, C.Ss.R.
Noted retreat director Thomas Santa answers questions about the special practice of making a retreat.
ISBN: 1-59471-052-X / 192 pages / $12.95 / Ave Maria Press

Available from your local bookstore or from **ave maria press**
Notre Dame, IN 46556 / www.avemariapress.com
ph: 1.800.282.1865 / fax: 1.800.282.5681
Prices and availability subject to change.

Keycode: FØTØ5Ø6ØØØØ